Hannes Werthner

Qualitative Reasoning

Modeling and the Generation of Behavior

Springer-Verlag Wien New York

Univ.-Doz. Dipl.-Ing. Dr. Hannes Werthner
Institut für Statistik, OR und Computerverfahren
Universität Wien, Österreich

Printed in Germany

Typesetting: Camera ready by author
Printing and Binding: Druckerei zu Altenburg, D-04600 Altenburg

Printed on acid-free and chlorine-free bleached paper

With 70 Figures

Library of Congress Cataloging-in-Publication Data

Werthner, H., 1954–
Qualitative reasoning : an approach to modeling and behavior generation / Hannes Werthner.
p. cm.
ISBN 0 387-82579-7
1. Artificial intelligence. 2. Human behavior — Simulation methods. 3. Reasoning. I. Title.
Q335.W44 1994
006. 3—dc20 94-12105 CIP

ISBN 3-211-82579-7 Springer-Verlag Wien New York
ISBN 0-387-82579-7 Springer-Verlag New York Wien

To my parents

Why "Qualitative Reasoning"?

The history of natural sciences is full of attempts to explain the human being through mechanistic models interpreting man as a machine and to build machines that imitate (the description of) human thinking and acting. Computers are, to some extent and under a certain point of view, the not completely satisfying outcome of this search. Nevertheless, computers require problems to be well defined and operations to be guided by algorithms. In contrast, human thinking, acting and communication is able to integrate uncertainty, missing information, contradictions, poor descriptions and associative relationships. In reality, very few problems are quantitatively well defined. The usage of computers requires human representations to be translated by means of formalisms into well defined descriptions. One computer-based approach which tries to integrate these different levels of problem situations - from well defined to vaguely structured - is that of decision support systems. It was precisely the work in the development of such systems - in connection with the building of knowledge-based simulation environments - that motivated my engagement in qualitative reasoning. I believe that this field of research is a possible way to improve problem formulation and the automatic translation into well defined formalisms. Thus, qualitative reasoning may help to express poorly defined problem situations, support the solution process and lead to a better interpretation of the final results.

I attempt to contribute to qualitative reasoning research by putting the existing different approaches into a common framework. The work classifies the most important methods and seeks for differences and correspondences. Different approaches will be described, distinguished and interpreted, taking into account relationships to other fields of research as well. Additionally, I will also present a new approach based on influence diagrams and Markov chains. I understand qualitative reasoning as an interdisciplinary approach, relating fields such as computer science, software engineering and programming paradigms, simulation and system theory, artificial intelligence and cognitive science. And qualitative reasoning deals with philosophical problems such as causality, which are at the starting point of every research activity. Consequently, I will also look at these different areas under the point of view of qualitative reasoning, although a profound discussions of all these topics is beyond the scope of this work. On the other hand, modeling and generation of dynamic behavior - which I see as the central areas of qualitative reasoning - are discussed in some detail and enriched by new ideas and approaches. I think that in these tasks, particularly in modeling, qualitative reasoning may provide for important contributions.

Acknowledgements

I want to express my gratitude to a number of people whose support was critical for this publication. Andrea Bonarini, Karl Fröschl, Liliana Ironi, Herbert Prähofer and Andrea Rizzoli made useful suggestions and critiques on a first draft. I owe a special note of thanks to Roy Leitch and Peter Struss for their important comments on the final draft and their encouragement. The various and extensive discussions with Giorgio Guariso and Martin Hitz often helped to clarify my ideas. Special thanks to all of them for giving their time, their thoughts and their colleagueship. I would also like to thank Georg Gottlob, Jimmy Schimanovich and A Min Tjoa for their continuous moral support - an indispensable element for everybody engaged in a work of this nature. In particular, I am grateful to Willi Grossmann, whose critical eye discovered several errors and misunderstandings in former drafts. His critiques contributed decisively to improve the quality of this work - especially his positive way of expressing them. I am, however, the only responsible for any errors this work may still contain. My special thanks go to Hedi Riegler; she was extremely helpful in reading the manuscript. And last but not least I would like to thank Irene Horejs for both her editorial advice and her warm companionship and support - not only during this period of academic work.

Contents

Structure of the Work

This publication proceeds partly in a historical perspective. In our opinion this approach allows best to illustrate both the principles of qualitative reasoning and its progress. We consider the original works which have established the field as best suited to cover and to differentiate qualitative reasoning. All further developments and results can be related to these early contributions.

Hence, the first part gives an overview, identifies the basic assumptions, describes the roots of qualitative reasoning and presents several fields of application.

Part II introduces the three main approaches of qualitative reasoning. In the first chapter of this part we concentrate on the basic modeling techniques and the respective results of the reasoning process, a detailed discussion of the implementations and reasoning techniques of these approaches is delayed to the final chapter of part II. Between these two chapters we provide a description of the different dimensions of qualitative abstraction and discuss the respective qualitative operations.

Part III treats advanced topics and introduces some new concepts. It both illustrates and manifests the rapid development in qualitative reasoning toward an applicable field of research. Particularly, the problems of ambiguity and uncertainty are discussed. In all these cases, techniques are presented in order to bypass limitations of qualitative reasoning. For that purpose a new concept will also be introduced. Furthermore, we discuss the problem of causality and its relevance in qualitative reasoning, taking a pragmatic and implementation-oriented point of view. We conclude part III with a chapter that provides, on the basis of graphs, a common framework for a further interpretation of the main techniques. In addition, this representation will allow to discuss the possibilities of integrating the different qualitative reasoning approaches.

Part IV puts qualitative reasoning into a broader framework and confronts it with other areas of research such as system theory, cognitive science and expert systems. This comparison shows that the applied concepts are very similar, at least on a conceptual level.

In part V we present several approaches to model building. In this discussion we deal with methods to build models from scratch as well as model bases and the related selection problem in such bases. These bases not only store concrete models but also the information about models. These approaches constitute the most recent advances in qualitative reasoning.

The last part not only provides concluding remarks but also identifies and proposes promising areas of further research.

Finally, we want to point out that this work attempts to concentrate on the underlying views, the basic concepts of qualitative reasoning and their development. Mathematical and technical descriptions are only used when necessary. We think that it is important to provide a rather complete and coherent picture of this new area of research and to stress its main advantages as well as its shortcomings. The reader should get a feeling that, in order to tackle the problems of modeling and behavior generation, a set of different methods may be necessary among which qualitative reasoning may play an important role.

Part I

Introducing Qualitative Reasoning

In the first part we introduce qualitative reasoning in a rather descriptive way. We will show several fields of application, give a short history and present its basic principles.

1. Instead of a Definition

The term *qualitative reasoning* has been used synonymously with *naive physics*, *qualitative physics* or *qualitative simulation*. In the following we will use the notion of qualitative reasoning since it is more general than the term qualitative physics. But we will also distinguish qualitative reasoning from qualitative simulation [Bobrow 84]. In our interpretation qualitative reasoning incorporates two central tasks: to identify the structure of a system, i.e. modeling, and to derive and to explain its dynamic behavior. To fulfill this latter task, simulation is just one - albeit the most prominent - possibility.[1]

A frequently published example to demonstrate necessary qualitative features of a problem description and its solution is that of a household robot which is to pour coffee into a cup [Forbus 88]. Suppose the "knowledge" this machine requires in order to fulfill its task. It has to prevent spilling, to consider the amount of coffee, to estimate roughly the distance between cup and carafe, etc. Another, simpler, example might be a container filled with some liquid, e.g. water, above a heat source. We want to know what can happen in principle in such a situation: if the flame is low, an equilibrium will be established and the water temperature will remain constant; if the flame is high enough, the water will begin to boil; and if it is not reduced, the water eventually evaporates.

Fig. 1: A filled container above fire; Can the liquid inside the container evaporate ?

The reasoning activities, necessary in such a situation, are typically interpreted as being qualitative. At first sight human beings seem to have some coarse descriptions of a situation as well as some rules for its change or temporal development. The imitation of qualitative

[1] In this work we will use the term simulation in two different meanings: it stands either for the mechanism of generating the dynamic behavior of a system or for the entire field of simulation as an area of system theory. In the latter case it also deals with the task of modeling. The concrete meaning will become clear through the context.

reasoning activities requires the consideration of several aspects, as illustrated in the previous example [Rajagopalan 86]:

- Humans understand basic concepts which can be applied to different situations. The concept of heat transfer, for example, explains how both the container and the water become hotter.
- Humans establish a cause-effect chain of changes. One can increase, for example, the water temperature by increasing the temperature of the heat source.
- Humans realize that interesting things happen around critical points. If the flame is high enough, the water will begin to boil.
- Humans are able to reason about changes over time. We can order events on the time axis, for example water begins to boil before the container may begin to melt.
- Humans can reason from particular points of views and at different levels of detail. We can identify what is important, e.g. in our example no reference is made to the shape of the container.

And finally we are satisfied with qualitative results - at least at the beginning. There is no extra need for a detailed quantitative information. We can conclude that both tasks, i.e. the organization of knowledge and its usage in the derivation of future states, are fundamental. A description just in the form of a set of equations seems not to be sufficient or adequate. In cases as the previous ones humans do not use differential equations to answer specific questions or to react to specific situations. We use some simpler patterns to perform reasoning activities. Based on "common-sense" knowledge other, more specific, knowledge may be applied. For example, in practice it is impossible to describe the creation, the form and the flight of a soap bubble entirely by a set of a numerical equations. The human observing such a bubble cannot even solve a set of differential equations because they are not available. Nevertheless, we are able to derive the probable future states of the bubble, e.g. the position in the next moment, its probability of being destroyed or its change of color.

Furthermore, the feature of being qualitative can also be seen as not being quantitative, neither in the description nor in the solution process. If in the previous case of a container above a heat source the question is 'Can the water start to boil ?', we may easily answer with 'Yes' based on pure qualitative insights. However, when the question 'Will the water start to boil ?' is asked, quantitative information, for example about the temperature of the heat source, will be necessary. Thus, both forms, qualitative and quantitative, do not contradict each other. Qualitative knowledge can be seen as a layer on top of the quantitative one and may even guide the application of quantitative knowledge. In fact, looking at an engineer performing a quantitative simulation, this person seems to use some qualitative patterns in advance to select the way of structure representation and the simulation algorithm. Thus, qualitative reasoning is also an attempt to model the knowledge of why and how we do something, it aims at writing programs that formalize and implement such rather vague type of knowledge. Hence, this new approach stems from two, interwoven, motivations [Weld and de Kleer 90a], [Williams and de Kleer 91]:

- Modeling real world situations and human artifacts in order to support the reasoning activities of persons such as engineers. The scope of the process is a model of the real world and references to numerical models or models which may be formulated with fair accuracy may exist. However, the necessary information is either not available or these models are too complex or too slow to provide the desired answer. Moreover, there may not even be the need for an exact quantitative solution, or, on the contrary, the desired result should already have a qualitative form. This aspect may also be called cognitive world modeling.

- Imitating human, mainly engineers', thinking. Also in this case a model of reality exists but it is just an instrument to study the reasoning process of man. We may use the term cognitive self-modeling in this case. Both levels together may provide qualitative reasoning with capacities for modeling which are most probably superior to those of other approaches.

Under a different point of view we could say that qualitative reasoning shifts the classical problem of modeling to a higher level as it incorporates and represents also the knowledge of the person who has to reason about physical mechanisms. This is new with respect to other approaches to formalize modeling in fields such as system theory. It is important to underline that qualitative reasoning tries to build a model of both the real existing system and the representational and reasoning primitives of the human who tries to model this system. Thus, "the heart of the qualitative reasoning enterprise is to develop computational theories of the core skills underlying engineers', scientists', and just plain folk's ability to hypothesize, test, predict, create, optimize, diagnose and debug physical mechanisms", as stated by [Williams and de Kleer, 1991]. However, in our discussion we extend the definition of the term physical mechanism to include not only man-made artifacts but also, for example, ecological systems. Moreover, it is clear that model building has to neglect aspects and attributes of reality, and that simplification and approximation are inherent features of mapping the "infinity of reality" to a finite description. Qualitative reasoning takes just a very radical point of view, it neglects most of the features and concentrates on just some important entities and relationships.

Qualitative reasoning deals also with the general knowledge humans possess to apply more specific knowledge ("what we know prior to knowing"). This "common-sense" knowledge is also general in that sense as it is applicable to several specific situations; once having found a qualitative mental model for the flight of an object, this can be applied to different distinct objects, hence also to a soap bubble. Thus, qualitative reasoning deals with generic descriptions, it provides prototypical portrays which treat entire classes of specific situations. This shows a similarity to the frame based approach in knowledge representation as presented by [Minsky 81].

In addition to the previously mentioned modeling problems and tasks, the following two problems are tackled by the qualitative reasoning approach (see also [Forbus 88]):

- The resolution problem: numerical solutions require knowledge - in form of data, structure, techniques - which very often is not available. This is also the case where an accurate model of reality may be available but the necessary information is not. Low resolution and partial information has to be incorporated and represented.
- The narrowness problem: numerical simulation provides precise answers to precise questions and assumptions. But very often one needs an alternative or wants to have a solution for an entire class of problems, in such cases single predictions are not sufficient.

However, the term qualitative is not reserved for the approach represented in this work, qualitative reasoning is not the only field of natural science which uses qualitative methods. In fields such as system theory, for example, the detection of qualitative behavior of dynamic systems is of central importance, though the structural description and behavior generation primitives are different. Furthermore, qualitative reasoning has to be distinguished from so-called "qualitative computer research" approaches in social and human science, as described by [Fielding and Lee 91]. These applications denote the daily usage of computers together with "simple" databases, statistical software or hypertext implementations in order to improve the results of social science research both quantitatively and qualitatively. However, such "qualitative computer research" has no relation with our field of study.

Finally, we see qualitative reasoning also close to decision support systems and the decision process formalized in these systems. Decisions may be ordered along a continuous line, starting with well-known structures, methods and data on the one side and ending up with no or little structure, no data and methods on the other (see also [Bonczek et al. 81], [Guariso and Werthner 89] and [Travé-Massuyès 92]). Decisions on a low and short-term level can often be compiled in advance together with their structure and data. On the other hand, decisions on a high, long-term and strategic level are often qualitative in nature. Thus, the embedding of qualitative models in such systems would support the decision maker. Furthermore, humans look for causal explanations. This is exactly what qualitative reasoning attempts to provide: the possible future behavior and its causal explanation, derived from an identified simple structural description.

Figure 2 summarizes the discussion of this chapter by drawing a general framework of qualitative reasoning.

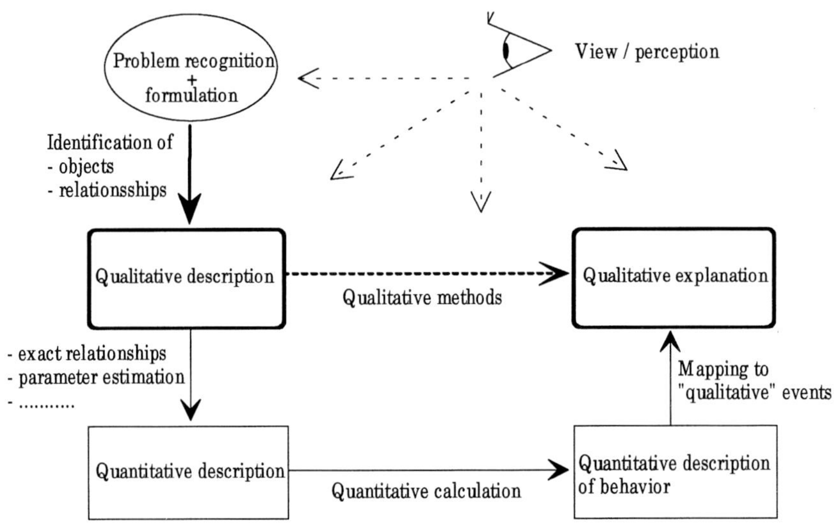

Fig. 2: General framework of qualitative reasoning

Qualitative reasoning, the upper part of Fig. 2, represents an attempt to automate the process of modeling. The figure illustrates that also in the "traditional" case a qualitative description of reality is necessary. Qualitative reasoning, dealing with both modeling and the derivation of qualitative behavior by means of qualitative methods, may represent an abbreviation when a qualitative interpretation of a system's behavior is looked for. Such a qualitative explanation consists of a time ordered sequence of well-distinguishable events (such as water starts to boil or to freeze), expressing how and why something happens. Furthermore, the step from a qualitative to a quantitative model might be very time consuming and expensive, especially when extensive measurements are required. In addition, in complex cases such as ecological problems, quantitative models may not be available and qualitative reasoning represents a first step to identify an exact structure. A qualitative layer on top of a quantitative one helps to identify and select an appropriate quantitative model. Such approach may, therefore, be used to manage assumptions about models and their usage in an explicit way. As already mentioned earlier, in many cases - in particular when a qualitative model can predict that some physical system may reach a state which has to be prevented anyway - a rough and qualitative description of behavior will be sufficient. The figure also shows that one has to consider human perception, i.e. how humans represent and treat real world objects, how they reason on a qualitative level. Approaches in qualitative reasoning can, thus, be classified with respect to such views.

2. Tasks of Qualitative Reasoning

In the following we present a list of the most common tasks which can be tackled with qualitative reasoning (see also [Bobrow 84], [Fishwick 89] and [Forbus 88]). This list does not pretend to provide a complete and exhaustive definition of the single tasks of application, but we want to supply a short description of the applicability of qualitative reasoning in different fields. However, we want to mention that qualitative reasoning is not the only approach to solving these problems. But it is applicable in all these cases, even when either accurate quantitative models are not known, or they are too complicated for the desired solution, or the necessary knowledge is not entirely available. In most of the cases it is assumed that some structural information is available. Qualitative reasoning represents, however, a specific approach as it allows for the treatment of new and unforeseen situations:

- *Diagnosis:* Given one or more structural descriptions of a device and maybe some fault models (i.e. how a device behaves assuming a specific fault), the task is to detect whether a fault has occurred, to identify the fault and to locate the faulty components ([de Kleer and Williams 87], [Reiter 87]).

- *Monitoring:* Given is a structural and behavioral model of a complex device, for example involved in some industrial processes. The task is to monitor the device's behavior and to check for malfunctions. This point is closely related to the above one, its central job is the mapping of a continuous data stream to relevant events and their qualitative description.

- *Design and modeling:* Given are the design specifications of an artifact, the task is to verify whether the actual behavior of this artifact - deduced from the description of the designed structure and some known parameters - shows the desired pattern and remains within some well and a priori defined ranges. This task is also closely related to simulation, i.e. to derive a future scenario based on a description of the topical situation.

- *Interpretation:* Given is a structural description of a device which allows to infer its dynamic behavior. In addition, a sequence of observations about the system is available. Furthermore, at the moment of reasoning the system is in some known state. Interpretation is now the task to interpret this situation and to conclude how and why it happened [Forbus 87].

- *Structure identification:* Given are some data observed as output of a real system. Furthermore, a modeler has an idea about the possible structure of this real system and its behavior. The task is to identify this structure by building a qualitative model and to reproduce by means of this model the pattern of the given data [Guariso et al. 92].

- *Explanation:* Given is a sequence of states as the description of the behavior of a system. The task of qualitative reasoning is to interpret this sequence, to deduce the cause-effect relationships.

The following list of application areas such as business and planning, traffic control, design of engines, diagnosis of electronics, fault detection in process control, applications in medicine, provides the impression that qualitative reasoning has already reached the state of practical usefulness and maturity (see also [Milne and Travé-Massuyès 92] as a good survey of practical applications):

- the system DIAPASON to monitor fluid separation column in nuclear reprocessing plants [Leyval and Ledoux 91],
- modeling and analysis of a cooling circuit for power generation at ABB Swiss [Sugaya 89],
- support of the troubleshooting process for analog systems at IBM France [Dague et al. 87],
- support of the design steps of electrical motors and other devices [Kiriyama et al. 91],
- diagnosis of faults in continuous process control, an ESPRIT project [Bertin et al. 90],
- an application in the area of business, e.g. to model and detect problems in cash flow [Baily et al. 91],
- modeling and analysis of a marine steam power plant [Govindaraj 87],
- qualitative simulation of a chemical reactor system [Oyeleye and Kramer 89],
- an assistant used in medicine for the interpretation of ECG [Kirby and Hunter 91],
- support in the identification process of problems in the cardiovascular system [Downing 91],
- analysis of fatigue and fracture problems in steel bridges, a system named CRACK [Roddis and Martin 92],
- prediction and analysis of deformation phenomena of materials, regarding elasticity, viscosity and plasticity ([Capelo et al. 91], [Capelo et al. 93]),
- application in medicine and medical diagnosis ([Ironi et al. 90], [Lanzola et al. 90]).

3. Basic Principles

Qualitative reasoning deals with the modeling of *dynamic systems* and describes their structure and behavioral changes in time.[2] In a *rationalist* view of the world it is assumed that a simplified structure of a system, i.e. entities and whether they are related or not, can be well identified as it is either given or it can be derived from somewhere. However, no notion of an explicit empirical test about the correctness of a structure exists. The structural description, together with some behavioral primitives, is used to derive the dynamic behavior of the system. A further basic principle is the - implicit or explicit - notion of *causality*. Qualitative reasoning derives causality from a behavioral description even if in "reality" - in a real situation or in a physical device - causality cannot be observed or expressed directly. This "desire" for causality derives from the fact that humans "normally" use causal dependencies in the explanation process to describe situations. Moreover, such cause-effect chains have also a pragmatic meaning, once identified (or assumed) they can be used to determine the sequence of steps in calculating values of variables.

Another underlying principle of this approach is a certain reductionism, as also expressed in the basic principles outlined below. Nevertheless, this introduction of reductionism - focusing on the formalization of common-sense daily knowledge - seems somehow paradoxical. Indeed, modern physics tends to use rather observer-dependent approaches and realizes - as in quantum physics - that things do not exist independently from the human observer and that relationships may have a rather complex form. A similar discussion can be observed in computer science (see for example [Coy et al. 92]). The following basic principles of qualitative reasoning can be identified:

Compositionality: The structural description of a physical device or of a situation is an assembling of single basic descriptional entities which can be connected by well-defined interconnections. These basic entities may be either some physical components of a device or some abstract objects such as processes. The respective assemblies in turn may also be composed in a hierarchic manner. The basic entities have attached descriptions of their behavior in the form of local laws. The behavior of the overall device or situation, i.e. the assemblies of single parts, follows cogently from the respective individual behaviors of the basic entities. Behavior is defined as the observable change of state.

Locality: Effects are local, the only way an effect can be propagated is via interconnection, either physical or abstract one, to other parts. Such effects can be localized; they are important to deduce a causal explanation.

Function: Function has to be separated from behavior. Human artifacts have specific functions which can also be described as the mapping from the behavior to the goal (purpose) of a device. For example, the finger of a clock moves around 360 degrees (behavior) and indicates the time (function). If two things have the same function they may be interchanged in some assembling (a digital and an analog watch, for example).

Class-wide assumptions: Qualitative reasoning assumes, similar to the object-oriented programming paradigm, that distinct objects can be grouped into a unique class, representing

---

[2] A dynamic system is described by a tuple $\langle T, U, X, Y, \delta, \lambda\rangle$ where T denotes the time base, U the input value, X the state and Y the output value set. δ, $U \times X \times T \rightarrow X$, is called the state transition and λ, $U \times X \times T \rightarrow Y$, the output function. In the continuous case, for example, $T = \mathbf{R}$ and $X = \mathbf{R}^n$. For a detailed discussion see IV.1.

just the common features. Hence, each qualitative description denotes an entire class. Thus, laws for one component are generic and not specific for a particular object.

No-function-in-structure: A model should be described by its structure and behavioral primitives, the overall behavior follows from this description. The description of a basic component of a device should not anticipate the function of the entire device in order to ensure modularity. In connection with the principle of locality it is stated that laws for one component must not refer to any other component.

Reduced quantity space: Values of variables, normally based on real numbers, are mapped to qualitative values, represented by reduced and at least partially ordered sets of values.[3] These sets may vary from small ones with just three members {+, -, 0} - denoting the positive, the negative range and zero - to bigger ones with more members - typically three to seven on both the positive and negative axis. These qualitative values represent intervals - crisp or overlapping - on the real number line. But the quantity space may also consist of a variable number of members, ordered according to their magnitudes or other quantities defined beforehand, so-called landmark values. On these qualitative value sets, also called quantity spaces, special operations, based on interval arithmetic, have to be defined, resulting in ambiguous situations because of the qualitative representations.

Reduced relationships: Between variables, describing attributes of objects, only a reduced set of relationships is available. However, not only simple algebraic operations are defined, but also complex functional dependencies may be used. These functional dependencies normally are of a simple, either positive or negative monotonic form with respect to the qualitative value representation. Additionally, qualitative derivative relationships are defined as the main mechanisms responsible for the changes of state.

Reduced representation of time: Since qualitative reasoning deals with generic descriptions of situations and their time-dependent evolution, it only produces a time ordered sequence of well distinguishable events. It is described what may happen before, at or after some occurrence, but no exact information about specific time points or duration is available. This corresponds with the reduced representation of quantities.

These last points reflect the low level of information, which is either not available or not put into the model. And these principles denote the fact that qualitative reasoning maps continuous processes to discrete sequences of states with a finite and discrete state space. It aims at providing a compact qualitative description, concentrating on the relevant points. This fits in well with the basic objective of qualitative reasoning to build models of the real system with respect to the cognitive processes of the human modeler, since the perception of what is relevant depends on the latter. The principles of no-function-in-structure, locality and compositionality, on the other side, are important for modeling and allow for constructing a whole out of single components. These principles are frequently applied in natural science, for example in computer science structured programming obeys these principles to ensure modularity in the software engineering process. They are, however, explicitly ignored in new research fields such as molecular computing. [Conrad 92], for example, distinguishes between programmable and non-programmable self-assembling structures. The latter are said to

[3] It should be noted, however, that also in "classical modeling" continuous variables have to be mapped to a finite set of discrete values as soon as the model has to run on a digital computer. Thus, continuous system simulation on a computer does not exist. From this point of view qualitative reasoning with its reduced value set represents just one extreme of a well-known circumstance.

possess a multiplicity of interactions and to have more computational search power. In this approach, which is beyond our discussion, it is suggested that structure holds a key to intelligence as well.

4. A Short History

The works of [Hayes 79] and [Hayes 85a] stand at the origin of the approach to formalize everyday common-sense knowledge and to introduce the term Naive Physics. It is stated that one of the central problems in AI is that of efficient search strategies in a discrete problem space. For the evaluation of search strategies a sufficiently large test bed is necessary. Thus, the formalization of common-sense knowledge regarding the physical environment of man would provide such a large test bed.[4]

The works of [de Kleer 75] and [de Kleer 77] describing NEWTON and qualitative reasoning in mechanics are other important and seminal contributions. Their main scope is the formalization of "pre-physics" knowledge. The prototypical application deals with the roller coaster problem, i.e. the movement of a cart on a track. Rather than to exactly solve the quantitative equations, it is important to understand the problem, to know when and how to apply which formula or model and to formalize qualitatively the possible outcomes, e.g. the cart flies away or it finishes a circle. A further, and until today one of the most important areas of application, is that of electronic circuits, the simulation of their behavior or the diagnosis in the case of faulty behavior [de Kleer 79]. Another important piece of history is Forbus' FROB program [Forbus 80], dealing mainly with spatial reasoning in the two-dimensional space, whereas de Kleer's roller-coaster application only took into consideration the dimension of time.

The most wide-spreading works were published in 1984 [Bobrow 84] with the work of [de Kleer and Brown 84], [Forbus 84] and [Kuipers 84]. The seminal volume 24 of the Artificial Intelligence journal in 1984 had a deep influence on the scientific community and presented in a very compact way the state of the art and the different approaches used in qualitative reasoning. Three approaches - ontologies or views (as indicated in Fig. 2) of reality and relationships between entities within these realities[5] - were presented by the different authors:

- *Device-centered ontology* [de Kleer and Brown 84]: A device is seen as an assembly of connected components. Behavioral constraints - derived from general physical laws - govern the behavior of the device.

- *Process-centered ontology* [Forbus 84]: Processes are the basic primitive, they influence and change objects, i.e. the values of their variables. These variables describe the attributes of individuals which participate in a specific situation.

- *Constraint-based ontology* [Kuipers 84]: This ontology differs in its approach to modeling, it refers directly to existing mathematical descriptions. A device or a situation is described by a set of variables and qualitative differential equations (QDE). These qualitative equations, which constrain a system's behavior, are derived from known or presumed equations, given in a canonical form.

Apart from and also earlier to this development in the artificial intelligence community, other areas such as mathematical analysis, system theory, economics or automatic control were engaged in qualitative system analysis. Comparative statics can be mentioned as an important

---

[4] It is interesting to note the implicit assumption that the description of the physical environment is not a problem. It seems that the modeling problem does not exist in this not very simple case.

[5] Ontology is defined by [Strawson 59] as the conceptual definition and cataloguing of entities and relationships composing the mind representation of the real world.

development of this kind in economics [Ritschard 83]. This technique may be used to predict qualitatively the direction of change of some endogenous variables given the direction of change of exogenous variables and the signs of the partial derivatives of the corresponding system of equations. In the automatic control community interest was laid on the derivation of qualitative system properties - such as stability - from system characteristics [Travé-Massuyès and Kaszkurewicz 86]. These studies focused mainly on linear systems. Thus, qualitative reasoning is not new and not an exclusive benefit of AI.

After the publication of volume 24 of Artificial Intelligence qualitative reasoning developed into an autonomous field of AI. Several workshops were, e.g. Lugano 1990 or Austin 1991, and are still organized. Today qualitative reasoning is a must in international conferences on AI and it has demonstrated its practical usefulness in different areas - as described earlier. In this development, interest turned more and more toward the problem of modeling. In the early works it was nearly always assumed that the structure of a system can be completely identified - the works were based on well-known examples - and emphasis was put on the demonstration of the power of the applied reasoning methods. In these early cases, modeling was easy, however it is exactly this task where qualitative reasoning may provide its most important contribution.

In the last years criticisms on the recent development in the field have emerged [Williams and de Kleer 91] and a discussion about this approach has been launched between the simulation and AI community [Fishwick and Zeigler 91]. Several editions of collected papers, for example [Weld and de Kleer 90], [Fishwick and Luker 91] and [Faltings and Struss 92], have been published. Yet, up to now no standard textbook has been written. Hence, no agreement on the notation and even the semantics of different terms exists in this field. Such deficiency, however, may at the same time indicate the strength of qualitative reasoning. As an interdisciplinary approach it is steadily attracting researchers from different fields. Furthermore, qualitative reasoning has demonstrated its ability to contribute to other areas, for example, classical fields of AI such as expert systems have been improved by the introduction of time and deep structure, or the importance of structuring knowledge on different levels has been recognized in simulation.

Qualitative reasoning deals with the qualitative description of dynamic systems, taking also into consideration human cognitive representations. The qualitative description may or may not include causal relationships. These relationships - together with the qualitative description of variables - are used in an algorithmic process to generate the time-dependent behavior in the form of a discrete sequence of states. This result corresponds to a causal explanation of the system's behavior. Thus, it can be stated that qualitative reasoning also participates in the creation of a cognitive theory of non-numerical process descriptions which can be mapped onto a digital computer.

Part II

The Basics of Qualitative Reasoning

This part describes the basic approaches used in qualitative reasoning as well as the underlying qualitative calculus and the different dimensions of mapping a quantitative model onto a qualitative one. Additionally, we provide a first classification of these methods. We separate the description of the modeling perspectives of the respective approaches in the next chapter from the detailed discussion of their specific reasoning techniques in chapter II.4 in order to underline the basic principles and their differences. However, also short descriptions of the reasoning mechanisms are provided in the first chapter. We use the following notation: if x denotes a variable or quantity in a numerical model, [x] or x denotes its qualitative equivalent. The same is true for operations: addition becomes ⊕, multiplication ⊗ and so on.[6]

1. The Main Approaches

In the following we will present the three main ontologies, their modeling perspectives and their way of representing the results of their reasoning processes; the latter most will also be described shortly. In this discussion we will concentrate on the classical presentations of these techniques and will use the examples demonstrated originally. We think that they still provide the best illustration of the basic principles, their similarities and differences. Subsequent and recent developments will be discussed later.

1.1 The Device-centered Ontology

This approach of [de Kleer and Brown 84] concentrates on the description of physical devices, where a device is seen as a set of individual components and conduits. The latter denote connections between components. Components may only be connected by means of so-called terminals or nodes. Interconnected components constitute a larger component, which in turn may be connected to other components. Thus, the modeling approach is a hierarchical one, starting with the simple and basic components. Electricity or material such as liquid may flow in these devices. Both modeling primitives, components and conduits, have associated sets of confluences which are multivariable linear equations, each parameter being either a qualitative variable or the qualitative derivative of a variable. These equations constrain the elementary behavior of the modeling primitives. Behavior is described in terms of the attributes of the processed material. For example for fluid, attributes are pressure and volumetric flow; for electricity, voltage and current; for translational conduits, force and velocity. Further attributes may describe physical properties of a device such as the area available for flow.

The entire set of confluences depicts the single components, their interconnections and the processing of material. The last one represents the qualitative counterpart of Kirchhoff's law for current and voltage. The so-called no-function-in-structure principle is respected, as

---

[6] Furthermore, we also use lower case letters to denote a quantitative boundary value of an interval and *italics* (e.g. *l*) to denote a qualitative landmark. We will extend this notation when necessary and try to keep consistent. However, this will be a hard task since up to now - as already mentioned - no largely accepted and consistent notation exists.

confluences describe only the behavior of the respective part, i.e. component or conduit, they do not state any function about the entire device. Confluences which describe the processed material obey this principle since they can easily be extended or limited by the number of participating physical parts. The entire set of confluences provides a description of both the static and dynamic features of a device and are based on physical laws. Given such structural description of a device and the laws of its components, the scope of this approach is to produce a total envisionment which contains the set of all possible future states of the system and the possible transitions between these states. This result of the reasoning process corresponds to a causal explanation of the overall behavior.

Real numbers are mapped to qualitative values by means of the operator [ ]. [x] (or x as already stated) indicates the qualitative value of variable x with the set of possible values {+, -, 0}, thus []: $\mathbf{R}^+ \rightarrow +$, $\mathbf{R}^- \rightarrow -$ and $\{0\} \rightarrow 0$. Supplementary to the information about its sign, a variable is further described by the qualitative value of its derivative, written as ∂x. ∂x denotes [dx/dt] and may also take any value from the set {+, -, 0}, indicating whether variable x is increasing, decreasing or not changing at all. Thus, ∂ describes the dynamics of the system, its change in time and the direction of change.[7]

The operations ⊕ and ⊗, the qualitative counterparts to addition and multiplication defined on **R**, are defined on this limited value set. The table for addition is not completely filled, the symbol ? denotes an open result. Thus, the sign algebra of the device-centered approach is not closed with respect to addition. Since + indicates (0, ∞) and - (-∞, 0), the operation + ⊕ - has no result.[8]

⊕	+	-	0
+	+	?	+
-	?	-	-
0	+	-	0

⊗	+	-	0
+	+	-	0
-	-	+	0
0	0	0	0

The following example from [de Kleer and Brown 84] and [de Kleer and Bobrow 84] may explain this approach in some detail:

[7] It should be noted that the symbol ∂ denotes an operator, whereas ∂x describes a qualitative feature of the variable x. As we will see in the following, the value of ∂x is not obtained by differentiating variable x, but by using qualitative information about the variable itself, i.e. value differences at two subsequent time steps, or about other variables.

[8] Subtraction can be expressed by including the negative of a quantity, i.e variable: -[-x] = [x].

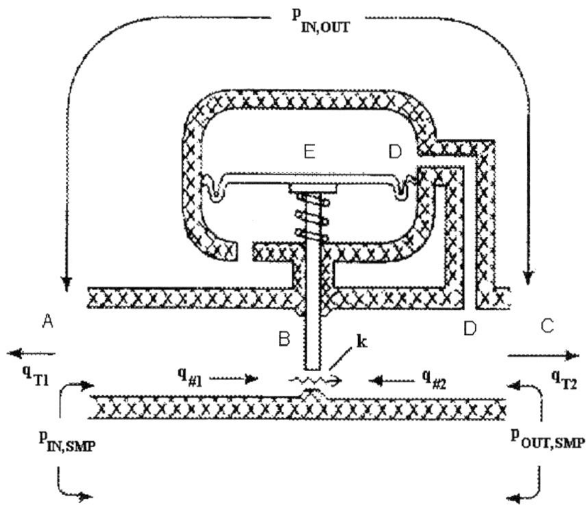

Fig. 3: Pressure regulator

The pressure regulator in Fig. 3 has to maintain a constant output pressure at point C even though the supply (at point A) and the load (at point C) may vary. Variable $q_{\#1}$ denotes the flow into the valve, $p_{IN,OUT}$ the pressure drop across the valve, and k the area available for flow with respect to the valve's position. The subscripts already refer to Fig. 4, showing the topological structure of this device. The arrows in Fig. 3 denote the directions of flow or point to the respective reference points for pressure-like variables. Such variables need a common sump, thus the sump SMP has to be introduced. The meaning of the remaining variables will be explained later when the entire set of confluences of the pressure regulator is described. A causal explanation of the work of the regulator may be given as follows:

An increase in source A increases the pressure drop across the valve (B). At this point the flow is proportional to the pressure, hence, it will also increase. This flow, in turn, will increase the pressure at C. The latter is sensed at D, causing the diaphragm (E) to move down against the spring pressure. This downward movement tends to close the valve and thus to reduce the flow. Now that the flow is restricted, the output pressure will increase much less than it would have otherwise. The central idea is that the device senses its own output to adjust its behavior. Such systems show the feature of oscillation due to the delay in sensing, the following qualitative description is able to detect such an oscillating behavior without any quantitative analysis.

Introducing the notion of a so-called mode of operation, we can derive three major modes: the valve working, closed or totally open.[9] These three different working modes result in three different sets of constraining confluences (if the condition is satisfied then the confluences of a mode are valid):

OPEN:	if $k = k_{MAX}$,	then	$[p_{IN,OUT}] \equiv 0$,	$\partial p_{IN,OUT} \equiv 0$
WORKING:	if $0 < k < k_{MAX}$,	then	$[p_{IN,OUT}] \equiv [q_{\#1}]$,	$\partial p_{IN,OUT} \oplus \partial k \ominus \partial q_{\#1} \equiv 0$
CLOSED:	if $k = 0$,	then	$[q_{\#1}] \equiv 0$,	$\partial q_{\#1} \equiv 0$

[9] The original literature also uses the notion of state, which is misleading as we will see in the following.

Hence, in the mode of operation "working", i.e. if the area of flow is greater than 0 and smaller than k_{MAX}, then the two constraints are valid: $p_{IN,OUT}$ and $q_{\#1}$ are qualitatively equal; the qualitative changes of the values of pressure and the flow area minus the qualitative change of the flow sum up to 0. Qualitative equality ≡ of two expressions has to be read as [x] ≡ [y] is satisfied if [x] and [y] evaluate to the same sign or one of [x] and [y] evaluates to "?".[10] The motivation is the following: if we assume that x and y are two quantitative expressions which contain some variables and that x = y, then consequently [x] ≡ [y]. If we assign values to the variables of x and y, then the respective qualitative values are also assigned to their qualitative representations. If both [x] and [y] are non-ambiguous, i.e. different from "?", they must be equal, x and y having the same sign. However, if one qualitative expression produces an undefined result, i.e. "?" (for example, + ⊕ -), then nothing can be stated about the result of the underlying quantitative expression, it may have any sign. Therefore, it may be compatible with any other one. In other terms, qualitative equality expresses the possibility that two terms be equal. However, it should be noted, that with respect to the defined qualitative mapping [] and the operation tables, the symbol "?" may only appear as the result of a qualitative operation; a distinct qualitative variable used in a qualitative expression always has a well-defined qualitative value.

The constraining equation of the pressure regulator in the mode "working" can be obtained in the following way, based on a well-known physical equation describing the flow through an orifice and the following rules:

$[a \times b] \rightarrow [a] \otimes [b],\ 0 \oplus [a] \rightarrow [a],$
$0 \otimes [a] \rightarrow 0,\ [+] \otimes [a] \rightarrow [a],\ [-] \otimes [a] \rightarrow [-a].$

$q = \gamma k \sqrt{\frac{2p}{\rho}}$, where $p > 0$, γ is the discharge coefficient of the orifice and ρ is the mass density of fluid. Qualitative transformation, based on the above rules, results in
$[q] \equiv [\gamma] \otimes [k] \otimes [(2p/\rho)^{1/2}] \equiv [+] \otimes [+] \otimes [(2p/\rho)^{1/2}] \equiv [p]$.[11]

To obtain the constraints on the derivatives, the original equation has to be differentiated
$dq/dt = \gamma\, (2p/\rho)^{1/2}\, dk/dt + \gamma k/\rho\, (\rho/2p)^{1/2}\, dp/dt.$

Qualitatively this corresponds to
$\partial q \equiv ([+] \otimes [(2p/\rho)^{1/2}] \otimes \partial k) \oplus ([+] \otimes [k] \otimes [(\rho/2p)^{1/2}] \otimes \partial p)$, thus
$\partial q \equiv ([p] \otimes \partial k) \oplus ([k] \otimes [p] \otimes \partial p)$
and with $k > 0$ and $p > 0$ $\partial q \equiv \partial k \oplus \partial p$ is obtained, which is written as $\partial p \oplus \partial k \ominus \partial q \equiv 0$.

In order to deduce the oscillating behavior of the device, a more detailed description of the pressure regulator is given, distinguishing the individual components sensor, spring, valve and mass of the valve. The respective conduits are named IN, OUT, and FP. The conduits IN and OUT transport fluid, the conduit FP force. This is shown in Fig. 4, the structural counterpart of Fig. 3. It identifies the individual parts as well as their assembling by means of conduits. The valve's mass is represented by a separate object with mass. T_1 and T_2 are terminals to the external world. The lettering #1 and #2 denote terminals of the valve, the

---

[10] Qualitative equality may, in fact, be interpreted as an intersection of intervals, where "?" denotes the interval $(-\infty, \infty)$; see chapter II.2.

[11] In this case k (area of flow) is substituted by + since it is positive in the mode working.

unnamed bottom terminal of the valve controls how much area is available for the flow and how much force is exerted by the spring. Terminal "-" of the pressure sensor is attached to the regulator output, terminal "+" to the reference SMP. Increased pressure results in less area available for flow. Pressure-like variables have a common reference; for electricity it is represented by the ground, for fluid systems by the main sump. In the following we will use this figure to provide a more detailed description of the pressure regulator in the mode "working".

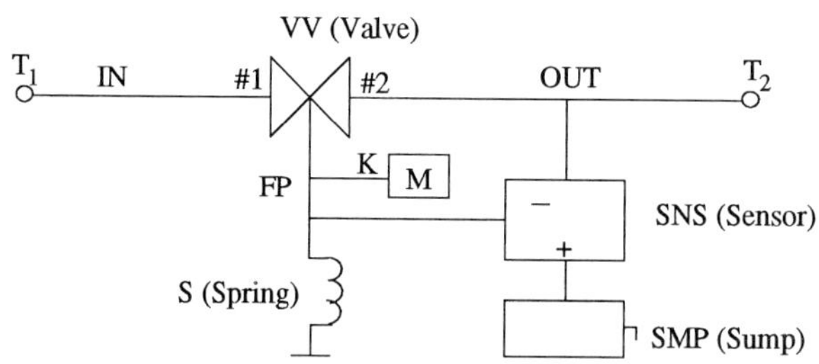

Fig. 4: Topological description of the pressure regulator, identifying components and connections

These individual parts have their annotated local confluences. Two general rules are assumed to be valid which refer to the processed material and which are used in the assembling process. The first one is the so-called condition of continuity. It states that conduits, i.e. interconnections, conserve instantaneously flowing material: what is entering at one side has to exit at the other, the sum of flows in conduits connected at one point having to be zero. This corresponds to Kirchhoff's law of current. The second rule is the condition of compatibility and resembles Kirchhoff's law of voltage. It states that - since components, in contrast to conduits, may also store something - gains and losses (for example of voltage or also pressure) around any loop in a device have to be equalized. These laws also hold for fluid or translational forces. For example, the condition of continuity for force states that, since connections (where two or more physical objects attach) are massless, forces at any connection sum up to zero. These rules have a modular form, enabling easy modification of structures. However, it should be noted that modeling still constitutes a problem, because the modeler has to design the network which describes the device and to decide which of the confluences are fundamental for the respective components and interconnections.

The following constraining equations of the pressure regulator can be identified, following general descriptions used in physics. They are attached to the individual components and connections and obey the mentioned conditions. The subscripts refer to the respective terminals and conduits (see Fig. 3 and 4):[12]

Valve's mass M: The effect of force on an object with mass m is f = ma. Since the mass m is always greater than 0, it follows that [f] = [dv/dt], where variable a denotes acceleration and v velocity. This is written as

$$[f_{K(M)}] \equiv \partial v_{FP}.$$

$f_{K(M)}$ being the force pushing the valve's mass upward and v_{FP} being the upward velocity of the valve. v_{FP} is directly related to k, the area available for flow.

[12] The coordinate system is chosen so that open positions of the valve correspond to positive values, closing activities to negative values.

Spring S: The model of the spring has a dual form of the previous model of an object with mass, i.e. f = cx. This is derived from the so-called Hooke's law (the tension in a spring is proportional to its extension: f = -cx), c being a constant and positive, x denoting the position. Since the direction of the velocity is inverted and points upward, the sign is changed. By differentiating this equation (df/dt = dx/dt), by using v instead of dx/dt and by using the qualitative notion the following confluence is obtained, where the force $f_{\#1(S)}$ pulls the spring upward:

$$\partial f_{\#1(S)} \equiv [v_{FP}].$$

Valve VV: This confluence follows directly from the previous confluence of the pressure regulator in the mode "working", however, $[v_{FP}]$ is used instead of ∂k:

$$\partial p_{IN,OUT} \oplus [v_{FP}] \ominus \partial q_{\#1(VV)} \equiv 0.$$

$p_{IN,OUT}$ is the pressure drop from input to output and $q_{\#1(VV)}$ the flow from terminal #1 into the valve. Additionally, a load is connected to the pressure regulator, $p_{OUT,SMP}$ denoting the pressure at the output side:

$$\partial q_{T2} \ominus \partial p_{OUT,SMP} \equiv 0.$$

Sensor SNS: The force pushing the valve's mass and the force pulling the spring vary inversely with the output pressure:

$$\partial p_{OUT,SMP} \oplus \partial f_{\#1(S)} \oplus \partial f_{K(M)} \equiv 0.$$

Confluence due to compatibility condition: $\partial p_{IN,OUT} \oplus \partial p_{OUT,SMP} \ominus \partial p_{IN,SMP} \equiv 0.$

Confluences due to continuity condition: $f_{\#2(S)}$ pulls the spring in the opposite direction of $f_{\#1(S)}$:

$$\partial f_{\#1(S)} \oplus \partial f_{\#2(S)} \equiv 0.$$
$$\partial q_{T1} \oplus \partial q_{\#1(VV)} \equiv 0.$$
$$\partial q_{\#1(VV)} \oplus \partial q_{\#2(VV)} \equiv 0.$$
$$\partial q_{T2} \oplus \partial q_{\#2(VV)} \equiv 0.$$ [13]

This is the entire set of constraining equations which describe the respective components and connections. They can be used to derive the behavior of the entire device. The states of the system are described by the combinations of values of selected qualitative variables. The state variables, i.e. those variables which describe the state of the system, are chosen from the set of mixed confluences. These are confluences where both qualitative variables and derivatives are contained. The non-derivative variables are chosen since their values describe the state of the system. In our case, these are the two variables v_{FP} and $f_{K(M)}$, denoting the velocity of and the force on the valve's mass. Thus, the state of the system is described by the state of valve. Since the value set contains only three members, the total set of states is finite and can be easily identified. The combination of their values creates a state space of nine members.

This is described in the following table, where also the values of the respective derivatives at the specific states are shown, assuming an input signal of $\partial p_{IN,SMP} \equiv$ "+", an increasing pressure at the source.

[13] A similar set of constraining equations can be identified, correlating the magnitudes of the variables, e.g. $[q_{\#1(VV)}] \oplus [q_{\#2(VV)}] \equiv 0$. But they are not used in the reasoning process about the dynamic behavior.

State State specifications	1 $v_{FP} = 0$ $f_{K(M)} = 0$ 1	2 $v_{FP} = 0$ $f_{K(M)} < 0$ 1	3 $v_{FP} < 0$ $f_{K(M)} < 0$ 1 2 3	4 $v_{FP} < 0$ $f_{K(M)} = 0$ 1 2 3	5 $v_{FP} < 0$ $f_{K(M)} > 0$ 1 2 3	6 $v_{FP} = 0$ $f_{K(M)} > 0$ 1	7 $v_{FP} > 0$ $f_{K(M)} > 0$ 1	8 $v_{FP} > 0$ $f_{K(M)} = 0$ 1	9 $v_{FP} > 0$ $f_{K(M)} < 0$ 1
∂q_{T1}	-	-	- - -	- - -	- - -	-	-	-	-
∂q_{T2}	+	+	+ + +	+ + +	+ + +	+	+	+	+
$\partial q_{\#1(VV)}$	+	+	+ + +	+ + +	+ + +	+	+	+	+
$\partial q_{\#2(VV)}$	-	-	- - -	- - -	- - -	-	-	-	-
$\partial p_{IN,OUT}$	+	+	+ + +	+ + +	+ + +	+	+	+	+
$\partial p_{OUT,SMP}$	+	+	+ + +	+ + +	+ + +	+	+	+	+
$\partial f_{\#1(S)}$	0	0	- - -	- - -	- - -	0	+	+	+
$\partial f_{\#2(S)}$	0	0	+ + +	+ + +	+ + +	0	-	-	-
$\partial f_{K(M)}$	-	-	- 0 +	- 0 +	- 0 +	-	-	-	-
∂v_{FP}	0	-	- - -	0 0 0	+ + +	+	+	0	+

The qualitative values of the derivatives in the respective states can be derived as follows: in state 1, $\partial f_{\#1(S)}$ is 0 as v_{FP} is 0. As $f_{K(M)} = 0$, also $\partial v_{FP} \equiv 0$. The other values follow from the propagation of the values of the variables by means of the respective confluences, i.e. those qualitative values assigned to variables which are not contradictory to the set of confluences. This assignment procedure corresponds to the simultaneous solution process of a set of algebraic equations and uses a combination of a constraint propagation and a generate-test procedure. It is based on the qualitative operation tables previously defined. However, since the defined qualitative algebra is not closed with respect to addition, multiple solutions exist. In state 3, for example, $\partial f_{K(M)}$ may have all three possible values for satisfying the set of confluences and therefore three so-called interpretations of this state exist. The concept of qualitative equality is critical for this procedure: given a confluence of $\partial a \oplus \partial b \equiv 0$ and ∂a having a value of "+", ∂b has to be "-", since $+ \oplus - \equiv ?$, which is the only possibility to satisfy the qualitative equality, i.e. $? \equiv 0$.[14]

[14] However, when satisfying a constraint of the form $a \oplus b \oplus c \equiv 0$, additional rules are necessary: if a is "+" and b is "-", this results in ?. Now c may have any value to satisfy the constraint. But this needs rules like $? \oplus - \equiv ?$, $? \oplus + \equiv ?$ and $? \oplus 0 \equiv ?$, which are not described in [de Kleer and Brown 84]. See also the discussion in chapter II.3.

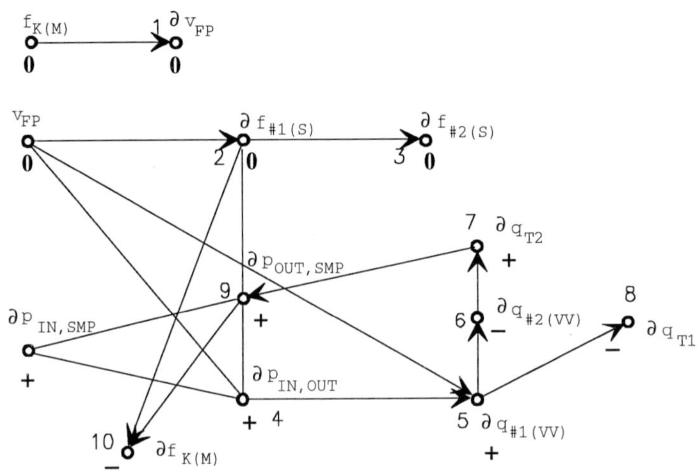

Fig. 5: Value assignment procedure in a set of confluences

The values of the state variables and of the respective input variables serve as starting points and are propagated by means of the constraining equations to the other variables. Arcs denote the direction of value propagation. Lines without arrows indicate that variables are related by confluences, but no influence occurred along this line. Numbers refer to the sequence of propagation steps. If not enough information to assign values to variables is available, the propagation within a state gets stuck (e.g. node 4 of Fig. 5). In this case all possible value assignments have to be considered. To reduce these ambiguous situations, heuristics are applied which give reasons for assumptions about unknown values of variables. For example, in Fig. 5 at node 4, the component heuristic is used in the confluence $\partial p_{IN,OUT} \oplus [v_{FP}] \ominus \partial q_{\#1(VV)} \equiv 0$ to set $\partial p_{IN,OUT}$ to "+"; consequently, at node 5, also $\partial q_{\#1(VV)}$ is set to "+". Without such heuristics the set of possible assignments, i.e. interpretation, would be much greater.[15] These heuristics are

the *component heuristic:* if something acts upon a component and nothing else is known, the component reacts as if the others things were negligible,

the *conduit heuristic:* if some component forces things into or sucks things out of the conduit, the pressure rises or drops respectively, and

the *confluence heuristic:* if some, but not all, variables of a confluence are known, propagate the values of the known variables as if the unknown variables had a value of zero. This represents a generalization of the previous two heuristics.

Based on the previous table and the qualitative values of the derivatives, the following envisionment graph can be produced. The graph denotes a discrete representation of the state space, indicating with circles instantaneous states and with squares states which exist for some time interval. The behavior of a continuous process is thus described in a compact form, concentrating on its qualitative features. States with an instant duration at interesting points interchange with states which summarize several, but "uninteresting", behaviors. The arrows denote state transitions. They follow from the signs of the derivatives of the state variables:

---

[15] Solving the set of confluences without the use of these assumption - just by a "normal" value propagation and generate-test procedure - would result into 5 interpretations for states 3, 4 and 5 and three interpretations for states 7, 8 and 9 with additional values assigned to the respective qualitative derivatives.

for example, since in state 1 $\partial f_{K(M)}$ is negative and $f_{K(M)} = 0$, it follows that $f_{K(M)}$ immediately has to become negative. State 2 is, thus, an immediate successor of state 1.[16]

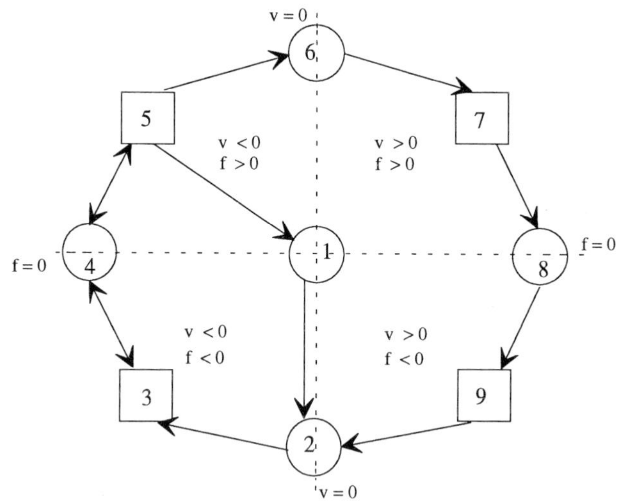

Fig. 6: Envisionment graph describing the potential behaviors of the pressure regulator

This envisionment graph shows the dynamic behavior of the press regulator under the assumption of an input $\partial p_{IN,SMP} \equiv$ "+" and a frictionless spring. This envisionment graph allows for answering a question like 'May such a pressure regulator show an oscillating behavior ?', which is indeed the case. Thus, qualitative analysis gives the correct answer. However, the graph indicates all possible behaviors; they are equally likely, none can be excluded. For example, in state 3 the value of the force on the valve is ambiguous. The closing of the valve could reduce the output pressure enough to equal the force of the spring, causing a transition to state 4. On the other hand, the rise in the input pressure could continue to dominate behavior and thus the output continues to rise. Thus, it cannot be concluded whether a state transition occurs or not. Furthermore, no information about time durations is given, it is just shown that instantaneous states are followed by states which last for some time, the real behavior might be compressed or stretched. The state diagram is a complete description of all possible behaviors - including, however, also non-valid ones - of a generic device. By refining the description, we would obtain more specific behaviors: for example, setting the input to zero would result in a permanent oscillation or adding friction to the description of the spring would show that oscillation eventually damps out.

The envisionment graph looks much like a finite state automaton, the directed arcs and the respective interpretations specify conditions under which a transition may occur. The construction of the graph and the deduction of the transitions correspond to the generation and explanation of behavior. It is based on specific rules (derived from mathematical analysis; they are valid for the other approaches as well; see also chapter II.3.). Such rules can be listed as follows:

Continuity rule:[17] each variable changes "continuously". A variable cannot change in one step from + to - (and vice versa), it has to pass the value of 0 first,

[16] In state 3 a transition may only happen if $\partial f_{K(M)} \equiv$ "+".

[17] This rule has to be distinguished from the condition of continuity, resembling Kirchhoff's law of current.

Limit rule: only an increasing (decreasing) variable $\partial x \equiv +$ (-) can produce state transitions. Furthermore, only if $\partial x \neq 0$, x may move to the distinguished value of zero,

Equality change rule: if $\partial x \neq 0$ and $[x] \equiv 0$, then the state terminates immediately, as denoted by circles in the previous envisionment graph,

Epsilon ordering rule: any change with respect to the above rule occurs first, if [x] changes to 0 and [y] changes from 0, then [y] changes first,

Contradiction avoidance rule: contradictions arise if confluences cannot be satisfied, i.e. no assignment of qualitative values to variables satisfies the confluence. If a state is contradictory, a transition to it is impossible,

Causality rule: a component will not change state unless it is acted upon.

The entire reasoning process works as follows: initially, the state space is created, then, based on the values of the state variables, the confluences are resolved, possibly resulting in several interpretations per state. Based on the values of the derivatives of the state variables, the state transitions are identified thereafter. In this sense the qualitative description of a variable's derivative defines the change in time. And finally, specific ordering rules may filter some of the available transitions. Thus, we can identify two main steps: first, the value propagation within one state, i.e. determining all sets of values which satisfy the confluences; and secondly, the identification of state transitions. These two steps correspond to intra- and interstate behavior, respectively.

The transition to neighboring states can be interpreted as following a causal path, a path along time. In a transition to subsequent states it is obvious what happens first, thus, what is influencing and what is being influenced. In contrast, no time step occurs during the propagation process within a state, causal influences cannot be identified. This is due to the implicit notion of confluences, even if these confluences are derived from explicit functions (see, for example, the derivation of $\partial p \oplus \partial k \ominus \partial q \equiv 0$). To maintain the notion of causality also in this circumstance, [de Kleer and Brown 84] define the concept of "mythical causality", which - together with the mentioned heuristics - forms the base of their value propagation mechanism. They assign causality to the sequence of value assignment steps as shown in Fig. 5. This sequence - together with the sequence of state transitions - is used to provide a causal explanation, to describe how the physical device works. However, this causal interpretation needs a rather "philosophical" motivation: to satisfy a constraining equation within a state, some time step below a noticeable grain size is virtually assumed. If a constraint has the form $a \equiv b$ and a has changed its value, b will change as well. But as a is influenced "earlier", it takes some time until b changes, at least at some causal level of explanation.[18]

[18] In the case of simultaneous feedback loops this approach may break such loops by inserting a "mythical" time delay. Such a delay allows to distinguish between cause and effect (see also chapter III.1).

1.2 The Process-centered Ontology

This approach represents a more abstract point of view. Reality is described by a set of objects and processes which may change the situation, i.e. state, of such objects [Forbus 84]. In addition, the relationships between objects, also called individuals and described by means of variables, may have a very complex form. Due to the concept of a process and the specific relationships between variables, this ontology - contrary to the device-centered approach - allows for the modeling of causal influences. All influences on variables stem from processes, these being the only primitives which may change the state of individuals.

Variables are described by both amount (A) and derivative (D), which may have additional information about magnitude and sign. The functions A and D map from variables - also called quantities - to numbers:

A_m magnitude of the amount,
A_s sign of the amount,
D_m magnitude of the derivative,
D_s sign of the derivative.

This representation contains more information than the previously described approach. In addition to the signs, also information about magnitudes is integrated. The latter information consists of the relationship of these magnitudes with magnitudes of other variables or with previously defined distinguishable values, also called limit points. These magnitudes form a partially ordered quantity space as shown in the following figure:

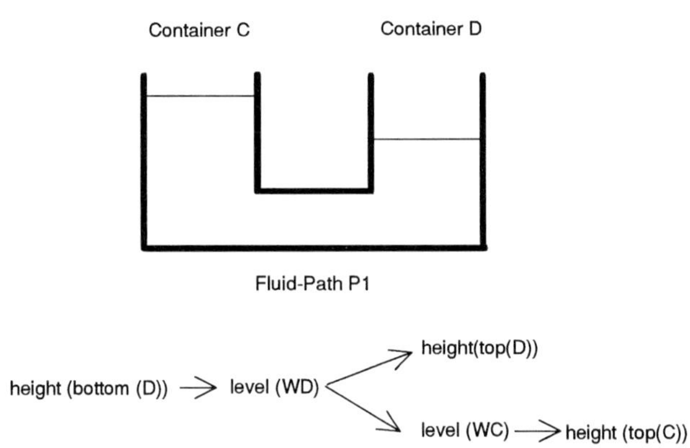

Fig. 7: Two connected containers and their partially ordered quantity space[19]

The letter W indicates the water in the respective container - WD being the water in container D - and the arcs the partial ordering relationship. Functions such as height or level denote mappings from the respective objects to their attributes, i.e. variables. Thus, this quantity space is described by a finer grain size and also a more flexible qualitative value set than that of [de Kleer and Brown 84], taking into account that multiple and previously known information about relationships between variables exists. Qualitative operations for signs such

[19] In the following notation we will use helvetica in the process-centered approach. In addition, predicates and relations (such as Fluid-Path) are capitalized, functions (e.g., level) are in lower case, sorts (e.g., *piece-of-stuff*) are written in italics, variables (e.g., p) in lower case and distinct objects (e.g., WD) in upper case letters. As we will see, names of views as well as processes can be thought of as relations or predicates on individuals.

as ⊕ and ⊗ are defined as before, however, in the case of ambiguous results, the information about the magnitudes of variables can be used. Operations on amounts, i.e. numbers, are straightforward.

Similar to the device-centered ontology this approach starts from individual objects and variables which describe their attributes. However, it includes supplementary concepts such as views, processes and histories. A view describes a specific situation in which some objects may be, indicating the relationship between individuals and their qualitative variables. The individuals must exist before a view may become active. A process may change these relationships, it represents the only primitive to change the state of a device or a situation. A history describes the trajectories of the single individuals and indicates the change of the entire system. These concepts introduce an explicit notion of time. Individuals cooperate when their histories meet, i.e. when processes create relationships between them. Thus, histories describe the behavior of individuals and not just of single variables. The following view describes the situation where some stuff is in a container:

```
Individual View Contained-Stuff (p)
    Individuals
      con a container
      sub a substance
    Preconditions
      Contain-Substance(con,sub)
    QuantityCondition
      A[amount-of-in(sub,con)] > 0
    Relations
      There is p ∈ piece-of-stuff
      amount-of(p) = amount-of-in(sub,con)
      made-of(p) = sub
      location(p) = inside(con)
```

A view is active when its preconditions and quantity conditions are valid. Preconditions and quantity conditions can be distinguished as follows: the former describe the physical (material) condition for a valid view, whereas the latter represent the time-varying entry points. They contain statements about inequalities between variables as well as whether other views or processes are active. In other terms, valid preconditions wait for the respective quantity conditions to activate a view. Quantity conditions may be changed dynamically by processes, whereas preconditions are beyond the reach of processes. Relations define what is imposed between variables of the participating individuals. A view can be seen as a means that describes the state of some individuals of a system, which is more complicated than just a combination of single variable values.

The previous description of view Contained-Stuff(p) can be translated into the following logical notation (showing just the time invariant part):[20]

```
∀ c ∈ container ∀ s ∈ substance
   Container(c) ∧ Substance(s) ⇒
      (∃ VI ∈ view-instance
      con(VI) = c ∧ sub(VI) = s
      ∧ (∃ p ∈ piece-of-stuff
         location(p) = inside(c) ∧ made-of(p) = s))
```

[20] The time-dependent part describes that the view is active whenever quantity conditions and preconditions hold.

Names of individuals are used as selector functions, VI denoting a distinct realization of a general view. The following statement defines *piece-of-stuff*, assigning variables (i.e. quantities) to the object. This is done by means of functions which map objects to quantities using the relationship Has-Quantity. Furthermore, a piece of stuff is made of some substance and is placed at some location:

$\forall$ p $\in$ *piece-of-stuff*
    Has-quantity(p,amount-of) $\wedge$ Has-Quantity(p,volume)
    $\wedge$ Has-Quantity(p,pressure) $\wedge$ Has-Quantity(p,temperature)
    $\wedge$ Substance(made-of(p)) $\wedge$ Place(location(p))

Now it is possible to define a process describing the flow of contained liquid from one container (where the attribute pressure is higher) to the other. A fluid path is aligned if it has no valve or if all valves are open. The flow exists as long as there is a pressure difference, then the process stops. A process looks much like a view with its additional part of influences. Since a process has to start in a state and leads to or creates a new one, this similarity is obvious.

<u>Process</u> Fluid-Flow (src,dst,path)
  <u>Individuals</u>
    src a *substance*
    dst a *substance*
    path a *fluid-path*
  <u>Preconditions</u>
    Fluid-Connected(src,dst,path)
    Aligned(path)
  <u>QuantityCondition</u>
    Contained-Liquid(src)
    Contained-Liquid(dst)
    A_m[pressure(src)] > A_m[pressure(dst)]
  <u>Relations</u>
    Let flow-rate be a quantity
    flow-rate α_{Q+} (A_m[pressure(src)] - A_m[pressure(dst)])
  <u>Influences</u>
    I + (amount-of(dst), A_m[flow-rate])
    I - (amount-of(src), A_m[flow-rate])

The notion of a process Fluid-Flow introduces two operators: x α_Q y states that variable x is qualitatively proportional to y, the sign on the symbol Q indicates whether this relationship is negative or positive. It can also be seen as an indirect influence from y to x. I(x,y) says that y directly influences x. This introduces the notion of causality, the direction of value propagation. Thus, a process is the construct which, by means of the operator I, changes the values of some variables and, in consequence, changes the situation. Operator I may also be interpreted as a differential operator, i.e. dx/dt = y, being responsible for the time advancement. All changes are due to processes. Variable flow-rate is defined as a quantity which is independent from any individual.

The process of reasoning in the process-centered ontology can be defined as follows:
firstly, identify the existing individuals, relationships and quantity conditions to create the set of active views and processes. Secondly, look at the D_s values, i.e. sign of derivatives, of variables where only variables with derivatives $\neq 0$ change. Then resolve the direct (I) and afterwards the indirect (α_Q) influences, assigning new values to the D_s of the respective variables. In the next step look whether some variables - due to the signs of their derivatives - pass a threshold, i.e. change valid predicates and relationships in the quantity space of

processes and/or views. In such a way the overall structure may change since new processes and views may become active. More than one change may occur - ambiguous situations are possible - due to the fact that i) the quantity space is not totally ordered; ii) a process most probably will influence more than one variable and, thus, more than one limit point may be reached; or iii) there may exist more than one process, which may cause multiple or conflicting changes. Similar rules to the device-centered approach derived from mathematical analysis are used to guide this process and to reduce ambiguity. In addition, this ontology proposes a more specific and modified version of the equality change rule: a process structure lasts over an interval of time unless a change away from equality occurs. In addition, a change toward equality may also last just for an instant if it constitutes only the reverse of a previous change away from equality.

All possible subsequent states have to be considered. Finally, an analysis of the situation is produced which contains the valid processes, the engaged individuals and the limit hypothesis. This presentation takes the form of a state diagram, where states are described by active views and processes as well as the engaged individuals. Transitions denote changes between states, induced by the quantity conditions of processes as well as views. Also in this case a state transition diagram is produced, denoting the entire set of possible behaviors. The propagation is - on a semantic level - similar to [de Kleer and Brown 84]. Values are propagated by means of the operators α_Q and I within a specific process structure (intrastate behavior); when some threshold limits are reached, the process structure, i.e. state, changes. Ambiguous situations may occur and all possible continuations which cannot be eliminated have to be considered.

In our example the process Fluid-Flow and the view Contained-Stuff have been defined up to now. Since a Contained-Stuff may be solid, gas or liquid, but process Fluid-Flow is only defined for liquids, a view Liquid is introduced, stating that a stuff is liquid when it is neither solid nor a gas and its temperature is in the respective range. Both quantities t-melt and t-boil introduce limit points in the quantity space to distinguish the different valid views. Views Solid and Gas are defined similarly.

```
Individual View Liquid (p)
    Individuals
      p a piece-of-stuff
    QuantityCondition
      ¬(A[temperature(p)] < A[t-melt(p)])
      ¬(A[temperature(p)] > A[t-boil(p)])
      ¬Solid(p)
      ¬Gas(p)
    Relations
      volume(p) αQ+ amount-of(p)
      t-boil(p) αQ+ pressure(p)
```

Since we have defined the views Contained-Stuff and Liquid, we are able to describe the view Contained-Liquid. Levels of contained liquids are related to their amount, and the pressure of a container liquid to its level. In defining an individual view Contained-Liquid a concept similar to the concept of multiple inheritance of the object-oriented paradigm is applied, using the names of active processes and views in the quantity conditions.

<u>Individual View</u> Contained-Liquid (p)
  <u>Individuals</u>
    p a *piece-of-stuff*
    con a *container*
  <u>QuantityCondition</u>
    Liquid(p)
    Contained-Stuff(p)
  <u>Relations</u>
    Has-quantity(p,level)
    level(p) = level-in(con,p)
    level(p) α_{Q+} amount-of(p)
    container(p) = con
    pressure(p) α_{Q+} level(p)

The individuals with their attributes, views and processes defined so far are general descriptions and deal with non-instantiated names for individuals. They describe the domain of discourse and form a so-called process vocabulary. The study of a distinct situation with concrete objects instantiates abstract individuals with concrete objects, in our case WC and WD, the water in the two containers. The general description - classes in the case of an object-oriented notation - can be instantiated into active views and processes. This takes also into consideration the valid quantity and preconditions of active views and processes. In our example, asking what might happen in the case of two connected containers filled with water, qualitative reasoning creates the following limit analysis, where the following is assumed:

Container(C)
Container(D)
Fluid-Path(P1)
Fluid-Connected(C, D, P1)
Contains-Substance(C, WC)
Contains-Substance(D, WD)
level-in(C, WD) > level-in(D, WD)

Moreover, implicit assumptions are that fluids are of the same kind, that containers have the same form and that they are open. The following is carried out for both containers: level-in(C, WC) leads to level(WC) which gives pressure(WC). Process Fluid-Flow becomes active due to A_m[pressure(WC)] > A_m[pressure(WD)]. The following limit hypothesis (LH) is performed, where PS denotes the active process structure and IS denotes participating individuals. The signs of the derivatives of the attributes of both individuals WC and WD are shown - together with the responsible views and processes - in the sequence they are deduced:

Process Fluid-Flow:	D_s[amount-of(WC)] = - 1	D_s[amount-of(WD)] = 1
View Liquid:	D_s[volume(WC)] = - 1	D_s[volume(WD)] = 1
View Contained-Liquid:	D_s[level(WC)] = - 1	D_s[level(WD)] = 1
View Contained-Liquid:	D_s[pressure(WC)] = - 1	D_s[pressure(WD)] = 1

IS: {WC, WD}
PS: {Fluid-Flow(WC,WD)}

↙ ↘

LH: A[pressure(WC)] = A[pressure(WD)]
IS: {WC, WD}
PS: {}

LH: A[amount(WC)] = 0
IS: {WD}
PS: {}

Fig. 8: Limit analysis of the two connected containers

This result corresponds to a state transition diagram, including all possible states and transitions due to the qualitative values of the derivatives. As in the case of the device-centered approach, this description concentrates on the qualitatively important features. The first possibility is obvious, i.e. the water levels in both containers and therefore the respective pressures reach an equilibrium. However, in principle it is also conceivable that object WC may completely disappear, since all its derivatives have negative signs. But in the concrete example this cannot happen because the values have to pass a point where the values of both pressures are equal, which will necessarily be detected due to the quantity space of Fig. 7. Thus, the second arrow of the limit analysis is misleading.[21] This discussion makes also clear a fundamental difference to the device-centered approach of [de Kleer and Brown 84]. The magnitude A denotes a concrete numeric value which might be unknown; however, due to the defined quantity space it can be used to determine its relationship to other values in a quantitative expression like A[pressure(src)] - A[pressure(dst)]. Furthermore, this approach assumes that causal influences can already be identified in the modeling phase and thus these causal relationships can be used both in the model description and the reasoning process.

[21] We leave this arrow in order to be consistent with the original description in [Forbus 84].

1.3 The Constraint-based Ontology

This approach differs from the others as it refers directly to well-known mathematical descriptions of dynamic systems in the form of differential equations. It starts from these equations, which exactly describe a given physical situation ([Kuipers 84], [Kuipers 86]). Based on this description, qualitative differential equations are is deduced, using some basic qualitative primitives representing operators and functional relationships. It does not provide modeling primitives like basic components or processes as in the other approaches. Since the focus of this approach is behavior generation, this method fits best into the notion of qualitative simulation. The set of qualitative values consists of non-overlapping intervals which cover the whole range of interest. The boundaries of these intervals are constituted by so-called landmark values of a variable. However, not all of them need to be known at the beginning.

Variables are described by functions of time, i.e. f: $[a,b] \to \mathbf{R}^*$ with $[a,b] \subseteq \mathbf{R}^*$ and $\mathbf{R}^* = \mathbf{R} \cup \{-\infty, +\infty\}$.[22] It is assumed that f is continuous on [a,b] and continuously differentiable on (a,b) and that it has only a finite number of critical points in any interval [a,b], i.e. the set $\{t \mid f'(t) = 0, t \in [a,b]\}$ is finite. Furthermore it is assumed that both limits $\lim_{t\downarrow a} f'(t)$ and $\lim_{t\uparrow b} f'(t)$ exist and f′(a) and f′(b) are defined to be equal to these limits. Such functions are also called reasonable functions.

Every function f has associated a set of landmark values which has to contain f(a), f(b), 0 and the value of f(t) at each critical point and may include additional values, this set being ordered (we use italics to denote landmark values): $l_1 < l_2 < \ldots < l_n$. The time points which correspond to landmark values are called distinguished time points. In addition, so-called corresponding values of two functions f and g are defined: these are landmark values p and q if there is some t $\in$ [a,b] with $f(t) = p$ and $g(t) = q$. The qualitative state QS(f,t) of f at some point t is described by a pair ⟨`qval`, `qdir`⟩ where

$$\texttt{qval} = \begin{cases} l_i & \text{if } f(t) = l_i \text{ (a landmark value)} \\ (l_i, l_{i+1}) & \text{if } f(t) \in (l_i, l_{i+1}) \end{cases}$$

$$\texttt{qdir} = \begin{cases} inc & \text{if } f'(t) > 0 \\ dec & \text{if } f'(t) < 0 \\ std & \text{if } f'(t) = 0 \end{cases}$$

The qualitative state of f is either an entire interval for all values of t in the respective domain or a well-defined landmark value at a distinguished time point. Both types of states strictly interchange. This corresponds to a qualitative description where important situations, such as passing a landmark value or reaching an extreme value, are emphasized and all other events inbetween are summarized. The qualitative behavior of f on [a,b] can be defined as the sequence $QS(f,t_0)$, $QS(f,t_0,t_1)$, $QS(f,t_1)$, ..., $QS(f,t_{n-1},t_n)$, $QS(f,t_n)$. States at distinguished time points and states between such time points interchange. A system is now a set $F = (f_1, \ldots, f_m)$ of functions f_i: $[a,b] \to \mathbf{R}^*$, as previously defined. The set of distinguished time points of F is the union of all such time points of the respective functions. The qualitative state of F of m functions is now a tuple of the individual qualitative states:

$QS(F,t_i) = [QS(f_1,t_i), \ldots\ldots QS(f_m,t_i)]$ and

---

22 $-\infty$ and ∞ are added for being used as explicitly defined landmark values.

$$QS(F,t_i,t_{i+1}) = [QS(f_1,t_i,t_{i+1}), ...QS(f_m,t_i,t_{i+1})].$$

If t_i and/or t_{i+1} are not such distinguished time points of some function f_j, then t_i and the interval (t_i,t_{i+1}) must be in some interval (t_k,t_{k+1}), with t_k and t_{k+1} being distinguished time points. Then $QS(f_j,t_i)$ and $QS(f_j,t_i,t_{i+1})$ are defined as being the same as the containing $QS(f_j,t_k,t_{k+1})$. Thus, the overall behavior of F can be written as

$$QS(F,t_0), QS(F,t_0,t_1), QS(F,t_1), ...QS(F,t_{n-1},t_n), QS(F,t_n).$$

During the simulation new landmark values can be generated, which are those values of a variable x where `qdir` of x becomes *std*, i.e. x has reached a - previously unknown - extreme value. This approach is able to generate new points in the qualitative value space which create new intervals and thus qualitative values. At the end of a simulation the set of landmark values consists of the initial set of landmarks plus all dynamically identified extreme values. This corresponds to a view where a user can state some of the important values he is interested in, however, the system also provides information about important events he did not identify in advance.

The example of the two containers may be used again, denoting the left container with C and the right one with D. The engaged objects are described by qualitative variables, i.e. reasonable functions. The change of these variables describes the behavior of the entire system. Simulation starts when the initial equilibrium situation is disturbed by an input, i.e. water filled into the container C. The following figure is the graphical representation of the relationships between the variables and some basic qualitative operators.

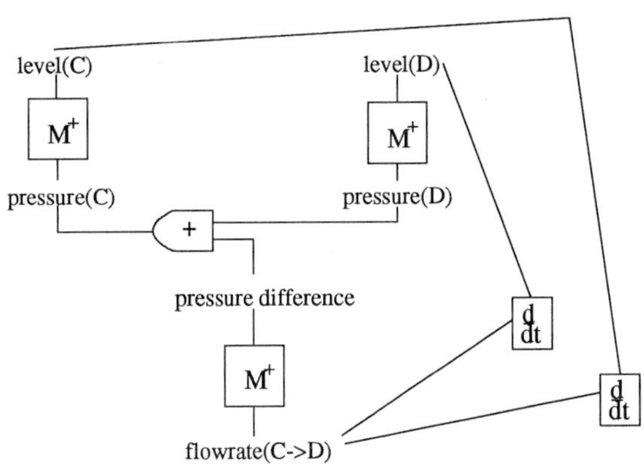

Fig. 9: Connected containers C and D, described by the notion of [Kuipers 86]

The basic functional dependencies are M^+ and M^-, which express either an increasing or a decreasing monotonic relationship, similar to α_Q of the process-centered approach. The predicate $M^+(a,b)$ is true for a, b: $[m,n] \rightarrow \mathbf{R}^*$ iff $a(t) = h(b(t))$ for all $t \in [m,n]$, h has its domain $b([m,n])$ and range $a([m,n])$, it is differentiable and $h'(x) > 0$ for all x in the interior of the domain. Note that it is assumed that $a(m) = h(b(m))$ and $a(n) = h(b(n))$.[23] These values n and m may serve to divide a non-monotonic relationship between two functions into well behaving monotonic pieces. In addition, predicates denoting the operators ADD(a,b,c), MULT (a,b,c) and MINUS(a,b) are defined. For example, ADD(a,b,c) on a, b, c: $[m,n] \rightarrow \mathbf{R}^*$

[23] Moreover, $M^+(a,b)$ does not imply that a and b are monotonic functions on [n,m]. $M^+(2 \sin t, \sin t)$ holds on $[0,2\pi]$ with $h(x) = 2x$.

holds iff a(t) + b(t) = c(t) for every t ∈ [m,n]. The other operators are defined in a similar way. The predicate DERIV(a,b) denoting the differential operator holds iff a′(t) = b(t) for every t ∈ [m,n]. It is responsible for the dynamic behavior of the described system. These predicates can be satisfied by several value assignments to the engaged variables and ambiguous situations may occur. The interpretation of Fig. 9 in the form of constraints is straightforward:

M^+(pressure(C), level(C))
M^+(pressure(D), level(D))
ADD(pressure(D), pressure difference, pressure(C))
DERIV(level(C), flowrate(C->D))
DERIV(level(D), flowrate(C->D))
M^+(flowrate(C->D), pressure difference)

The lines of Fig. 9 do not define any directions. This fact indicates that causality is not imposed directly and that the propagation mechanism does not use causal influences. However, the differential operator DERIV is a directed connective between two variables, denoting a causal influence as well. The result of simulating the system is described by the following behavior representation, showing the sequence of qualitative states of the single variables, which is similar to classical simulation studies.

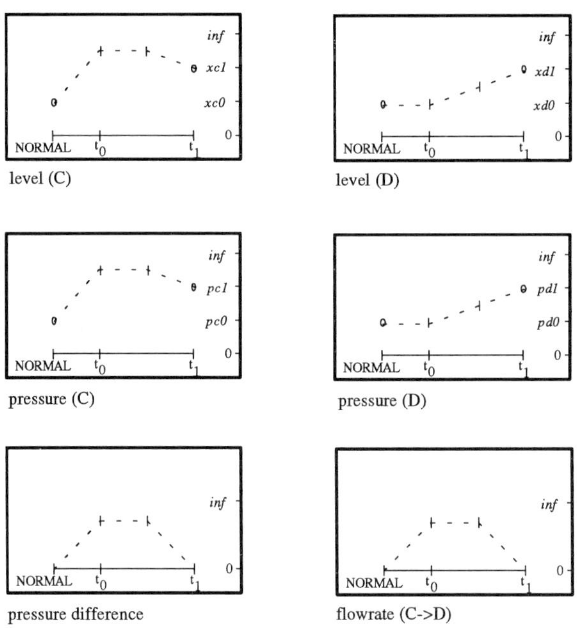

Fig. 10: Trajectories of the variables describing the two connected containers C and D

At the beginning, the set of landmark values for the respective variables is given, i.e. for level of C: 0, *xc0* and *inf*; for pressure of C: 0, *pc0* and *inf*, and so on. At time t_0 an amount of water is added to C. One of the possible results of the qualitative simulation is that the system returns to an equilibrium. It shows that this equilibrium is reached at new landmark values which are created for both variables level and pressure of the two containers, i.e. *xc1*, *xd1*, *pc1* and *pd1*. However, it is not stated how long it will take. Other, spurious, solutions produced by the algorithm are not shown. These are behaviors which do not correspond to any feasible behavior of the real system. The positions at the horizontal axis indicate time with the values of NORMAL, t_0, the interval (t_0,t_1) and t_1. The first time point is NORMAL and denotes, that at the beginning, the system is in a state of equilibrium. The interval (t_0,t_1) is represented as tick-marks on the qualitative trajectory. The qualitative values remain the same for the entire interval. The corresponding quantitative values remain within the intervals defined by two landmarks. The above sequence of states also represents a causal explanation of behavior by telling when and why something happens. The figure differs from the other approaches in so far as it shows just one trajectory, one behavior, whereas the others describe the whole state space and thus all possible behaviors.

The algorithm QSIM of [Kuipers 86], the implementation of this approach, generates behavior, starting from a description based on qualitative constraints. In the dynamic behavior time points and time intervals have to interchange, i.e. $QS(f,t_i) \Rightarrow QS(f,t_i,t_{i+1})$ and $QS(f,t_i,t_{i+1}) \Rightarrow QS(f,t_{i+1})$ as already described. Based on this fact and the general rules outlined in the description of the other ontologies as well as the continuous change of variables, it is not possible for a variable to change directly from ⟨`qval`,*inc*⟩ to ⟨`qval`,*dec*⟩; it must pass ⟨`qval`,*std*⟩ in any case. The algorithm generates all behaviors which are consistent with the constraining equations and works as follows (for a detailed discussion see II.4.1):

Denote with ACTIVE a list of those states which have to be considered. At the beginning, the only member is the initial state, the algorithm iterates until this list is empty (or the resources of the computer are totally exhausted). Select one state out of ACTIVE. Generate for each variable of this state all possible transitions. That means that all possible successor states that do not violate continuity are generated. After this step, the constraints are used to filter out the contradictory ones, i.e. those which do not satisfy the constraints and their predicates. This is done in several steps. During the first step, each constraint is checked individually against these transitions. Then a pairwise filter is applied - if some constraints share arguments, they must be consistent. Finally, global filters are used - for example check for cycles, if one is found this state can be deleted as well. Afterwards all remaining states are put into the list ACTIVE. By applying two main steps - state transitions and constraint satisfaction - this method works similar to the other approaches. However, the algorithm uses a generate-test strategy and works "backward". It produces all successors and excludes those which are inconsistent. It produces ambiguous behavior and not all spurious states, i.e. denoting states which are in "reality" impossible, can be eliminated. However, by this way of generating behavior, QSIM lies on the conservative side, i.e. it does not miss real existing solutions and expels only the obviously contradictory ones. It can be shown that this algorithm is complete insofar as it generates all possible behaviors with respect to the modeled system. But it also creates behaviors that do not correspond with the real system. However, it follows that, if just one solution exists, this is the correct one.

2. Correspondences and Differences

All three approaches discussed in the previous chapters deal with dynamic systems and their behavior described in the form of state variables and state transitions. However, we can position them on different levels. QSIM of [Kuipers 86] can be seen as a reasoning technique, whereas the other two approaches are more general and also include the task of modeling. Simulation constitutes just one part of their work. Based on this distinction it would, in principle, be possible to map structural descriptions used by the other approaches onto a description using qualitative differential equations. QSIM could then be applied as a reasoning method.

Both the device- and the process-centered approach support a bottom-up point of view in modeling. They start with elementary primitives, which can be further assembled. These basic units are assumed to exist, their origins are not described. The formal descriptions of these pieces have to obey specific rules to maintain both availability for flexible integration into different environments and modularity. The constraint-based approach directly derives its qualitative constraints from mathematical descriptions. Correlated with modeling is the problem of identifying the objects which constitute a system. The process-oriented approach identifies individuals such as containers, liquids, springs, etc. They are described by means of attributes such as pressure, temperature, level, etc. The variables which are used in the reasoning process denote these features. The device-centered ontology is similar, however it identifies topological components and the connections between them. In this "architecture" material flows and may be stored or modified. The components and the processed materials possess attributes such as pressure, velocity, etc. These attributes again are subjects of the reasoning process. The difference between the two ontologies consists in their different conception of an elementary object. The device-centered approach - viewing everything like a machine - uses a very concrete and "hardware-oriented" approach, the other view is a more general one and additionally includes abstract and behavior objects. It also shows a similarity to the object-oriented paradigm by using the concept of inheritance. The constraint-based view directly deals with variables, which describe a system. We cannot identify participating objects on this descriptional level. Thus, we can distinguish the following modeling ontologies: the device-centered approach uses as structural elements components and conduits, connectivity is achieved via terminals. In the process-centered approach, objects and processes can be identified as basic entities. Model composition can be done via shared objects. The constraint-based approach uses variables and constraints, communication is performed via shared variables. [Bredeweg and Wielinga 88] position these three different approaches as points on a continuum, starting from concepts which support physical modeling, such as the process-centered ontology, and ending with a form corresponding to well-known mathematical descriptions, e.g. the constraint-based approach.

In the approach of [Forbus 84] and its concept of processes, the fundamental piece of knowledge is already included in the modeling step. It compiles the direction of influence, i.e. the causal relationships, directly into the model. In contrast, the device-centered ontology relates the variables merely by means of constraining relationships; causal chains are not compiled. Causality is a result of the reasoning process, it is used in the output interpretation phase. The constraint-based view also relies on non-causal constraints, however it implicitly uses directed influences by means of the predicate DERIV, which represents a differential equation. [de Kleer and Brown 84] explicitly rely on the locality principle, effects can only be propagated when two components are connected. In the process-centered approach, two objects may interact when one variable of one object influences a variable of another object by means of a process. In the constraint-based approach, the principle of locality cannot be identified straightforward. Since this description already represents a mathematical model, one has to refer to the original physical model.

The representation of values is based on intervals and ordinal relationships. This is a very abstract form of description, concentrating on specific and emphasized values, which are also used as interval boundaries. The defined calculus is necessarily very limited. The system defined by means of such qualitative descriptional primitives represents a whole class of systems, i.e. a qualitative model can be seen as an abstraction of several distinct quantitative models. Thus, the solutions produced represent also the set of solutions of the entire class. If more than one solution, i.e. behavior, of the system exists, all of them might be possible. The central problem of qualitative reasoning is - due to its abstract form of representation - that solutions may be generated which do not represent a "real" solution. This, however, implicitly assumes the existence of a quantitative reference model, which in real application cases may not exist.

The three approaches use different representations of values, i.e. mappings from the real numbers to a reduced quantity space. Whereas the device-centered ontology only uses the positive and negative range and, as specific point, the value of zero, the process-centered ontology additionally introduces a partially ordered relationship between values of variables and other landmark values, assuming the knowledge of magnitudes. The constraint-based approach is different as it can create new qualitative values during simulation. The process- and the constraint-based approaches integrate more knowledge than the device-centered approach and are easier extendible to incorporate more information when available. Moreover, there is a further distinction on a philosophical or interpretational level, which results in different operational procedures. The device-centered approach uses only signs and does not assume that most or at least some of the information might be available. For that reason the operations of $\oplus$ and $\otimes$ need a special treatment. Furthermore, the notion of qualitative equality is necessary in the value assignment process. The process-centered approach takes the value of a variable and relates it to other, already known, quantitative information. In some sense this approach assumes a concrete value, which can be directly used in a quantitative manner. Thus, normal addition and subtraction and relational operators such as "<", ">", "=" can be applied. The constraint-based view expresses such operators by means of logical predicates, assuming also distinct landmark values to define intervals. Although these values are not exactly known, their relationship to other values can be derived.

Functional relationships are modeled by $x \ \alpha_Q \ y$, M(x,y) and $[x] \equiv [y]$. Also in this case the representation of the device-centered approach is weaker than in the other two cases. The only information to be derived is whether two variables have the same sign. The other approaches do not know the exact shape of a relating function, but due to the defined quantity space and the corresponding values, more information is available. All three techniques use information about both the magnitude of a variable and its derivative in the form of `qdir`, D_s, or ∂. They indicate the qualitative direction of change, i.e. their values $\in$ {+,0,-}. The treatment of these values is similar in all three approaches and based on a qualitative algebra. Additionally, first order differential equations of the form $x' = y$ are modeled as I(x,y), DERIV(x,y) and $\partial x \equiv [y]$. They are - on a semantic level - the generative primitives. Whereas the first two approaches possess dedicated primitives, the device-centered approach directly relates a derivative with a variable. Moreover, its confluences may contain more than one derivative.

In the following we will use the example of a frictionless spring to exemplify these different representation techniques and to distinguish between their results. All three techniques will be applied to this common problem. Such a system is described by the following equation:

$\frac{\partial^2 x}{dt^2} = -kx$, with x being the spring's extension from its natural length d. k is calculated on the basis of the mass and the natural length d and determines also the frequency of the system [Borrie and Burghes 81]. The so-called Hooke's law is applied, which states that the tension in a spring is proportional to its extension. The solution is a permanently oscillating harmonic motion with
$x(t) = d\cos(\sqrt{k}t+\beta)$, where β denotes the translation of the curve from the origin.

Due to the available predicates, the approach based on qualitative differential equations separates the above formula into three constraints:

DERIV(x,v), DERIV(v,a) and M^-(a,x), with v being the velocity and a the acceleration. This is derived from f = m * a and f = - k * x. Mass m can be neglected, since it is always positive - we take the qualitative form -, and variable a is substituted for variable f, therefore, the three constraints constitute a valid description.

At the beginning variable a has the landmark set $\{-\infty, 0, \infty\}$, v the set $\{-\infty, 0, v^*, \infty\}$ and x the set $\{-\infty, 0, \infty\}$. The simulation starts with the initial values $a_0 = 0$, $v_0 = v^*$ and $x_0 = 0$ and proceeds for one cycle using specific transition rules as described in chapter II.4.1. For example, for variable a the following sequence of states is produced (see Fig. 11), starting with $QS(a, t_0) = \langle 0, dec\rangle$: $QS(a, t_0, t_1) = \langle(-\infty,0), dec\rangle$, $QS(a, t_1) = \langle a_1, std\rangle$, i.e. it detects the new landmark a_1, $QS(a, t_1, t_2) = \langle(a_1,0), inc\rangle$, $QS(a, t_2) = \langle 0, inc\rangle$, $QS(a, t_2, t_3) = \langle(0,\infty), inc\rangle$, $QS(a, t_3) = \langle a_2, std\rangle$, i.e. the next landmark value a_2 is discovered, $QS(a, t_3, t_4) = \langle(0,a_2), dec\rangle$. The simulation discovers similar landmarks for the other variables. However, having arrived at interval (t_3,t_4) the simulation has three possibilities to continue, none of these alternatives can be eliminated by the filtering mechanism:[24]

	behavior 1	*behavior 2*	*behavior 3*
$QS(a,t_4)$:	$\langle 0, dec\rangle$	$\langle 0, dec\rangle$	$\langle(0,a_2), dec\rangle$
$QS(v,t_4)$:	$\langle v^*, std\rangle$	$\langle v_2, std\rangle$	$\langle v^*, inc\rangle$
$QS(x,t_4)$:	$\langle 0, inc\rangle$	$\langle 0, inc\rangle$	$\langle(x_2,0), inc\rangle$

Thus, it branches depending to whether v reaches its initial value at the same time (behavior 1), later than (behavior 2) or earlier than x (behavior 3). The first behavior corresponds to the desired permanent oscillation, the other two represent spurious solutions. In the trajectory of behavior 3 a supplementary time step is introduced to reach the respective boundary values. Since the qualitative representation ignores relevant information - it does not include the quantity k and thus loses information about the frequency and the amplitude -, the spurious results are not astonishing. Due to M^-(a,x) a and x must proceed simultaneously. No such limiting condition or local knowledge on v exists. The following figure shows another feature of this approach: dependent on a distinct initial value - in our case v* - it creates distinct

---

[24] These behaviors of a, v and x correspond to the three different sets of I-transition rules $\{I_6, I_2, I_3\}$, $\{I_6, I_8, I_3\}$ and $\{I_7, I_3, I_4\}$ which remain after all filtering steps. These rules and the filtering mechanism are described in more detail in II.4.1.

trajectories in the time space. The applied rules to generate behavior directly incorporate time: the equations are used to filter non-feasible interpretations. The vertical short lines on the time axis of Fig. 11 indicate time points, the qualitative values between two such points are valid for the entire interval.

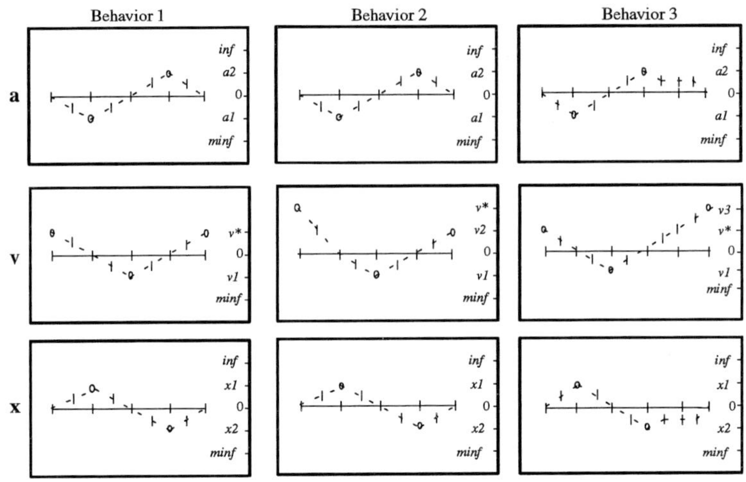

Fig. 11: The constraint-based approach generates three different behaviors of the frictionless spring

Before we can apply the process-centered approach we must define a process vocabulary describing motion, acceleration and elastic objects being stretched, compressed or relaxed. This is different from the previous method and represents a different modeling perspective. We define the following two basic processes:

Process Motion (m,dir)
  Individuals
    m an *object*
    dir a *direction*
  Preconditions
    Free-Direction(m,dir)
    Direction-Of(dir,velocity(m))
  QuantityCondition
    A_m[velocity(m)] > ZERO
  Influences
    I + (position(m), A[velocity(m)]) *(1)*

<u>Process</u> Acceleration (m,dir)
  <u>Individuals</u>
    m an *object*
    dir a *direction*
  <u>Preconditions</u>
    Free-Direction(m,dir)
    Direction-Of(dir,netforce(m))
  <u>QuantityCondition</u>
    A_m[netforce(m)] > ZERO
  <u>Relations</u>
    Let acc be a quantity
    acc α_{Q+} netforce(m) *(2)*
    acc α_{Q-} mass(m) *(3)*
    Correspondence
      ((acc ZERO) (netforce(m) ZERO)) *(4)*
  <u>Influences</u>
    I + (velocity(m), A[acc]) *(5)*

Correspondence ((acc ZERO) (netforce(m) ZERO)) indicates that an acceleration of zero corresponds to a force of zero, which is similar to the corresponding values of [Kuipers 84]. Direction-Of (dir,q) is true when dir equals A_s[q], where dir is a one-dimensional direction along an axis with values -1 and 1. Free-Direction(m,dir) states that there is no immobile object directly against object m in direction dir. acc α_{Q+} netforce(m) and acc α_{Q-} mass(m) qualitatively model the equation $f = m \times a$. The processes Motion (m,dir) and Acceleration (m,dir) correspond to the processes of moving and accelerating an object m into direction dir. The influencing operators I are similarly defined to the predicates DERIV in the previous case.

In addition, we need a description of views to describe the different situations of an elastic object n:

<u>Individual View</u> Elastic-Object (n)
  <u>Individuals</u>
    n an *object*
  <u>Preconditions</u>
    Elastic-Substance(made-of(n))
  <u>Relations</u>
    Has-quantity (n, length)
    Has-quantity (n, internal-force)
    Has-quantity (n, rest-length)
    D_s[(rest-length(n)] = 0
    internal-force(n) α_{Q+} length(n) *(6)*
    Correspondence
      ((internal-force(n) ZERO) (length(n) rest-length(n))) *(7)*

<u>Individual View</u> Relaxed (n)
  <u>Individuals</u>
    n an *object*
  <u>QuantityCondition</u>
    Elastic-Object(n)
    A[length(n)] = A[rest-length(n)]

<u>Individual View</u> Stretched (n)
  <u>Individuals</u>
    n an *object*
  <u>QuantityCondition</u>
    Elastic-Object(n)
    $\mathbb{A}$[length(n)] > $\mathbb{A}$[rest-length(n)]

<u>Individual View</u> Compressed (n)
  <u>Individuals</u>
    n an *object*
  <u>QuantityCondition</u>
    Elastic-Object(n)
    $\mathbb{A}$[length(n)] < $\mathbb{A}$[rest-length(n)]

These views describe an elastic object and its respective specializations. Hooke's law is modeled within the view Elastic-Object. Forces into an object (pushing) are negative, forces directed outward (pulling) are positive. Thus, the sign of proportionality is positive. Now we can consider a block B (an instantiation of m) connected to an elastic object spring S (an instantiation of n). We assume that

length(S) α_{Q+} position(B) *(8)*
Correspondence ((length(S) rest-length(S)) (position(B) ZERO)) *(9)*
netforce(B) α_{Q-} internal-force(S) *(10)*
Correspondence ((internal-force(S) ZERO) (netforce(B) ZERO)) *(11)*

These proportionalities and correspondences are used to model the communication between object B and spring S. The final limit analysis looks as follows, VS denoting view structure and PS process structure:

1	VS:	{STRECHTED(S)}
	PS:	{ACCELERATION(B,-1)}
2	VS:	{STRETCHED(S)}
	PS:	{ACCELERATION(B,-1), MOTION(B,-1)}
3	VS:	{RELAXED(S)}
	PS:	{MOTION(B,-1)}
4	VS:	{COMPRESSED(S)}
	PS:	{MOTION(B,-1),ACCELERATION(B,1)}
5	VS:	{COMPRESSED(S)}
	PS:	{ACCELERATION(B,1)}
6	VS:	{COMPRESSED(S)}
	PS:	{MOTION(B,1), ACCELERATION(B,1)}
7	VS:	{RELAXED(S)}
	PS:	{MOTION(B,1)}
8	VS:	{STRETCHED(S)}
	PS:	{ACCELERATION(B,-1), MOTION(B,1)}

Fig. 12: Limit analysis of the frictionless spring

Reasoning starts with the spring being stretched, i.e. $\mathbb{A}$[length(S)] > $\mathbb{A}$[rest-length(S)]. Now, the procedure is as follows (we use italic numbers to denote the engaged proportionalities, correspondences and influences and the symbol $\rightarrow$ to denote propagation steps):

→ *(7)* A[internal-force(S)] > 0 → *(10)* A_m[netforce(B)] > 0 ∧ A_s[netforce(B)] = -1 → state 1
→ *(4)* A[acc] < 0 → *(5)* D_s[velocity(B)] = -1 → state 2
→ *(1)* D_s[position(B)] = -1 → *(8)* D_s[length(S)] = -1 → *(6)* D_s[internal-force(S)] = -1 → A[length(S)] = A[rest-length(S)] → *(7)* A[internal-force(S)] = 0 → *(11)* A[netforce(B)] = 0 → state 3
→ *(1)* D_s[position(B)] = -1 → *(8)* D_s[length(S)] = -1 → A[length(S)] < A[rest-length(S)]
→ *(7)* A[internal-force(S)] < 0 → *(10)* A_m[netforce(B)] > 0 ∧ A_s[netforce(B)] = 1→ state 4.

The other states follow similarly. States 1, 3, 5 and 7 have an instant duration, corresponding to the situations where the spring's position is at its extreme values or corresponds to the rest-length.

The explanation could be as follows: The stretched spring exerts a force on B. Therefore, process acceleration is active, which is represented by the first state. However, by the influence of acceleration on the velocity of B, process motion starts immediately afterwards (state 2). Thus, state 1 has just an instant duration. This moves the block. Since we assume that the position of B is proportional to the length of S, this length also starts to decrease, as does the spring's internal force. The next limit point is reached when the length of S equals its rest-length, changing S from being stretched to being relaxed (state 3). The view relaxed has an instant duration, changing immediately to view compressed (state 4).

The correspondence of netforce(B) and internal-force(S) represents the necessary communication between the two objects. The limit analysis shows the oscillating behavior. We could add a state 9 with view relaxed and no active processes, which would correspond to a non-moving spring as an initial condition. By introducing this state, the entire state space could be described. This analysis produces no spurious solutions. Different from the previous approach, however, information is also poorer. Both the positive and the negative range are not refined, therefore there is no indication how large an oscillation is or how faraway the block would move. This could be done by introducing further critical landmark values and by properly adapting the process vocabulary. However, similar to the constraint-based approach, spurious solutions would be introduced. This reasoning method works also in two steps; however, the descriptional primitives and the applied techniques differ. The description directly includes the time-dependent behavior by the notion of processes.

Using the device-centered approach, the system can be described by two confluences:
$\partial x \equiv [v]$ and $\partial v \equiv -[x]$. This looks similar to the description of the constraint-based approach. But the second constraint - denoting Hooke's law - combines two constraints of the former approach. This is possible as the device-centered view enables the creation of more complex descriptions based on algebraic equations. The following states can be created:

State	1	2	3	4	5	6	7	8	9
State specifications	$v = 0$ $x = 0$	$v = 0$ $x < 0$	$v < 0$ $x < 0$	$v < 0$ $x = 0$	$v < 0$ $x > 0$	$v = 0$ $x > 0$	$v > 0$ $x > 0$	$v > 0$ $x = 0$	$v > 0$ $x < 0$
∂x	0	0	-	-	-	0	+	+	+
∂v	0	+	+	0	-	-	-	0	+

The values of the derivatives follow from the value assignment with respect to the two confluences, i.e. solutions of the two algebraic equations. By analyzing the derivatives of the respective states the following envisionment graph can be created:

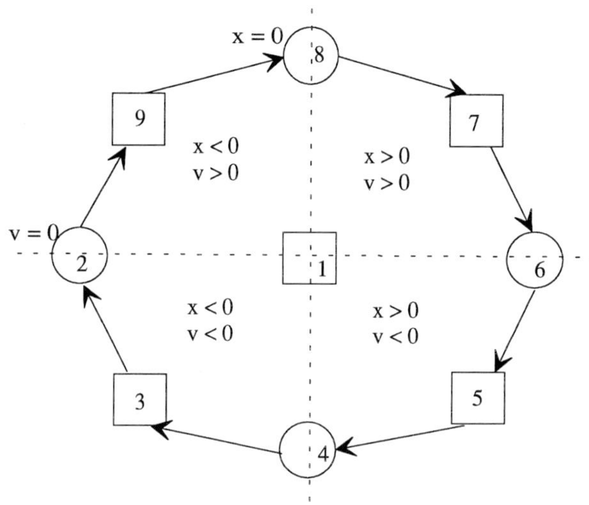

Fig. 13: Envisionment graph of the frictionless spring

This graph shows the same behavior as in the previous case, the spring may either oscillate or remain in the quiescent state. The behavior does not contain any ambiguous case, but the information provided is also poor.[25] This is due to the fact that both the positive and negative range are mapped onto just one qualitative value. The envisionment graph follows from an interpretation of the derivatives which are valid within a state. Thus, it interprets and analyzes the states and does not explore the state space. However, also in this case the reasoning process proceeds in two steps, i.e. first it satisfies the constraints within the states and deduces the possible transitions afterwards.

Although, on a semantic level, all three approaches can be interpreted as behavior generating, these algorithms are not constructive. They work in an exploratory and rather defensive way. Since the defined operators do not uniquely determine their results, all possible combinations of values which satisfy the constraints have to be considered. In order to guarantee all existing solutions of a set of constraints, they generate all possible solutions and exclude just the contractory ones. They do not touch the infeasible ones due to the lack of information. The produced set of solutions, represented either in the form of a limit analysis, an envisionment graph or trajectories, cannot distinguish between its different members. All of them are possible. No measure exists to favour one or some of them. This is the greatest weakness of qualitative reasoning: The selection of the "right" solution has to be done by means of some external knowledge.

In principle, all three approaches use a state space description which divides the space into a finite set of discrete cells. All local trajectories inside one cell are summarized, concentrating on a representation where behavior is described by an interchanging sequence of cells and boundary values. The latter have to be passed in an instant, it is not possible to deduce how long a behavior inside one cell will last. We can draw a fundamental distinction between

[25] However, it has to be mentioned that the description in form of an envisionment graph might not be sufficient to decide whether or not a qualitative state will be left; for example, in the case of multiple interpretations inside a state (as in the case of state 3 in the envisionment graph of the pressure regulator). Moreover, it might also be argued that a state which lasts for an interval can only be left if Zenon's paradoxon is excluded.

envisionment and behavior generation. The envisionment graph represents all possible behaviors in the form of sequences of states. It allows for answering 'Can it happen ?' questions. In the case of an envisionment graph it is fundamental that the number of states is finite and that the set of states can be enumerated. The approach of [Kuipers 86] is different, as it allows for the dynamic creation of new qualitative values, i.e. cells in the state space. The nodes, i.e. states, of an envisionment graph can be created before behavior generation. Whereas the envisionment graph displays all possible behaviors of a system, in the approach of [Kuipers 86] just one trajectory through the state space is searched for. In addition, the generation of trajectories has to explore and determine the state space. This trajectory depends on concrete starting and input values. We can state this difference also in another form: the device-centered approaches analyzes the state space, whereas the constraint-based approach explores it. However, since qualitative simulation may produce several solutions, the final result is also a whole set of solutions.

The discretization of the state space differs, [de Kleer and Brown 84] using only signs, whereas the approach of [Kuipers 86] has a finer grid. We think that [de Kleer and Brown 84] cause some misunderstandings with their notation, since they denote both the general mode of operation, such as working normal or not working at all, and the distinct description of a system's state with the term state. One could differentiate them by using a hierarchic distinction, putting the first on a general and the latter on a lower level of "states". Since both approaches of [de Kleer and Brown 84] and [Kuipers 86] only use signs to denote derivatives, they have problems with the description of time. They are able to describe what will happen and the sequence of well-distinguished events, but nothing can be stated about the duration of states.

The representation of [Forbus 84] uses the concept of histories, which describes the succession of values of variables - describing objects - over time as well as the time sequence of engaged processes and views. Thus, all histories together describe the time behavior of a system. A state is represented by the set of active views and processes which contain the valid predicates and relationships between variables and critical values. Since it has, similar to the constraint-based approach, a set of several landmark values, it also has a more detailed subdivision of the state space. However, when the process structure changes, new participating individuals may be inserted and thus the description of the state space may change as well. The general modes of operation of the device-centered approach look similar, since in different modes different sets of equations may be valid. In the process-centered approach, the representation of time is still weak, nothing can be said about durations and time spans, just the relationships between events can be deduced. [Forbus 84] cannot tell how long an influence will last or a process will be active even if the concept of events is used.[26] However, this approach has an advantage since it incorporates information about the magnitudes of derivatives, i.e. the speed of change.

In the reasoning mechanism of all three approaches two interchanging steps can be distinguished: the intrastate and interstate behavior [de Kleer and Brown 84]:

Intrastate behavior: This behavior denotes the mechanism of satisfying the constraining equations within one state. The system enters a state with some known values from the previous state and values of those variables which were responsible for the state transition; or - in the case of [de Kleer and Brown 84] - the propagation of values starts with the already

[26] [Forbus 84] uses the concept of an event to indicate something which happens instantaneously and changes something.

identified values of state variables. Afterwards, the values of the other variables have to be determined. Ambiguity may occur because several value assignments to variables may be valid.

Interstate behavior: This indicates the transition to one or more next states. In the case of the device-centered approach the next state can be identified by the qualitative values of the derivatives. In the constraint-based approach new successor values are generated by means of the continuity rule and the time-dependent transition rules. Thereafter, the set of new successor states is identified. In the process-centered view the set of possible successor states depends on the variables which pass certain threshold values. In the case of ambiguity several transitions may occur.

The interstate behavior can be interpreted as the causal explanation of the behavior of a system. It reflects time and links successive states, where the predecessor state can be identified as the cause and the successor state as the effect. The intrastate behavior does not possess this property. It is just based on a constraint satisfaction mechanism, producing a new value of a specific variable based on the values of other variables, and it cannot be inferred that these variables are causally linked. However, a difference between the device-centered and the constraint-based view can be seen: the constraint-based approach of QSIM creates all possible values for the next time step by applying the continuity rule - on the basis of the current value of the variables and their derivatives. Only then the constraining equations are used to filter out impossible solutions. The creation of all possible successor values prevents the algorithms to get stuck, when there is not sufficient information available to satisfy a constraint. The different values of variables which satisfy the constraining equations also represent some assumptions for the continuation of the process. If, for example, in a constraint `a + b = c`, only one value is known, for example `a` as being positive with a positive derivative, then all combinations of values of `b` and `c`, together with their derivatives, based on the previous values and consistent with the addition constraint, have to be considered. The device-centered approach, on the other side, solves its set of algebraic equations; only in the case of ambiguity heuristics are used to supply further information. However, also in this approach spurious solutions may remain. Time-dependent rules are used only in the analysis of state transition, i.e. in the construction of the envisionment graph.

We can summarize the following distinctions between the three approaches:

	Device-centered	Process-centered	Constraint-based
modeling perspective	topology of device	processes	mathematical description
structural elements	components and conduits	objects and processes	variables
quantity representation	signs	signs and magnitudes; partially ordered quantity space	landmarks; dynamically created intervals
descriptional form	algebraic equations	processes	QDE
reasoning orientation	assumption-based propagation (interpretation)	limit analysis (construction)	filtering (exploration)
produced result	state-space description	state-space description	trajectory

Since a qualitative model represents an entire class of quantitative models, its results denote - besides spurious solutions due to missing information - all possible behaviors of these models.[27] A central problem that remains is how to distinguish between several valid solutions which correspond to different quantitative models and non-feasible, invalid spurious results which have no "real" counterpart. However, even with this weakness, we think that a major strength of qualitative reasoning is its capability to differentiate possible behaviors from impossible ones, i.e. to partition the space of solutions, based on very little information. Such a qualitative description of the solution space may constitute the starting point for a further, maybe quantitative, investigation. This could be done on the basis of a well-elaborated and structured description of knowledge which allows for the selection of some of its pieces and for more specific reasoning activities when desired.

[27] This shows - at least on a semantic level - some similarity to the concept of sensitivity analysis. Qualitative values, i.e. intervals, correspond to wide ranges of possible parameter and variable values. They could also be interpreted as an entire set of admissible "if - then" questions.

3. Dimensions of Qualitative Mapping

A qualitative model represents, as already stated, an abstraction of an assumed to exist quantitative construct, regardless of its physical existence. Four dimensions of such abstraction can be identified:

- the representation of the attributes of individuals (variables and their values), together with related algebraic operations,
- the functional and differential relationships,
- the representation of time in the dynamic behavior, and
- the structural elements.

In the following we will show that, along all these four dimensions, information is lost. Or the other way around, it may also provide an idea of how qualitative reasoning may be used, when a specific form or amount of information is not available. Still, we can state that, by following these mapping processes, distinct individual behaviors will become members of an entire set of behaviors. The "correct" behavior will always be included, although not easy to identify. Even worse, this set may contain solutions which do not correspond to any of the original quantitative models. However, since the "real" behavior is always included in the set of all resulting behaviors, we can classify qualitative mapping as an abstraction.

a) The Representation of Qualitative Values and Related Algebraic Operations

This represents, to some extent, the basic decision in qualitative modeling, since the choice of qualitative value representation also determines the power of applied reasoning methods, i.e. algebraic operators and functional/differential relationships, and the significance of time. Real numbers are mapped onto a limited set Q of qualitative values, since information in the form of real numbers is either not available or not useful. In the following the representation of values and their rules of algebraic manipulation will be discussed together. Assuming an underlying quantitative model with real valued variables, the mapping q: $\mathbf{R} \rightarrow Q$, allowing to go from a numerical to a qualitative value, should possess - following [Struss 87] - properties such as

- Coverage: qualitative values should cover the whole range of interesting behavior.
- Finiteness: the set Q of qualitative values should be finite, but not necessarily previously determined.
- Interpretation: it should be possible to interpret results in Q, i.e. there exists a mapping p: $Q \rightarrow P(\mathbf{R})$, which is compatible with q: $\forall\, x \in \mathbf{R}$, $x \in p(q(x))$, where P denotes the power set.
- Exclusiveness: qualitative values should not overlap $\forall\, a, b \in Q$: $a \neq b \Rightarrow p(a) \cap p(b) = 0$.
- Varying granularity: if two variables x and $y \in \mathbf{R}$ stand for similar things and denote similar properties of an object, then the qualitative values should also be "similar": $q(x) = q(y)$.
- Ordering: Q should be ordered, at least partially, i.e. $\forall\, x,y \in \mathbf{R}$: $x < y \Rightarrow q(x) \leq q(y)$.

In the following we will discuss - based on [Struss 87] - three different forms of representation and the respective properties and limitations. All these alternatives are based on intervals. None of them has all the mentioned properties:

i) The first case to be considered is based on an extension of the sign algebra as defined in [de Kleer and Brown 84]. The landmark set L consists of $\{-\infty,0,\infty\}$. The set of intervals I is $\{(-\infty,0), [0,0], (0,\infty)\}$, which corresponds to the set Q with the values {+, 0, -}. The operation of addition defined on these values is not closed as in the case of + ⊕ -, which is indicated by the symbol ? in the original operation tables of [de Kleer and Brown 84]. However, ? may also be interpreted as the entire range $(-\infty, \infty)$. In such a way it has a well-defined interpretation and may be added to Q ([Struss 87], [Williams 88]). Thus, in this first case, the set of intervals I is modified, i.e. $I = \{(-\infty,0), [0,0], (0,\infty), (-\infty,\infty)\}$. This set I corresponds to the modified set Q of qualitative values {+, 0, -, ?}. The operations of ⊕ and ⊗ can now be defined as follows:

a ⊕ b	+	-	0	?
+	+	?	+	?
-	?	-	-	?
0	+	-	0	?
?	?	?	?	?

a ⊗ b	+	-	0	?
+	+	-	0	?
-	-	+	0	?
0	0	0	0	0
?	?	?	0	?

By inserting the symbol ?, denoting an interval, both operations do not contain undefined results. ⟨Q, ⊕, ⊗⟩ shows the following properties for addition and multiplication: it is associative, commutative, 0 and + are the identity elements, and, furthermore, it is distributive. However, no inverse for addition exists. In contrast to the concept of qualitative equality, in this case equality is defined in the strict sense, i.e. a = b only if a and b have the same sign. In this case, a ⊕ b = 0 can only be satisfied by a = 0 and b = 0. Furthermore, no cancellation law for addition exists, i.e. a ⊕ b = c ⊕ b does not imply that a = c. However, the property of transitivity of equalities can be demonstrated.

This representation can be extended by defining the set of landmarks $L \subset \mathbf{R} \cup \{-\infty,\infty\}$. The set I of intervals is changed accordingly and can be written as $\{[u,u] \mid u \in L \setminus \{-\infty,\infty\}\} \cup \{(u,v) \mid u, v \in L \text{ and } u < v\}$. Note that also in this case an interval may include another one, therefore I (and Q) is not exclusive. Mapping q is obtained by mapping a real number to the smallest interval from I containing this value. The operations of addition, subtraction and multiplication on intervals are defined as in the following, they map $I \times I$ onto I (for convenience $\langle u,v\rangle$ denotes both (u,v) and $[u,u]$):

$$\langle u,v\rangle \oplus \langle w,z\rangle = \langle u + w,\ v + z\rangle$$
$$\langle u,v\rangle \ominus \langle w,z\rangle = \langle u - z,\ v - w\rangle$$
$$\langle u,v\rangle \otimes \langle w,z\rangle = \langle \min(uw,uz,vw,vz),\ \max(uw,uz,vw,vz)\rangle$$

Additionally, ∞ and $-\infty$ are included by defining $u + \infty = \infty$ and $u + -\infty = -\infty$ for $u \in L$. For the other operations ∞ and $-\infty$ are included by similar definitions. This representation possesses the properties of coverage and ordering. But this extension to more intervals eliminates the inverse for multiplication. Moreover, since for every $u \in L$ also $u + u$, $u + u + u$, etc. $\in L$, Q is not finite anymore. This is just the case for the limited set $L = \{-\infty,0,\infty\}$. The same is valid for varying granularity. Furthermore, problems with subtraction can be identified: from a ⊕ b = c it does not follow that a = c ⊖ b. If a = [1,1] and b = (1,2) it follows that c = (2,3), but (2,3) ⊖ (1,2) = (0,2). This would lead to the contradiction a ≠ a.

However, the operation of subtraction could also be stated to look for an x which satisfies a ⊕ x = b. But such solution may not even exist, e.g. (1,3) ⊕ x = (4,5). This can only be achieved, if the interval length of the sum is not less than the sum of the terms. Supplementary, it can be stated that, if a ⊕ x = b has a solution, it differs from x' = b ⊖ a. It can be shown that x ⊆ x', x restricts more than x'. Additionally, by using the extended set of landmarks L, ⟨Q, ⊕, ⊗⟩ is not distributive anymore.

ii) After these disappointing results we look at a representation which, different from the previous case, contains the approach of [de Kleer and Brown 84] as a specific case. We introduce a set E of elementary intervals, i.e. $E = \{[u,u] \mid [u,u] \in I\} \cup \{(u,v) \mid (u, v) \in I$ and there is no $z \in L$ with $u < z < v\}$. Thus, E contains only point intervals and the intervals between such points: In the following, we restrict possible solution to be elements of E, thus Q = E. In the device-centered approach $E = \{(-\infty,0), [0,0], (0,\infty)\}$. The qualitative operations are defined as in the previous case i). In representation i) Q is infinite, due to the assumption that I is closed with respect to addition. Now we have to state the following: If the set of all intervals I is closed with respect to addition and subtraction, then all open elementary intervals have the same length, i.e. $\forall\ (u,v) \in E$ the difference $v - u = d$ with $d \in \mathbf{R}$. It follows that the members of the landmark set L are equidistant and that L is homomorphic to the set of integers.[28] Therefore, both properties of finiteness and varying granularity are not obtained.

In this case ii) equality is defined as a ⊕ b ≡ c being satisfied if a ⊕ b ∩ c ≠ 0 with a, b, c ∈ Q, which corresponds to the notion of the device-centered approach. A qualitative confluence with expressions including qualitative operations on both sides is solved as follows: Both sides are evaluated obtaining intervals from the set of all intervals I. These intervals have to overlap, solutions are those elements of Q which yield a non-empty intersection.[29] This representation is exclusive and ordered, commutativity and associativity for addition and multiplication are provided. However, no inverse elements, excluding only one-point intervals, exist. Moreover, it is not distributive, i.e. a ⊗ (b ⊕ c) ≠ a ⊗ b ⊕ a ⊗ c. But it has the property of subdistributivity: a ⊗ (b ⊕ c) ⊆ a ⊗ b ⊕ a ⊗ c, for example in the case when a = (1,2), b = [1,1], c = [-1,-1]. Furthermore, if we want to include division by defining a ∅ b = $\langle u,v\rangle \oslash \langle w,z\rangle = \langle u,v\rangle \otimes \langle 1/z,1/w\rangle$, this would make L dense everywhere, obviously in contradiction to the qualitative view. Thus, division adds a further limitation, since addition already eliminated finiteness and subtraction created equidistant landmarks. One possible solution to this problem is represented by the device-centered approach with its restricted landmark set $L = \{-\infty,0,\infty\}$.

iii) A further solution would be to include only a finite number of intervals, defined by boundary values known beforhand such as critical points on the number line, e.g. boiling temperature. These points divide the number axis into a finite set of ranges, resulting in the set of landmarks $L = \{x_i \mid x_i \in \mathbf{R}$ and $i < \infty\}$. Q is now $\{(x,y) \mid x,y \in L, x < y\} \cup \{[x,x] \mid x \in L\} \cup \{(-\infty, x) \mid x \in L, x = \min(x \mid x \in L)\} \cup \{(x,\infty) \mid x \in L, x = \max(x \mid x \in L)\}$. The

[28] However, it should be noted that equidistant landmarks on one side of the real number line, for example on the positive side, are already obtained, if the set L contains one positive number u, because then u, $u + u$, $u + u + u$, etc. have to be added. Subtraction leads to equidistant values in both the negative and positive range and also in the case when two different values u_1 and $u_2 \in L$.

[29] For example, a ⊕ b ≡ c has - among others - the solutions over $L = \{-\infty, 0, \infty\}$: ((-∞,0), (-∞,0), (-∞,0)), ((-∞,0), (-∞,0), [0,0]), ((-∞,0), (-∞,0), (0,∞)).

result of an operation a op b, with op $\in \{\oplus, \otimes, \ominus\}$, is defined as $\langle \max (x \mid x \in L, x \leq u,$ where $\langle u,v \rangle$ = a op b), min $(x \mid x \in L, x \geq v,$ where $\langle u,v \rangle$ = a op b)$\rangle$, with op defined as before. Q is exclusive, finite, covers whole **R**, and is ordered. The results in Q possess an interpretation in **R**. If 0 and 1 are elements of L, [0,0] and [1,1] are the identity elements. However, now the property of associativity is lost: the result of a sequence of additions depends on the order of these operations. Taking $L = \{-\infty, -10, 0, 2, 4, 5, 8, 13, 16, 24, \infty\}$ and the operation $((2,4) \oplus (2,4)) \oplus (4,8) = (4,8) \oplus (4,8) = (8,16)$. But $(2,4) \oplus ((2,4) \oplus (4,8)) = (2,4) \oplus (5,13) = (5,24)$ yields a different result. Moreover, this presentation is not distributive.

The process-centered and the constraint-based approaches are close to this classification. In the first case, the landmark set is well-defined and does not change during the simulation process. In the second case, where qualitative values are represented by reasonable functions and which have only a finite number of critical points, the set of landmark values L contains the values of this function at its boundaries, the value of 0 and any, but finite number of other values. Moreover, L also includes the value of f at each of its critical point, i.e. where $f'(t) = 0$.

In the following table we summarize the properties of the respective representations, case i' corresponds to i, but with the restricted landmark set $L = \{-\infty,0,\infty\}$, representation ii' to ii with $L = \{-\infty,0,\infty\}$:

	i		i'		ii		ii'		iii	
	$\oplus$	$\otimes$	$\oplus$	$\otimes$	$\oplus$	$\otimes$	$\oplus$	$\otimes$	$\oplus$	$\otimes$
associative	x	x	x	x	x	x	x	x	-	-
identity	x	x	x	x	x	x	x	x	x	x
inverse	-	-	-	x	-	-	-	x	-	-
commutative	x	x	x	x	x	x	x	x	x	x
distributive	-		x		-		x		-	
coverage	x		x		x		x		x	
exclusive	-		-		x		x		x	
finite	-		x		-		x		x	
ordering	x		x		x		x		x	

In the previous techniques crisp intervals were used to represent values. The degree of vagueness - as the consequence of missing information, which qualitative reasoning tries to integrate - is shown by means of smaller or bigger intervals, depending on the existing knowledge. But it is assumed that the qualitative value is certain, even if the qualitative value is unprecise. For example, if some value is not exactly known, the range is widened until a qualitative value represents, with complete certainty, all numerical values it stands for. A further modification could also integrate the uncertainty that one numerical value may be represented by two qualitative values. This can be done by the concept of fuzzy sets [Yager et al. 87], which allows for defining the possibility that a value may be in two or even more intervals, not exclusively in one. In this approach a qualitative value is represented by a fuzzy subset of a set of numbers. This set is generated by a discretization of the numeric range of the variable. Fuzzy subsets may also have linguistic interpretations, e.g. small, medium and big. Boundary values define these basic intervals or fuzzy subsets. The union of all these sets is called the fuzzy quantity space. Approaches in qualitative reasoning based on this method define the membership function $\mu_A(x)$, which denotes the grade of membership of a variable x in a subset A, typically written as a tuple $\langle a,b,\alpha,\beta\rangle$ [Shen and Leitch 90]

$$\mu_A(x)=\begin{cases}0 & x<a-\alpha\\ \dfrac{x-a+\alpha}{\alpha} & x\in[a-\alpha,a)\\ 1 & x\in[a,b]\\ \dfrac{b+\beta-x}{\beta} & x\in(b,b+\beta]\\ 0 & x>b+\beta\end{cases}$$

Q is finite, covers the whole range of interesting behavior, and is partially ordered. It is implicitly assumed that there exists an upper and lower limit on the real number line, that the range of possible behaviors can be cut off in advance. Due to the fuzzy membership function, Q has now lost the property of exclusiveness.[30]

This discussion shows that all attempts to represent qualitative values and to define algebraic operations on Q lead to limited results, and, in consequence, to spurious behaviors. These are inherent basic limitations of qualitative reasoning rather than technical shortcomings which may be repaired, unless more information is added or the point of view is altered.

b) The Representation of Functional Relationships

Qualitative reasoning contains also the ability to represent functional relationships between qualitative variables. These are functional primitives such as M of [Kuipers 84] or α_Q of [Forbus 84]. They represent similar concepts and denote either increasing or decreasing monotonic constraints.

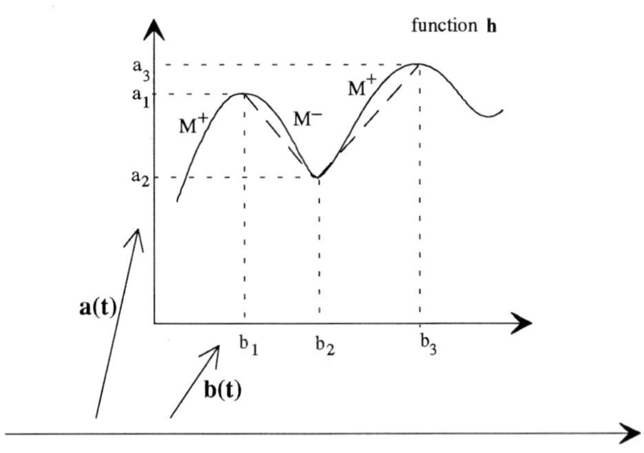

Fig. 14: Function h and relationships M(a,b)

The monotonic relationship M partitions a function h. Predicate $M^+(a,b)$ is true iff there is a function h with $h(b(t)) = a(t)$ and $h'(x) > 0$ for all x from the interior of the domain. Both

[30] The respective operations will be described in chapter III.3.

variables a and b are defined as continuous and differentiable functions and the respective boundaries of the intervals (domain and range) map. M^- is defined similarly. The difference between M and α_Q lies in the fact that M is a = f(b), whereas a α_Q b is defined as a = f(...,b,...), i.e. variable a is monotonically related to variable b all others holding equal. The modeling primitive M thus represents all functions which satisfy this condition. The detection and mapping of corresponding values, where the monotonic relationship changes, is critical to this approach in supporting the creation of homogeneous regions of functions [Chiu 89]. Thus, it is possible to divide a general function into subsequent pieces with the above mentioned properties. Additionally, M shows the property of invariance under a monotonic transformation. If variables x and y are positively (negatively) related, i.e. M(x,y) is valid, and both are transformed by w = f(x) and z = g(y), where f and g are monotonic functions, then w and z are still positively (negatively) related, i.e. M(w,z) is valid. This property can also be used in the process of structural simplification, as described later in this chapter.

If we treat such subsequent homogeneous pieces of a function as its linear approximation, we can interpret both operators M and α_Q as mapping from an entire set of functions - including the assumed real one - onto one of its members. This represents a valid interpretation, since continuous and differentiable functions can locally be approximated by linear ones. Thus, these monotonic constraints represent, under this point of view, a linearization. At least on a conceptual level this corresponds to the work of [Sacks 87], which also substitutes continuous and differentiable functions by piecewise linear approximations, in order to obtain qualitative as well as simple statements about these functions.

All operational primitives discussed up to now deal with static situations, where variables at the same moment of time are constrained by each other. The symbols I [Forbus 84], DERIV [Kuipers 84] and ∂ [de Kleer and Brown 84] relate variables at different time points. In classical simulation they can be seen as the driving forces of simulation and represent also the time advance function, since they indirectly involve the time to be calculated. The primitives I(x,y) and DERIV(x,y) represent differential equations of the form y = dx/dt. This relates the rate of change of a variable to the value of a variable, written in a discretisized form as $y_t = (x_{t+1}-x_t)/\Delta t$ and thus, $x_{t+1} = x_t + \Delta t * y_t$. In contrast, confluences like $\partial a \oplus \partial b \ominus \partial c \equiv 0$ relate all respective changes. Whereas, in classical simulation, the two representation modes produce solution strategies on very different levels of complexity, the constraints of qualitative reasoning, used for the value propagation algorithm, behave with similar complexity.

c) The Representation of Time

Similar to the discretization of continuous values of variables, qualitative reasoning maps the continuous phenomenon time to the discrete form of an interchanging sequence of well distinguished points and ranges on the time axis:

t: $\mathbf{R} \rightarrow T = \{[t_i, t_i] \mid t_i \in K\} \cup \{(t_i, t_{i+1}) \mid t_i, t_{i+1} \in K, t_i < t_{i+1}\}$ where K is a finite set of numbers.

Such a sequence is common to all approaches. The respective points on the time axis are identified by the occurrence of specific events, i.e. critical situations. Additionally, one should also note that the exact values of the respective t_i are not known, time is rather represented by an interchanging sequence of two types of time symbols. This sequence is used in the propagation mechanism of the different approaches. These mechanisms deduce the sequence of possible states and give a causal explanation of behavior by generating and interpreting such a sequence of states. Nevertheless, no quantitative information as to how long it will take to reach some specific situation is available. This is due to the fact that all approaches - to some extent [Forbus 84] may be excluded - represent the derivative of a variable just by the sign of a derivative. Based on this limited information one cannot derive any quantitative information about time. Qualitative representation cannot even decide which of two time intervals is longer; the real behavior might be either compressed or stretched. However, also with respect to this dimension a qualitative behavior represents an entire set of behaviors.

In contrast to traditional simulation, where the information about time determines state transitions, in qualitative reasoning the available qualitative information is used in the form of specific time ordering rules to exclude invalid transitions. In the following we provide an overview of such rules and some of their extensions. These follow from standard mathematical analysis and can be seen as their qualitative counterparts. The rules and their application are common to all approaches in qualitative reasoning, they are used to remove invalid transitions from the entire set of possible ones, after having completed the propagation of values. In the following it is supposed that variables are continuous and differentiable functions of time:

Intermediate value theorem: if function f is continuous on the closed interval [a,b], where a,b $\in$ **R**, and if m is some number between f(a) and f(b), then there is at least one point x $\in$ [a,b] for which the equality f(x) = m holds.

Alternating states: when using the notion of [Kuipers 86] of a sequence of alternating well-distinguished time points and intervals between these points, time can be described as a sequence $<.., t_i, (t_i, t_{i+1}), t_{i+1}, (t_{i+1}, t_{i+2}), ...>$, due to the interval representation of qualitative values. If a system is not quiescent, at least one of its variables has to change its value. If the current value of this variable is the boundary value of an interval, it has to leave this value immediately (the duration of this step is zero). In the opposite, the attaining of a boundary value lasts for some time interval, at least longer than to leave this value. Hence, only two types of state durations exist. Their alternation follows from the definition of qualitative states.

Continuity rule: if some function (variable) is positive (negative) at some instant, it will remain positive (negative) for an open interval immediately following this instant, i.e. $f(t_i) > (<) 0$ then $f(t) > (<) 0$ for $t \in (t_i, t_{i+1})$. Furthermore, if $f(t) = 0$ for $t \in (t_i, t_{i+1})$, then $f(t_{i+1}) = 0$.

The following figure explains this rule, where $a \ominus b = c$ at some instant of time t_1. $[a(t_1)] = +$ and $[b(t_1)] = 0$, using the notion of the device-centered ontology.

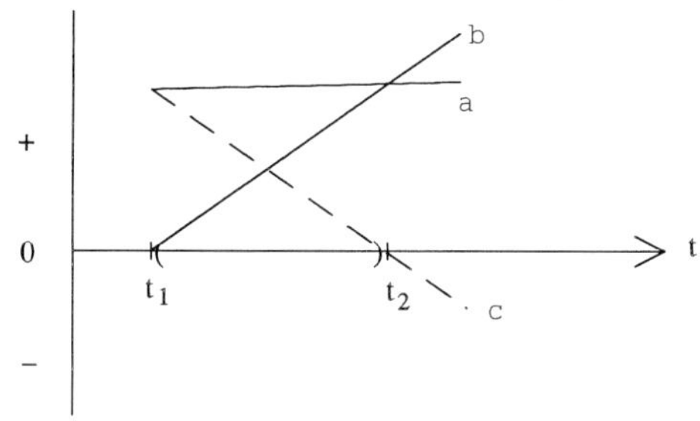

Fig. 15: Application of the continuity rule

Value propagation infers that $[c(t_1)] = +$. If b now takes on a positive value, i.e. $[b(t)] = +$, during the interval $t \in (t_1,t_2)$ and a keeps its old value, the value of c cannot be deduced anymore since $+ \ominus + = ?$ during the interval (t_1,t_2). The continuity rule, however, predicts that c has to remain positive during this interval.

Instant change rule: a change off zero takes only an instance, whereas a change to zero takes longer. If $f(t_i) = 0$ and $f'(t) > 0$ for $t \in (t_i,t_{i+1})$, then $f(t) > 0$ for $t \in (t_i,t_{i+1})$. Furthermore, if $f(t) > 0$ and $f'(t) < 0$ for $t \in (t_i,t_{i+1})$, then it may be that $f(t_{i+1}) = 0$. This rule is also called the transition off and transition to zero rule according to [Williams 84].

Equality change rule: this represents a generalization of the instant change rule by substituting the value of zero with fixed values $a \in \mathbf{R}$. If function $f(t_i) = a$, then changes off this value will happen in an instance (when $f'(t_i) \neq 0$). A change to this value will take some time. An exception is represented by the notion of [Forbus 84]. It states that a return to such a fixed value may also only last for an instant, when the variable previously changed away from this value in an instant of time as well.

Epsilon ordering rule: any change introduced by the equality change rule happens first. If $f(t_i) = 0$ and $g(t_i) > 0$ and $f'(t) > 0$ and $g'(t) < 0$ for $t \in (t_i,t_{i+1})$, then $f(t_x) > 0$ for t_x immediately after t_i and $t_x < t_{i+1}$. If g(t) now also becomes 0 at some time point t_y with $t_y < t_{i+1}$, it follows that $t_x < t_y$. This follows from the fact, that if $g(t) > 0$, then there is a number ε with $0 < \varepsilon < g(t_i)$. As g is a continuous function, it takes some time to reach 0. This rule allows for the sequential ordering of several possible transitions.

Additional rules may be defined as follows, based on the value representation of [de Kleer and Brown 84] and the notion of predicates of [Williams 84]. They are also valid for finer interval representations:

Equality
[a] = +/- [b]
Transition[31] (a) iff Transition (b)
Not-transition(a) iff Not-transition(b)

[31] The meaning of the predicates is obvious.

Monotonic relationship
a is a monotonically increasing (decreasing) function of b, i.e. $M^{+/-}(a,b)$
to-zero(a) iff to-zero(b)
Not-to-zero(a) iff Not-to-zero(b)

Sums and differences
[a] + [b] + [c] = 0 where [a] = [b] = -[c]
Transition(a) $\wedge$ Transition(b) $\rightarrow$ Transition(c)
Not-transition(a) $\vee$ Not-transition(b) $\rightarrow$ Not-transition(c)
Transition(c) $\rightarrow$ Transition(a) $\wedge$ Transition(b)
Not-transition(c) $\rightarrow$ Not-transition(a) $\vee$ Not-transition(b)

Products
[a] x [b] = [c]
Transition(a) $\vee$ Transition(b) $\rightarrow$ Transition(c)
Not-transition(a) $\wedge$ Not-transition(b) $\rightarrow$ Not-transition(c)
Transition(c) $\rightarrow$ Transition(a) $\vee$ Transition(b)
Not-transition(c) $\rightarrow$ Not-transition(a) $\wedge$ Not-transition(b)

d) The Representation of Structure

The identification and representation of structure is a central problem of modeling. An appropriate grain size has to be chosen, a specific point of view has to be taken, properties and entities of the real system have to be identified, necessarily some of them have to be ignored. It follows that the resulting model represents a simplification of reality, but this is not the central point. The problem is rather how large this deviation is allowed to be. In qualitative reasoning the identification of structure (isolation of the basic entities and their relationships) is guided by specific ontologies; i) one remains close to the physical components and their physical interconnections; ii) one describes prototypical situations and processes acting on them; iii) one just takes available mathematical descriptions and applies a qualitative mapping onto these equations.

Qualitative reasoning acts similarly to "classical" modeling. One may select a specific view and level of detail, depending on the purpose of the modeling task. When the level of description gained by the qualitative primitives is too detailed, these may be further aggregated. The structure may thus be further lumped. However, once a very lumped and simple description is reached after several steps of aggregation, the lost information cannot be regained, as this mapping process is homomorphic and not isomorphic. It is important to note that in the case - which is the normal one anyhow - that qualitative reasoning is applied because of lack of information, one has no exact measure of this missing information. This constitutes an additional difficulty to identify the "correct" behavior in the set of all behaviors obtained by qualitative simulation.

The following example, taken from [Kuipers 1984], shows the iterative aggregation from a detailed to a lumped structure. This is based on specific rules which can be applied to the different relationships, and also leads to a reduced number of quantities as well. In a double heat flow system, $temp_s$ denotes the temperature of the heat source, temp the temperature of the stuff in a pot and $temp_a$ the temperature of the surrounding air. This system can be described by the following equation dtemp/dt = $n(temp_s - temp) - m(temp - temp_a)$, where n and m are constants. This system moves to a stable equilibrium *temp** of the temperature of the stuff in the pot. If we denote with $difft_s$ $(temp_s - temp)$ and with $difft_a$ $(temp - temp_a)$, then the system can described as

ADD(temp, $difft_s$, $temp_s$)
ADD($difft_a$, $temp_a$, temp)
M^+(inflow, $difft_s$)
M^+(outflow, $difft_a$)
ADD(netflow, outflow, inflow)
DERIV(temp, netflow)

The constraint ADD(netflow, outflow, inflow), i.e. netflow + outflow = inflow, corresponds to netflow = inflow - outflow, thus ordering of the variables in this constraint is crucial. Figure 16 shows these constraints.

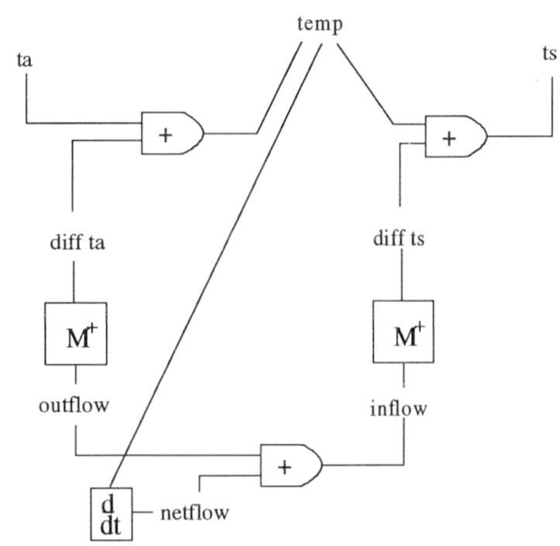

Fig. 16: Detailed description of the heat flow system

However, this description leads to an intractable branching, hence, this structure needs to be simplified in several steps. In a first step the following two rules are applied:
$x + y = z$ & constant (y) $\Rightarrow z = M^+(x)$, i.e. ADD($difft_a$, $temp_a$, temp) $\Rightarrow M^+$($difft_a$, temp), and
$x + y = z$ & constant (z) $\Rightarrow y = M^-(x)$, i.e. ADD(temp, $difft_s$, $temp_s$) $\Rightarrow M^-$($difft_s$, temp).These rules allow the mapping of additive constraints onto monotonic functional relationships. However, information about the magnitude of constant terms is lost.

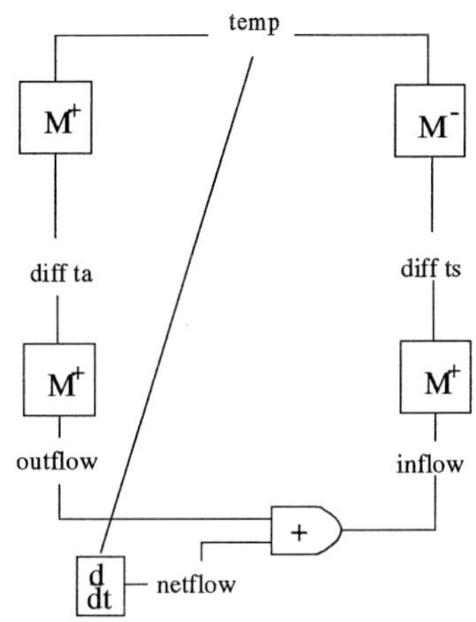

Fig. 17: Aggregation step one

In a further step, the respective successive functional constraints may be composed: $y = M^+_1(M^+_2(x)) \Rightarrow y = M^+(x)$, i.e. outflow = $M^+_1(M^+_2(\text{temp})) \Rightarrow$ outflow = $M^+(\text{temp})$, and $y = M^-_1(M^+_2(x)) \Rightarrow y = M^-(x)$, i.e. inflow = $M^-_1(M^+_2(\text{temp})) \Rightarrow$ inflow = $M^-(\text{temp})$. This creates the following result. But the boundaries of the respective ranges and domains of M_1 and M_2 have to correspond to each other.

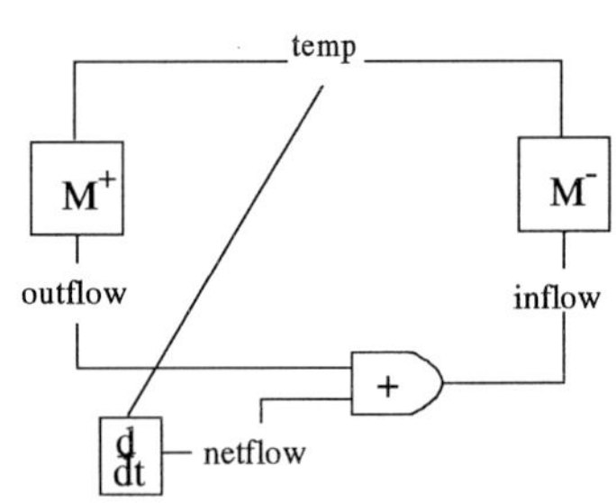

Fig. 18: Aggregation step two

Figure 19 shows the final result of this simplification process. The structure is obtained by means of the rule $y = M^-(x) - M^+(x) \Rightarrow y = M^-(x)$, i.e. netflow = $M^-(\text{temp}) - M^+(\text{temp})$, which is represented as ADD(netflow, $M^+(\text{temp})$, $M^-(\text{temp})$) in Fig. 18. Thus, we obtain netflow = $M^-(\text{temp})$, which corresponds to $M^-(\text{netflow,temp})$.

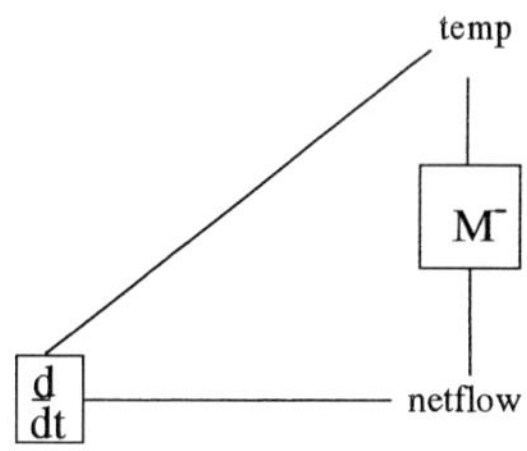

Fig. 19: Last aggregation step of the heat flow system

The final system can be written as
M^-(netflow, temp)
DERIV(temp, netflow)

This system is much less constrained, but it still represents a valid description. The number of variables and constraints is dramatically reduced, however, the original structure cannot be inferred from this final result. But, if we assume that both $temp_s$ and $temp_a$ are known as landmark values and that the initial value of temperature temp is in this interval, then the stable equilibrium *temp** will be identified. The specific scope of the modeling task as well as the power of the applied reasoning method have to determine the level of detail, i.e. how much information is necessary or how much may be ignored.

4. The Reasoning Techniques of the Main Approaches

In the preceding chapters the main approaches, their properties as well as limitations were introduced and presented. Since emphasis in the presentation of the main approaches, i.e. the device-centered, the process-centered and the constraint-based approach, was more on their modeling perspectives, the following discussion will concentrate on their reasoning mechanisms.

4.1 The Constraint-based Ontology

Due to the limited expressiveness of the used primitives, denoting values, algebraic operations and functional relationships, QSIM works backward to guarantee that all possible solutions to satisfy the constraints are exploited [Kuipers 86]. At each step QSIM generates all possible future transitions of the values of variables, which, in a second step, are reduced by a sequence of filtering steps. The constraining equations are used as filters and not for value generation. The possible transitions - based on the discrete representation of the state space - depend on whether the time duration of the current actual state is represented by an interval or by a point. The two respective classes of transitions are called P-transitions (from point to interval) and I-transition (in the reverse case). The following table enumerates all valid transitions in the chosen state space description, based on the fact that continuous variables must vary continuously:

P-transition	$QS(f,t_i)$	$\Rightarrow QS(f,t_i,t_{i+1})$	I-transition	$QS(f,t_i,t_{i+1})$	$\Rightarrow QS(f,t_{i+1})$
P1	$\langle l_j,std\rangle$	$\langle l_j,std\rangle$	I1	$\langle l_j,std\rangle$	$\langle l_j,std\rangle$
P2	$\langle l_j,std\rangle$	$\langle (l_j,l_{j+1}),inc\rangle$	I2	$\langle (l_j,l_{j+1}),inc\rangle$	$\langle l_{j+1},std\rangle$
P3	$\langle l_j,std\rangle$	$\langle (l_{j-1},l_j),dec\rangle$	I3	$\langle (l_j,l_{j+1}),inc\rangle$	$\langle l_{j+1},inc\rangle$
P4	$\langle l_j,inc\rangle$	$\langle (l_j,l_{j+1}),inc\rangle$	I4	$\langle (l_j,l_{j+1}),inc\rangle$	$\langle (l_j,l_{j+1}),inc\rangle$
P5	$\langle (l_j,l_{j+1}),inc\rangle$	$\langle (l_j,l_{j+1}),inc\rangle$	I5	$\langle (l_j,l_{j+1}),dec\rangle$	$\langle l_j,std\rangle$
P6	$\langle l_j,dec\rangle$	$\langle (l_{j-1},l_j),dec\rangle$	I6	$\langle (l_j,l_{j+1}),dec\rangle$	$\langle l_j,dec\rangle$
P7	$\langle (l_j,l_{j+1}),dec\rangle$	$\langle (l_j,l_{j+1}),dec\rangle$	I7	$\langle (l_j,l_{j+1}),dec\rangle$	$\langle (l_j,l_{j+1}),dec\rangle$
			I8	$\langle (l_j,l_{j+1}),inc\rangle$	$\langle l^*,std\rangle$
			I9	$\langle (l_j,l_{j+1}),dec\rangle$	$\langle l^*,std\rangle$

l^* indicates a new, at the beginning of the simulation unknown landmark value of a variable with $l_j < l^* < l_{j+1}$ and with a derivative value of *std*. These new landmark values may only be created in a transition from an interval to a point. The value of a derivative may only become zero at an instantaneous point. Even in the case that a derivative has a value of zero for an entire - open - interval, then it must also be zero at the boundary of the respective interval. The algorithm consists of the following steps:

- select an active state,
- for each variable determine the respective valid transitions based on the transition table,
- for each constraint generate the set of tuples of transitions of its arguments. Filter for all transitions inconsistent with that constraint,
- perform pairwise consistency filtering on the sets of tuples associated with the constraints,
- generate all possible global interpretations from the remaining tuples; if there is none, mark this behavior as inconsistent. Create new qualitative states as a result of each interpretation; mark them as successors of the current state,
- apply global filters on these states. Put any remaining states on the list of possible active states.

The example of a ball thrown up in a constant gravitation field may explain these steps [Kuipers 86]. The QDE description is the following one:

DERIV (y,v), i.e. $y'(t) = v(t)$,
DERIV(v,a), i.e. $v'(t) = a(t)$,
$a(t) = -g$ (constant)

with a being the acceleration, v the velocity and y the height of the ball.

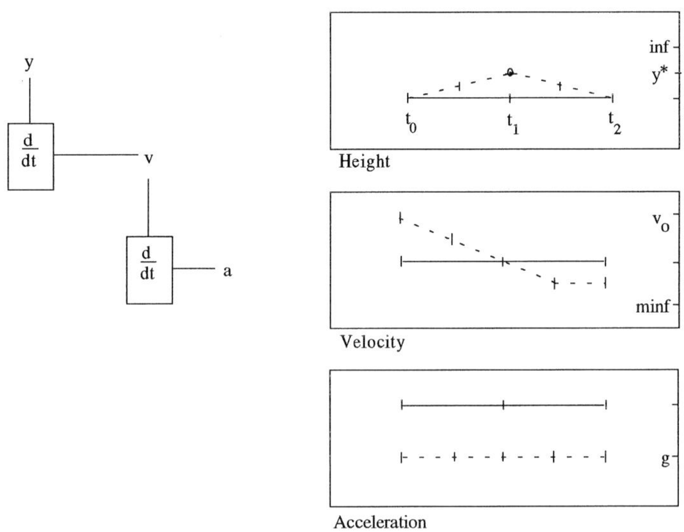

Fig. 20: Constraints and trajectories of throwing up a ball in a gravitation field [Kuipers 86]

When the simulation starts with the initial values $a_0 = -g$, $v_0 = v_0$ and $y_0 = 0$ and reaches the interval (t_0, t_1), this active state can be represented by:
$QS(a, t_0, t_1) = \langle -g, std \rangle$
$QS(v, t_0, t_1) = \langle (0, v_0), dec \rangle$
$QS(y, t_0, t_1) = \langle (0, \infty), inc \rangle$

Since time is represented by an interval, only I-transitions apply. By excluding a value of ∞ for y, transitions I2 and I3 may not occur for y. The following values are generated for the respective variables:

a	I1	$\langle -g, std \rangle \Rightarrow$	$\langle -g, std \rangle$
v	I5	$\langle (0,v_0), dec \rangle \Rightarrow$	$\langle 0, std \rangle$
	I6	$\langle (0,v_0), dec \rangle \Rightarrow$	$\langle 0, dec \rangle$
	I7	$\langle (0,v_0), dec \rangle \Rightarrow$	$\langle (0,v_0), dec \rangle$
	I9	$\langle (0,v_0), dec \rangle \Rightarrow$	$\langle v^*, std \rangle$
y	I4	$\langle (0,\infty), inc \rangle \Rightarrow$	$\langle (0,\infty), inc \rangle$
	I8	$\langle (0,\infty), inc \rangle \Rightarrow$	$\langle y^*, std \rangle$

In the next step, each constraint forms a set of tuples. All combinations of transitions of variables within the constraint are put together. Inconsistent transitions are eliminated (marked with x in the following list). Tuple (I4,I5) from DERIV (y,v), for example, would allow y to continue increasing, while v would have a value of 0. This is not consistent with the derivative constraint. Such constraint consistency filtering is based on criteria which are local to each constraint. Furthermore, the direction of change tuple must be consistent with the constraint. The following table, for example, defines the direction of change of c with regard to the directions of a and b for the constraint ADD (a,b,c). In the ambiguous case no result can be excluded, every result is possible. When generating all successors and excluding only the contradictory ones, all possible assumptions about values are maintained automatically:

a + b	*inc*	*std*	*dec*
inc	*inc*	*inc*	?
std	*inc*	*std*	*dec*
dec	?	*dec*	*dec*

In the next step of the algorithm, pairwise consistency filtering is applied (eliminating those which are marked with z in the following list). The pairwise consistency filtering mechanism looks at adjacent constraints which share an argument. If a tuple assigns a transition to a variable which is not assigned by any tuple associated with an adjacent constraint, then this tuple is deleted. This represents some kind of pattern matching, where, in the case that no corresponding subsequent tuple can be found, the tuple is removed. The tuple (I8,I5) of DERIV (y,v), for example, cannot find - after the previous filtering step - a related tuple starting with I5 in the constraint DERIV (v,a).

DERIV(y,v)		DERIV(v,a)	
(I4,I5)	x	(I5,I1)	x
(I4,I6)	x	(I6,I1)	
(I4,I7)		(I7,I1)	
(I4,I9)	z	(I9,I1)	x
(I8,I5)	z		
(I8,I6)			
(I8,I7)	x		
(I8,I9)	x		

Furthermore, if a value of a variable lies between two landmark values and is moving toward one of the landmarks, it may or may not reach this value during the next step. In the case that several variables are moving toward corresponding landmark values, constraints between those variables may filter out some of the possible behaviors. For example, if $M^+(f,g)$ is valid and both f and g are moving toward corresponding values, then either both or none of them will reach these values. Two landmark values p and q of the variables a and b are called corresponding values, if there is some $t \in [a,b]$ such that $a(t) = p$ and $b(t) = q$.

In the next step, global interpretations of the remaining tuples are created:

y	v	a
I4	I7	I1
I8	I6	I1

This step can be seen as a non-conflicting chaining of variable values and the generation of new potential qualitative states. In a last step, global filtering rules are applied to these states. Such filters are

- *No change:* If the new state is identical to the previous one, the latter is deleted, as its behavior is already described.

- *Cycle:* If the new state is identical to one of its predecessors, then a cycle is detected. This state does not need to be added to the list of further active states.
- *Divergence:* If any variable of a new state takes a value of ∞ or $-\infty$, then the actual time point must be the endpoint of a domain; this state is not put in the list of possible successor states.

With these rules only the new state

y	v	a
I8	I6	I1

remains, since the other state is identical to the old state. A unique successor state is found, defining also a new landmark for y, i.e. $y^* = y_{MAX}$, at time point t_1:
$QS(a, t_1) = \langle -g, std \rangle$
$QS(v, t_1) = \langle 0, dec \rangle$
$QS(y, t_1) = \langle y_{MAX}, std \rangle$.

4.2 The Device-centered Ontology

The device-centered ontology models a device in the form of components and conduits, the relationships between qualitative variables being described by means of algebraic constraints. Causal influences are not represented in the model. However, the resulting envisionment graph, the sequence of qualitative states, corresponds to a causal explanation of the device's behavior. The sequence of states is determined by the derivatives of the state variables. The calculation of these derivatives is based on a modified value propagation method which uses assumptions in the case of missing information to satisfy the set of confluences. This assumption-based - and based on the values of the state variables - assignment procedure happens within one state, thus no time step occurs. In this case, causal explanation represents a problem. [de Kleer and Brown 84] introduce the concept of mythical causality to get around this problem and assign causality to the sequence of assignment steps of their value propagation mechanism.

In the following we use the example of the pressure regulator of chapter II.1.1 to present an alternative method to deduce unknown values and to provide an "explanation of behavior" within one state, i.e. intrastate behavior. This has the form of a logical proof and is based on algebraic manipulations. It explains why the force pushing upward the valve starts to decrease ($\partial f_{K(M)} \equiv -$) as the input pressure begins to rise ($\partial p_{IN,SMP} \equiv +$).[32] In such a proof the sequence of inference steps does not represent a cause-effect chain, given facts and axioms and derived facts have to be true simultaneously. Thus, it explains why something happens, not how (in contrast to the concept of mythical causality, as presented in II.1.1), it does not represent a causal explanation. In the following variable v denotes velocity, q flow, p pressure and f force. The coordinate system is chosen in such a way that an open valve position corresponds to positive values, closing activities to negative ones.

[32] This is equivalent to the statement that the downward force on the valve starts to increase.

(1)	$\partial p_{OUT,SMP} \oplus \partial f_{\#1(S)} \oplus \partial f_{K(M)} \equiv 0$	Given
(2)	$\partial f_{\#1(S)} \equiv v_{FP}$	Given
(3)	$\partial q_{T2} \ominus \partial p_{OUT,SMP} \equiv 0$	Given
(4)	$\partial q_{\#2(VV)} \oplus \partial q_{T2} \equiv 0$	Given
(5)	$\partial q_{\#1(VV)} \oplus \partial q_{\#2(VV)} \equiv 0$	Given
(6)	$v_{FP} \equiv 0$	Specification of state 1
(7)	$\partial f_{\#1(S)} \equiv 0$	Substitution 6,2
(8)	$\partial q_{\#1(VV)} \equiv +$	Premise
(9)	$\partial q_{\#2(VV)} \equiv -$	Substitution 8,5[33]
(10)	$\partial q_{T2} \equiv +$	Substitution 9,4
(11)	$\partial p_{OUT,SMP} \equiv +$	Substitution 10,3
(12)	$\partial f_{K(M)} \equiv -$	Substitution 7,11,1

Central to this proof is the introduction of a premise - step 8 of the proof - to continue the process. By an indirect proof it can be shown that the premise of step 8, i.e. that the flow into the valve is increasing, necessarily holds. This is done by showing that $\partial q_{\#1(VV)} \neq +$ is contradictory if $\partial p_{IN,SMP} \equiv +$. However, such an explanation proof has disadvantages: the introduction of premises is somehow arbitrary and they have to be motivated by indirect proofs. The number of possible assignments of values to variables increases and it is hard to use indirect proofs in explanation. This motivated the concept of mythical causality and the use of heuristics to give reasons for assumptions (as assuming a value of "+" for $\partial p_{IN,OUT}$, from where the value of $\partial q_{\#1(VV)}$ follows directly from $\partial p_{IN,OUT} \oplus [v_{FP}] \ominus \partial q_{\#1(VV)} \equiv 0$, if $[v_{FP}] \equiv 0$). Such assumptions make the propagation mechanism more efficient.

It should be noted, however, that the steps of the previous proof could be continued to represent interstate behavior as well. If we use the knowledge that a non-zero value of a variable's derivative causes an immediate change of its value, therefore, if this value was zero it will become negative (step 13). Thus, we could conclude that in state 2 - following from line 14 - the valve starts to close, i.e. $\partial v_{FP} \equiv -$ (line 15).[34]

(13)	$f_{K(M)} \equiv -$	Applying 12 to a state where $f_{K(M)} \equiv 0$
(14)	$\partial v_{FP} \equiv f_{K(M)}$	Given
(15)	$\partial v_{FP} \equiv -$	Substitution 13,14

The use of the previously mentioned assumption heuristics differs from the approach of [Kuipers 86], where - from a semantic point of view - all potential values representing all assumptions are generated and only the impossible ones are filtered out. In contrast, [de Kleer and Brown 84] introduce such assumed values only when necessary and the results depend on the choice of these assumptions. Thus, different assumptions may produce different results, all of them valid only in the context of their assumed premises. A mechanism is needed to record these assumptions as well as the intermediate results. QSIM of [Kuipers 86] does not require such mechanism, since his list of potential active states corresponds to all potential next states of a system. Furthermore, QSIM tries to produce just one trajectory, whereas the device-centered ontology performs an analysis of the entire system.

[33] As already mentioned, the assignment of the qualitative value of "-" to the variable $\partial q_{\#2(VV)}$ is the only non-contradictory way to satisfy confluence 5, given that $\partial q_{\#1(VV)}$ is "+". This is based on the definition of qualitative operation $+ \oplus - \equiv ?$ (with respect to the addition table), where $? \equiv 0$ satisfies qualitative equality.

[34] However, this last step is not included in [de Kleer and Brown 84].

A mechanism which is able to deal with assumptions and to record intermediate states of the inferencing mechanism is the assumption-based truth maintenance system (ATMS) ([de Kleer 86a], [de Kleer 86b] and [de Kleer 86c]), which in principle is capable of considering simultaneously all assumptions to produce all solutions as desired in the envisionment process. The ATMS functions as a kind of a cache memory for all the inferences needed to generate the entire envisionment graph. This mechanism is widely used in the qualitative reasoning community, for example for diagnostic purposes (see also [de Kleer and Williams 87] or [Struss and Dressler 89]). A reasoning system with an ATMS shows the following architecture:

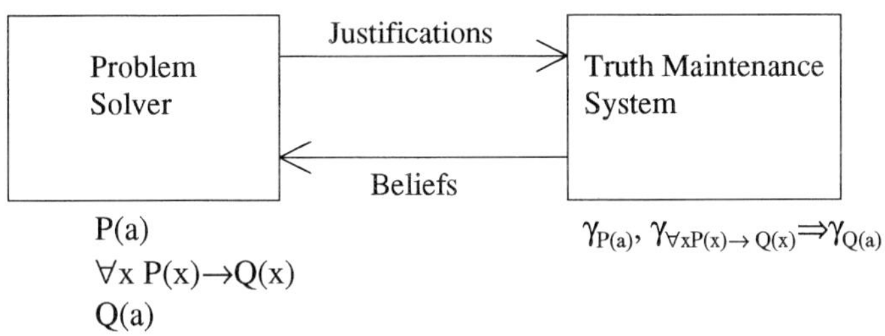

Fig. 21: ATMS architecture

The task of the maintenance system is to determine which data are believed and which are not. In addition, the problem solver takes into consideration the justifications for values derived hitherto. It is assumed that the problem solver contains all the knowledge and an inference mechanism. Every inference is communicated to the TMS. Problem solving is seen as a process of accumulating justifications and changing beliefs until some goal is satisfied. The TMS determines belief on the basis of the justifications that have been encountered until that moment, but it does not produce solutions. A TMS is based on propositional logics, using justifications as propositional axioms, and can be seen as a clever organization of storing intermediate results and their supporting environments. When, in the previous figure, the inference Q(a) is made, the TMS treats this expression as a propositional atom. Therefore, the two inference procedures work synchronously on the same expression, but they treat them differently.

The basic structure of an ATMS is a node which corresponds to a problem solver data, i.e. some fact. A justification describes how such a node is derivable from other nodes. A justification has three parts: i) the node to be justified, ii) the justifying nodes and iii) the problem solver's description of the justification, which is the rule in the form of an implication of how some consequent is inferred from its antecedents. This approach distinguishes between what is assumed and the decision to assume. An assumption denotes a decision to assume without any commitment as to what is assumed. An assumed datum is the problem-solver datum that has been assumed. Assumptions are connected to assumed data by means of justifications. Thus, assumptions can be managed independently. A set of assumptions forms a so-called environment. A node n is said to hold in an environment E, if it can be derived from E and the current set of justifications J,

$E, J \vdash n.$

In the case where $E, J \vdash \bot$, it is said that the environment is inconsistent.

Furthermore, the concept of context is introduced. It is the set formed by the assumptions of a consistent environment plus all nodes derivable from these assumptions. A context is characterized by an environment, if, from its set of assumptions, every node of the context can be derived. The task of an ATMS, provided with a set of assumptions and justifications, now is to determine the context of a node. A node is in the context, if it has at least one environment which is a subset of an environment characterizing the context. For this purpose, each node has a specific label that consists of the set of all environments associated with this node. All these labels are consistent and describe the assumptions on which each node ultimately depends. Unlike justifications, labels are built by the ATMS itself; justifications describe how the data depends on its immediately preceding antecedents. Thus, a node has the form

γ_{data} : ⟨data, label, justifications⟩.

In the following lower-case letters and γ_x represent nodes, upper-case letters denote assumptions. An ATMS contains four types of nodes: premises, assumptions, assumed nodes and derived nodes. A premise has a justification without antecedent and holds universally: ⟨p,{{}},{()}⟩. An assumption contains the environment mentioning itself: ⟨A,{{A}},{(A)}⟩. An assumed node with data x contains a justification mentioning an assumption: ⟨x, {{A}}, {(A)}⟩.

Finally, the node $\gamma_{w=1}$: ⟨w=1, {{A,B},{C},{D}},{(b),(c,e)}⟩ represents a derived node. It denotes that w = 1 is derived from either the node b or the nodes c and e. In addition, this fact holds in the environment {A,B}, {C} and {D}. Furthermore, the node $\gamma_{\perp}$: ⟨⊥,{},{...}⟩ represents falsity. Inconsistent environments are called nogoods.

Every consistent environment defines a context. There are $\binom{n}{k}$ environments having k assumptions, when the total number of assumptions is n. These environments can be grouped to form a so-called environment lattice. The following example shows the usage of the ATMS and the environment lattice with its basic operations. The assumptions are {A,B,C,D,E}, and the nogood is formed by the environment {A,B,E}. The following nodes are given:

$\gamma_{x+y=1}$:⟨x + y = 1,{{A,B},{B,C,D}},{...}⟩, indicated by dotted circles,

$\gamma_{x=1}$:⟨x = 1,{{A,C},{D,E}},{...}⟩, indicated by dotted squares.

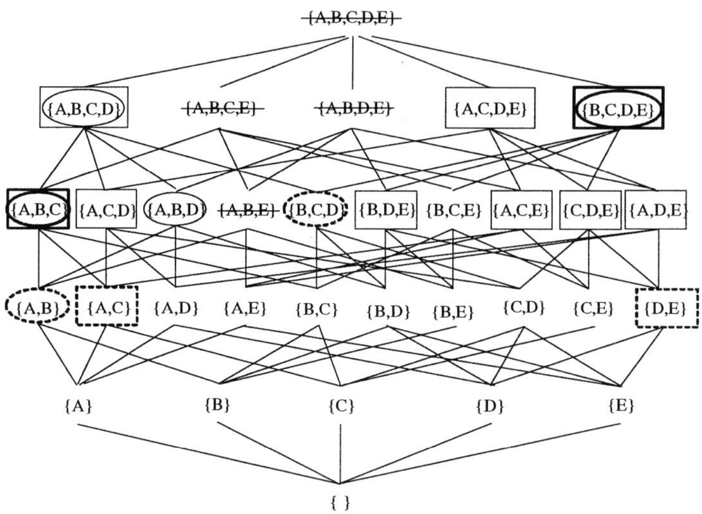

Fig. 22: Environment lattice in an ATMS [de Kleer 86a]

Super- and subset relations are defined by the respective lines. Any environment which allows the derivation of $\perp$ is nogood and is crossed out. All its supersets are also removed. If a data is in some context, it is also in its supersets. This is indicated by both circles and squares. In the above example, the label of the node $\gamma_{x+y=1}$ is the set of the greatest lower bounds of the circled nodes, i.e. {{A,B} ,{B,C,D}}.

It is now the problem solver's task to deduce from both facts x + y = 1 and x = 1 that y = 0, in consequence the justification $\gamma_{x+y=1},\gamma_{x=1} \Rightarrow \gamma_{y=0}$ is added.

The context of $\gamma_{y=0}$ is the intersections of the contexts of $\gamma_{x+y=1}$and $\gamma_{x=1}$. The node of $\gamma_{y=0}$ looks now as presented below. Its label is the set of the greatest lower bounds of the intersections (indicated by both bold circles and squares):
$\gamma_{y=0}$:⟨y=0,{{A,B,C},{B,C,D,E}},{($\gamma_{x+y=1}$,$\gamma_{x=1}$)}⟩

The ATMS guarantees that labels are
sound: no context will contain a data it should not,
complete: it is guaranteed that every context contains all data it should contain,
consistent: all inconsistent environments are identified and do not appear in labels, and
minimal: no environment of a label is a superset of any other environment of this label.

A not minimal label, for example, is {{A,B,C}, {A,B,C,D}, {B,C,D,E}}. This label can be reduced by removing {A,B,C,D}, which is subsumed by {A,B,C}. The algorithm to build labels, given a new justification by the problem solver, proceeds as follows:

- a new label is computed assuming that each antecedent node has a sound and complete label. These operations can be seen as set operations. If j_{ik} is the label of the ith node of justification k for consequent node n, a complete label for n is:
  $\cup_k \{x \mid x = \cup_i x_i \text{ where } x_i \in j_{ik}\}$, where x is an environment contained in the label. After removing inconsistent and subsumed environments, the label is sound and minimal.
- if the new label is the same as the old one, the procedure is finished.

- if the node is $\gamma_\perp$, each environment of its label is marked as nogood and all these inconsistent environments are removed from every node's label.
- if the node is not $\gamma_\perp$, then the updating procedure recurs to all consequent nodes to update the respective labels (i.e. adding environments).

The basic operations of an ATMS are simple set operations. The procedure guarantees that a label is formed by the complete, consistent, sound and minimal disjunction of environments under which a node holds. And if some environment of a node's label is a subset of a given environment, then its corresponding statement is believed under the assumptions of the given environment. Thus, to determine whether some node is valid, the ATMS merely verifies, whether the current environment is a superset of one of the environments in this node's label. Furthermore, a node with an empty label is believed in no environment (it is not member of any context), and a node whose label contains the empty environment is believed under every set of assumptions.

The device-centered ontology describes devices in the form of algebraic constraints and derives the behavior by identifying the state space and the respective state transitions by satisfying the constraints using several assumption heuristics. These assumptions can be managed by an ATMS. The causal explanation provided corresponds to the single steps of the value propagation mechanism. Thus, the causal arguments are very pragmatic and it might be argued that they explain more the flow of calculation than the cause-effect relationships in a device. A similarity with approaches in simulation exists on the level of the result in the form of an envisionment graph which corresponds to a compact description of the state space, but representational primitives and reasoning mechanisms are completely different.

4.3 The Process-centered Ontology

The process-centered ontology can be seen within both the perspective of modeling and the aspect of generating the time-dependent behavior. Causality is already introduced in the modeling phase. It represents an approach which explicitly addresses the modeling problem, as it provides a technique to produce a model of a real world situation. The central concept of [Forbus 84] is the notion of process. A process is not only the active part of a situation which changes everything, but represents also the distinction between active and passive parts. The concept of a process distinguishes this ontology from the other approaches, where influencing / active entities and modeled objects are mixed up. This concept has similarities with the object-oriented paradigm in software engineering and provides important hints regarding implementational issues.

The point of departure is a specific view structure, i.e. the identification of individuals engaged in a situation, their respective attributes, i.e. variables, and their relationships. This structure determines the active processes which will act upon or influence this situation. Active processes change values of the derivatives of variables, which in turn may change the derivatives of other variables by means of some other operators. This will be done until some threshold value is reached, detected by the limit analysis. When such threshold values are attained, the description of the situation, i.e. its state, changes. New participating objects may be detected and /or inserted. This task cannot be accomplished by the other approaches.

Two operators are fundamental:
- I(x,y), which means that variable y directly influences variable x, and

- $y \;\alpha_Q\; x$, which means that variable x indirectly influences variable y or that y is proportional to x, i.e. y = f(.....,x ,...).

It is assumed that a variable is either directly or indirectly influenced. Furthermore, it is subject to continuous change. To some extent, directly influenced variables can be considered as independent, because they are only influenced by processes, which can be seen as an external and independent construct; the indirectly influenced variables can be interpreted as dependent ones, as they are product of the value propagation process, which starts with directly influenced variables. Everything is caused by processes, they directly or indirectly influence variables, the latter by means of directly influenced intermediate variables. Semantically, the operator I represents the driving force of the simulation process as it incorporates time and models a differential equation.

Two variables cannot indirectly influence each other at the same time, i.e. $x \;\alpha_Q\; y$ and $y \;\alpha_Q\; x$ together are not allowed. Such feedback loops are solved by the insertion of directly influenced variables, because the operator I transfers time to the next point. It breaks such algebraic loops. This can be shown with the influence structure of the two container example, where I indicates not only a direct influence but also a time step. Thus, the feedback is ordered in time [Forbus and Falkenhainer 90].

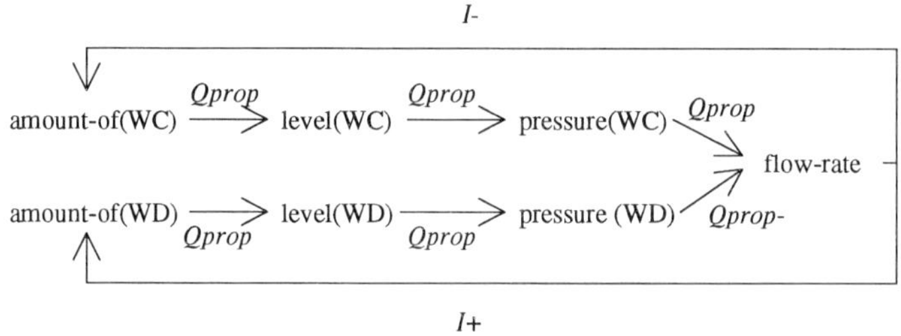

Fig. 23: Influence structure of the two connected containers example

The value propagation mechanism has to distinguish between the two influencing operators. The direct influences on a variable may be added up. A variable's change in time is the sum of all direct influences. Given the positive and negative influences on x_0 with $I^+(x_0,x_i)$ and $I^-(x_0,x_j)$, they result into

$\frac{dx_0}{dt} = \sum_i x_i - \sum_j x_j$, where x_i are all positively influencing and x_j all negatively influencing variables.

The signs of the respective derivatives D_s determine the direction of change. In the above example, there might occur an ambiguity as a consequence of the sign algebra. In such cases - if no information about magnitudes is available - assumptions have to be made about specific values, based on heuristics similar to those of [de Kleer and Brown 84]. These assumptions enable the process of propagation to continue for all assumed data.

The proportionality operator α_Q needs a more detailed consideration, since indirect influences do not add up. It is only known whether the functional relationship of α_Q is monotonic increasing or decreasing. In the case of

$x_0 \alpha_{Q+} x_1 \wedge x_0 \alpha_{Q-} x_2$ and $D_s[x_1] = 1 \wedge D_s[x_2] = 1$

the result is undefined. In the case that $D_s[x_1] = 1 \wedge D_s[x_2] = 0$ we can conclude that $D_s[x_0] = 1$. Thus, also in the case of indirect influences assumptions have to be introduced, each one producing different results of the propagation process.

The QPE (qualitative process engine) of [Forbus 86] represents the implementation of the qualitative process theory and is based on an ATMS architecture [de Kleer 86a]. This system keeps and manages the different assumptions necessary during the envisionment process. Such an ATMS can also be seen as a network of nodes. Each node represents a potential solution according to its distinct environment, i.e. initial assumptions. Thus, an ATMS represents a set of possible solutions, selecting one of its members depending on the initial choice sets. A choice set denotes a construct which comprises the problem solver's search space and provides the set of ATMS assumptions which form the base of a solution. [Forbus 86] calls this view an interpretation of an ATMS as a "many world database". One inserts into this network a particular set of assumptions and obtains a particular answer out of an entire set of possible ones.

The QPE is based on the closed-world assumption, for example all influences on a quantity are known in order to identify how it will change. It can be stated as an assumption about set memberships, i.e. the members that are known are indeed the only members. For each set requiring a closed-world assumption there is a stage in the solution process, where all the information needed is known. This assumption allows for the creation of so-called closed-world tables. Consider, for example, the following situation of three connected liquid containers and the respective flow processes according to pressure differences:

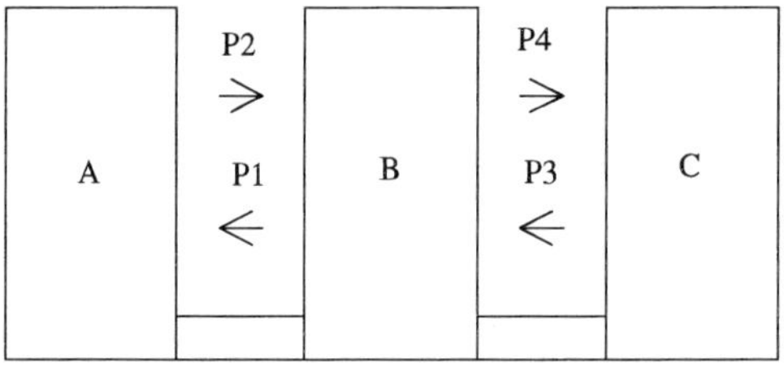

Fig. 24: Three connected containers and four potential processes

Once this structure is identified, the assumption that these are the only influencing entities enables closed-world tables to maintain the possible results of resolving these influences. The sets of consistent influences, i.e. active processes, are:

- {}
- {P1} {P2} {P3} {P4}
- {P1, P3} {P1, P4} {P2, P3} {P2, P4}

All other combinations are nogoods, for example {P1, P2}, since the pressure difference cannot instantaneously be negative and positive. Combinations of three active processes would contain nogoods and are inconsistent. Based on these sets, the influences can be resolved. This can be done in advance, before they are needed, already in the moment the structure is identified. In the following D_s denotes the direction of change of B's water:

{ }: $D_s = 0$ {P1}: $D_s = -1$ {P2}: $D_s = 1$ {P3}: $D_s = 1$ {P4}: $D_s = -1$
{P1, P3}: $D_s = ?$ {P1, P4}: $D_s = -1$ {P2, P3}: $D_s = 1$ {P2, P4}: $D_s = ?$

In ambiguous cases further information about the magnitude of the respective variables is needed. This final step is done at the moment when these tables are really used in the reasoning process, at that moment the necessary information is either available or provided by well-defined assumptions.

QPE looks for the entire set of solutions and produces a total envisionment graph. It breaks down its work into several phases, starting with a given scenario description and finishing with the limit analysis. On a technical level, QPE consists of a several times repeated sequence of different steps: i) a justify step generates justifications for conclusions and constraints that follow from a current set of facts; ii) a step to assume values for unknowns to continue the propagation; iii) an interpretation step to extend partial solutions.

The overall procedure of the QPE looks as follows:

expand the scenario model
Prototypical descriptions of views and processes form the base of QPE's work. In the first step, instances are generated which are valid for a given initial scenario description. The many world database interpretation allows for reusing the same instances in different situations, a generation of new instances is not necessary. All views and processes which may apply to the given scenario are created, their enabling conditions and consequences are installed. Closed-world tables are created and it is determined which specific parts of a domain model apply.

install initial assumptions
Preconditions and quantity conditions define the status of active processes and views. Furthermore, different choice sets, which should be explored, can be defined, i.e. solutions depend on the assignment of different values to variables. Each member of this set is also an assumption and used in the ATMS to update labels. The combination of all inequalities, which defines the quantity space in the qualitative process theory, forms the set of all possible states.

resolve non-ambiguous influences
In this step direct and indirect influences which are not ambiguous are resolved. Direct influences can be added with respect to their D_s values, indirect influences have to be resolved as described earlier. Ambiguous cases are left to be solved in a further step. The previously mentioned closed-world tables are used in this step.

construct initial solutions
This step represents an interpret cycle and constructs the initial set of solutions. The choice set includes alternatives for each pre- and quantity condition. Consistent combinations of alternatives are built from these sets. Each combination forms an environment. The consequences of these environments include the active process and view structure and the unambiguous results of influences.

resolve ambiguous influences
In this step ambiguous situations are resolved by identifying values for unknown D_s. This can, in principle, be done in two ways: either values for the respective sums of all negative

and positive influences are assumed or the combination of all assumptions for each possible pair of opposite influences is taken into consideration. However, this second alternative may result in an expensive procedure. In the case that there are N positive and N negative influences on a quantity, then N^2 inequalities - depending on the magnitudes of these influencing quantities - have to be considered. Fortunately, this procedure can normally be shortened. For example, if quantity x_0 depends on x_1 then x_1 should be considered before exploring x_0.

perform limit analysis

Limit analysis identifies the potential state transitions and determines their consequences. It is the conjecture that a set of inequalities will no longer hold and the system changes into a new state. A limit hypothesis LH is applicable to state S_i if the initial state of inequalities mentioned in LH holds in S_i. The next step is to find S_j, which results when applying LH to S_i. It has to be ensured that S_j is a result of LH. Furthermore, it has to be guaranteed that the transition is a valid one, based on state transition rules described previously. The final envisionment graph consists of the states and the possible transitions. Due to the applied ATMS, the envisionment graph represents all solutions.

The device-centered approach of [de Kleer and Brown 84] and the constraint-based approach of [Kuipers 86] are centered around total system descriptions. Their sets of equations describe the entire system. The process-centered approach of [Forbus 84] concentrates on individuals and their history. This approach is able to identify forces which act upon individuals, i.e. processes. However, in another aspect the device- and the process-centered ontology have common features; both approaches produce the entire set of future behaviors. Sets of inequalities or specific rules indicate which of these possible behaviors may occur in distinct situations.

Two fundamentally different techniques to generate behavior can be identified: the generate-test algorithm of [Kuipers 86] and the ATMS of [de Kleer 86a]. Both are able to handle ambiguous situations. The former puts all states into one set, the latter also records how they depend on specific assumptions. Furthermore, the ATMS-based approach analyzes relationships between known facts, i.e. states, and deals with a finite number of elements. The constraint-based approach generates new elements and their sequence. It iteratively increases the state space. This is also the reason why the approach of [Kuipers 86] looks very much like a classical simulation algorithm. In contrast, the ATMS represents a more general solution strategy and is not limited to the generation of envisionment graphs. And it explicitly represents the assumptions on which the final solutions depend.

However, it should be noted, that regardless of the specific aim - either envisionment or simulation - all behaviors shown in the final result are possible. All these approaches are unable to detect and to exclude solutions which are consistent with the supplied model description and the applied reasoning techniques but contradictory to "reality". They have no instrument to achieve this feature. This capability requires a level of knowledge which lies beyond these systems.

Part III

Advanced Topics

This part deals with topics such as causality, ambiguity and uncertainty, which were mentioned shortly in the previous chapters. Additionally, several approaches will be discussed which explicitly deal with these topics and, to some extent, manage to avoid the limitation of ambiguity.

1. Some Remarks on Causality

Causality represents a main theme in qualitative reasoning. Although it was discussed intensively, it was not explicitly referred to detailed discussions, for example, in philosophy. A rather pragmatic view was taken, motivating implementational issues, either coding causal influences directly into a model or giving reasons for the sequence of assignment steps and the introduction of assumptions. In the following we look at the approaches presented hitherto to see how they deal with the problem of causality. Moreover, other approaches will be described. The approach of qualitative reasoning toward causality is a rather empirical one which also explores how causal arguments appear in cognitive processes. The views and the respective manifestations obtained in this way, however, may differ from causality based on theories in natural science.[35] In principle, we can observe two ways how causality appears in the thinking process:

- People tend to think in causal schemes and implications. Human thinking relies on cause - effect chains, causes have to explain certain effects. For example, the reasoning of engineers fundamentally relies on causality, as shown by [Forbus and Gentner 1986].
- People expect results to be based on causal explanations. This phenomenon is important for the development of expert systems as well as decision support systems.

In order to be of use in a causal explanation of behavior, an argument has to meet three criteria:

- temporal order: causes and effects have to be ordered with respect to time,[36]
- locality (one of the basic principles of qualitative reasoning): a link between cause and effect has to be identified, and finally
- necessitation: a specific event, i.e. an effect, requires a cause.

Thus, a causal argument consists of a temporally ordered sequence of local causal interactions, each one forced by earlier ones in the sequence. A causal explanation describes a process much like a single, initial falling domino causing an entire sequence of dominos to fall. The following example shows the use of such arguments, especially the importance of temporal order. The two equations $s = i$ and $i = m$ might have the interpretation: if the power switch is on ($s = 1$), then current flows ($i = 1$), and furthermore, if $i = 1$, then $m = 1$ is also valid, the lamp lights (hopefully it is not broken). An equivalence relationship between the three variables s, i and m can be established. Hence, if one of these values is known, the others can be calculated. However, taking a causal point of view, considering the flow of

[35] Also theories in science are created by cognitive processes, but the discussion of this epistemological problem is beyond the scope of this work.

[36] However, temporal ordering depends on the observer. What can be in a time sequence for one, may happen simultaneously for another one.

some material, the relationship is s → i → m, because the switch enables the flow of current and, thus, turns the light on and not vice versa. The relationship is asymmetric and we can identify the elements of a causal argument. On a technical and implementational level, we have to take care when to use the property of symmetry. For example, in a situation where no change occurs on account of the fact that m = 1, it may be deduced that s = 1, i.e. when one sees the light on, one can deduce that the switch is on. In dynamically changing situations this equivalence cannot be applied.[37] Causality has to do with dynamic situation, a cause has to occur before an effect. Hence, the concept of causality only makes sense in the case of dynamic systems. In addition, it should be noted that the cause is necessary, but not sufficient, for the effect.[38]

In qualitative reasoning, according to the knowledge about the real system and the chosen ontology, either causal relationships - as influences - or only constraining equations are implemented. Using the differentiation of [Forbus and Gentner 1986] regarding the distinctions explicit versus implicit causal mechanisms and directed versus not-directed connectives between objects, the following classification of research approaches can be drawn:

Connectives	**Mechanisms** Explicit	Implicit
Directed	[Forbus 84] [Kuipers 84] [Weld 88] [Davis 89] [Guariso et al 92]	
Not-directed		[deKleer & Brown 84] [Williams 84]

Fig. 25: Causal connectives and mechanisms

The dense population of two cells is an obvious result of the fact that explicit mechanisms are correlated with directed connectives and implicit ones with not-directed connectives. The other two cells remain empty. We only show some of the published techniques and also include methods which will be discussed later in this part. It is interesting to note that an explicit and directed causal explanation is such a dominant concept, so that people even use it, when it does not represent an appropriate method [Forbus and Gentner 86].

The placement of the constraint-based approach of [Kuipers 84] in the directed/explicit cell is not straightforward. On a technical level, the relationships between its variables are only used in a constraining manner, on a semantic level, however, an operator like DERIV has a directed and explicit interpretation. The rules of this approach include the representation of time as well as the order of calculation in the case of functional relationships. The process-centered ontology, which is based on the causal directness hypothesis, stating that every change in situations is caused by some explicit mechanism, i.e. process, incorporates causal

[37] It is interesting to note that this distinction can also be expressed by the different interpretation of the symbol = as used in computer science. In addition to an equivalence relationship, this symbol denotes an assignment operation of values and addresses.

[38] In a logical view there exists an implication instead of an equivalence.

knowledge already in the modeling step. It compiles this knowledge and explicitly states which variables influence others by the operator I. The other basic operator, which denotes proportionality, represents the fact of being similar, of behaving in the same way.

The device-centered ontology of [de Kleer and Brown 84] relates variables by means of constraints, relating magnitudes and /or derivatives. In this approach, causality enters as the result of the reasoning process, thus it is introduced on another, higher, level. Taking as input a non-causal description, a causal chain of state sequences is derived. The explanation which is provided by this approach states how a specific situation follows another one. The advancement in time is implicitly described by a set of confluences which relate the derivatives of variables and constrain their values. Time is not explicitly introduced. Since quantities are only related with each other by means of algebraic constraints, there is the "philosophical" problem of explaining how influences occur, i.e. how variables change their values during the phase of intrastate behavior. For example, in the case of the constraint $\partial a \oplus \partial b \equiv 0$, the values of $\partial a \equiv +$ and $\partial b \equiv -$ would satisfy the constraint. If now one variable, for example ∂a, receives an new value, e.g. $\partial a \equiv 0$, the constraint is not satisfied anymore. However, ∂b also has to have the value of 0 to again satisfy the constraint. The concept of mythical causality is introduced to explain this assignment step, to tell how variable ∂b changes its value. However, the criteria of temporal ordering has to be relaxed. It is assumed that it takes an interval of time - at least some time - before the value, the information, reaches ∂b. This is called mythical time, which denotes the "technically negligible" interval of time during which a constraint may not be satisfied due to the assignment of a new value to one of the constraint's variables. It ends, when this value is propagated to the other variables and the constraint is again satisfied. On a technical level, it only describes the process of value propagation within constraints.

This process works with respect to the algebraic equations, the order of the value assignments to variables defines the "causal" relationship. Time is not considered on that level. The procedure can also be described by the following picture: the algebraic constraints form a kind of network where the nodes are the respective variables and the undirected arcs their relationships. Value propagation is now something like a wave originating from those variables which already have values assigned. This wave moves constantly outward until all variables are reached - very similar to a wave caused by a stone thrown into an initially calm lake. As a consequence, this procedure may also be seen as a specific answer to the question, how something is happening within a state. In the case of problems caused by missing values during value propagation, causal heuristics are used to assume values for unknown variables, i.e. the component, the conduit and the confluence heuristic.

Simultaneous feedback loops give rise to serious problems for causal explanations (see also [Williams 84]). Consider the following structure:

$$a + b = c$$
$$b = f(c)$$

If function f contains an integration step, i.e. time is involved, then the causal direction is parallel to the direction of time. No problem occurs. But in an algebraic situation the argument has to be modified. The necessitation and the temporal order criteria of a causal argument cannot be satisfied. However, in such case the dominant flow of some material can be considered to be assigned to the path that responds to the largest initial change. Human interpretations of these algebraic feedback situations justify such statement. Given a change in variable a, causality can be assigned to the flow from variable a to variable c, if $|f(c)| \ll |c|$, and from a to variable b, if |c| << |f(c)|, where << denotes "much smaller". In the former case, b becomes small with respect to c, thus, variable a mainly influences c. In the other case, the opposite argument is valid.

In the controversy of [de Kleer and Brown 86], [Iwasaki and Simon 86a], [Iwasaki and Simon 86b] about causality, the respective concepts of causal ordering [Simon 52] and mythical time were confronted. This discussion - characterized by misunderstandings as mentioned by [Weld and de Kleer 90a] - showed that, in principle, both methods are able to produce the same result. The main argument focuses on the solution of an underdetermined system of equations in which some variables are either interpreted as exogenous (Iwasaki & Simon) or assigned some values based on the assumption heuristics of (de Kleer & Brown). Therefore, causality enters in the modeling step (Iwasaki & Simon) and is thereafter compiled - it is assumed that it is normally clear which variables are exogenous -, or causal heuristics are used during the reasoning process to introduce missing values (de Kleer & Brown). In the latter case, the interdependence depends on the specific choice of heuristics and is not fixed beforehand.

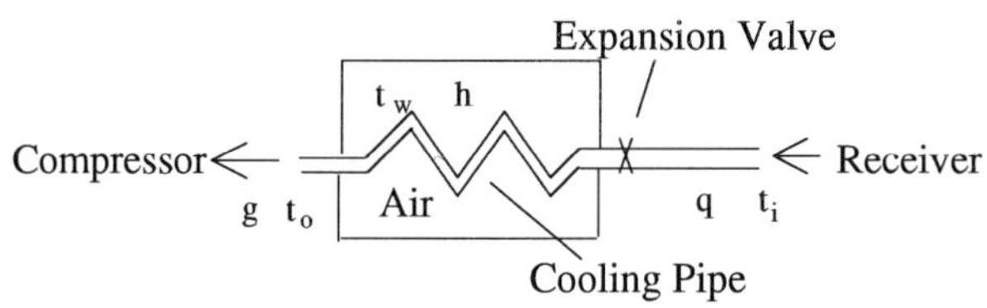

Fig. 26: Diagram of a refrigerator box

Fig. 26 shows a refrigerator box, t_i and t_o are the temperatures of the in- and outgoing refrigerant. t_w denotes the temperature of air in the chamber, t_c the condensing temperature of the refrigerants. h is the heat gained, p the pressure within the chamber of the refrigerant; q is the flow rate and g the ratio of vapor to total mass of outgoing refrigerant. The refrigerant that enters through the expansion valve is liquid, when it leaves the box its temperature is t_c, its form is either vapor or liquid or both. The system is described by the following equations, constants are left out:

$$h = t_w - t_c \qquad 1$$
$$h = gq - (t_i - t_o)q \qquad 2$$
$$t_c = f(p) \qquad 3$$
$$t_o = t_c \qquad 4$$

The first equation assumes that cooling is an instantaneous process. The method of causal ordering produces an asymmetric causal relation starting with a system described in an non-causal manner. The sequence of value assignment steps corresponds to the obtained causal order. Moreover, the system has to be described by means of so-called structural equations.[39] The equations are said to be structural, when each of them represents its own separate mechanism. The notion of a structural equation is similar to the component - interconnection description formalism of [de Kleer and Brown 84], as it only has to describe the important items and to separate them properly.

---

[39] But is not clear where structural descriptions are coming from. There are several heuristic principles which may be applied to identify a structural description. However, it should be noted that such heuristics again depend on the view of the human modeler.

The equations of the above example are underdetermined. The following variables are now defined as exogenous. Hence, their values can be assumed to be known:

$t_i = c_1$ 5
$q = c_2$ 6
$p = c_3$ 7
$t_w = c_4$ 8

The system of equations can be presented by the following matrix, showing on the left side the equation number and within the cells the respective engaged variables (marked by x).

	h	g	q	t_i	t_o	t_w	t_c	p
1	x					x	x	
2	x	x	x	x	x			
3							x	x
4					x		x	
5				x				
6			x					
7								x
8						x		

Those lines of the matrix with only one variable form a starting subset; beginning with this subset, the entire system of equations can be solved and the causal influences determined. Equation 7 allows to calculate variable p, inserting p into equation 3 gives t_c. Substituting this value into equation 4, the value of t_o is obtained. In equation 1 variable h can be calculated, because the value of t_w and t_c are known. Finally, everything is known to infer the value of variable g using equation 2. The matrix makes the set of linear equations explicit, the method is similar to the Gaussian method of solving such equations by applying proper rules like exchanging columns or rows. In this way the exogenous variables, they appear only once in the respective rows, determine the causal structure of the system:

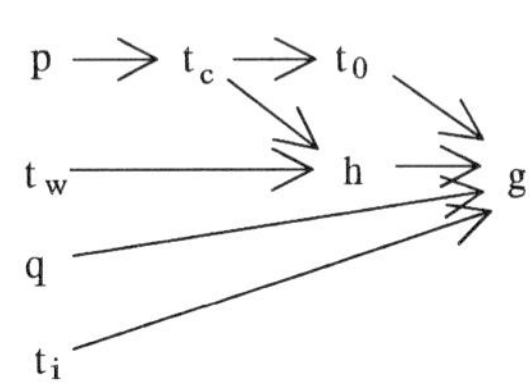

Fig. 27: Causal structure of the refrigerator box

A similar structure can be derived, when the concept of mythical time is used, the continuation of the propagation process depends on the choice of heuristics. Equations 1 to 4 are rewritten as qualitative confluences, both equality and operators have a qualitative interpretation:

$\partial h \ominus \partial t_w \oplus \partial t_c \equiv 0$ 1a
$\partial h \ominus \partial g \ominus \partial q + \partial t_i \ominus \partial t_o \equiv 0$ 2a
$\partial t_c \ominus \partial p \equiv 0$ 3a
$\partial t_o \ominus \partial t_c \equiv 0$ 4a

The value propagation process may proceed as follows:

$\partial p \equiv +$	initial disturbance, works like an exogenous variable	5a
$\partial t_c \equiv +$	substitute 5a in 3a	6a
$\partial t_o \equiv +$	substitute 6a in 4a	7a

At this stage the propagation mechanism is interrupted, further information is missing. The confluence heuristic is taken to continue the process:

$\partial h \equiv -$	setting $\partial t_w \equiv 0$ in 1a and substitute 6a in 1a	8a

The confluence heuristic is used once more:

$\partial g \equiv -$	setting $\partial t_i \equiv 0$ and $\partial q \equiv 0$ and use 8a and 7a in 2a	9a

The produced causal chain is the same as in the previous case, the application of the confluence heuristic justifies the assignment of zero to the unknown variables, which permits the continuation of the propagation process. A choice of other heuristics, i.e. setting other variables to zero, would produce other results. But both approaches, causal ordering and the device-centered approach, rely upon heuristic principles, either in the modeling or the reasoning phase.

The method of causal ordering produces an asymmetric relationship between variables through iterative substitution of quantities in equations, assuming that a correct structural description of the system is provided. However, this approach shows serious limitations in the case of feedback loops and needs further mathematical methods. The concept of mythical time and its heuristics, on the other side, justifies the assignment of values when and how it is necessary during the reasoning process. Thus, it represents a dynamic concept, applicable in the case of feedback.

Another approach, the qualitative resolution rule of [Dormoy and Raiman 88], shows a similarity with the theory of causal ordering and its process of iterative substitution. This rule defines a substitution procedure as well:

If x, y, z, a, b are qualitative quantities such that

$$x \oplus y \equiv a \text{ and}$$
$$-x \oplus z \equiv b$$

Furthermore, if x is different from ?, then

$$y \oplus z \equiv a \oplus b.$$

In this approach the concept of qualitative equality $\equiv$ is used. The algebraic operations are defined in a similar way as in case i) of chapter II.3 with the set of qualitative values Q = {+,0,-,?}. The condition on quantity x is necessary for this operation, because the qualitative resolution rule relies on two properties:

- Quasi transitivity of qualitative equality: if $a \equiv b$ and $b \equiv c$ and b differs from ?, then $a \equiv c$.
- Compatibility of addition and qualitative equality: $a \oplus b \equiv c$ is equivalent to $a \equiv c \ominus b$. This can be shown by case analysis.

If we apply the second property, the first and second line of the qualitative resolution rule can be written as $z \ominus b \equiv x$ and $x \equiv a \ominus y$. Assuming that x differs from ?, we can use the first property, i.e. $z \ominus b \equiv a \ominus y$. Using again the second property, $y \oplus z \equiv a \oplus b$ is obtained.

The method of causal ordering can also be applied to systems which are described by means of both algebraic and differential equations. If a dynamic system is described in an non-causal and structural form, the causal relationships between the variables can be derived (see also [Iwasaki 88], [Vescovi 91], [Iwasaki and Bhandari 88], [Skorstad 90], [Iwasaki 90a]). It is assumed that the differential equations are supplied in a canonical form, i.e. only one derivative exists in one equation and is written on the left hand-side of the equation. Variables occurring in the form of derivatives can be interpreted as being dependent, in the notion of [Forbus 84] they would be called influenced quantities. Hence, in this dynamic part of a system's description causality can be well identified. The causal ordering procedure has only to be applied to variables which do not appear as derivatives. This can be demonstrated using the following set of equations:

1 $f_1(x_1,x_2,x_4) = c_1$
2 $f_2(x_2,x_3,x_4) = c_2$
3 $dx_3/dt = f_3(x_2,x_5)$
4 $dx_4/dt = f_4(x_5)$
5 $x_5 = c_5$

The derivative dx_3/dt depends on both x_2 and x_5, dx_4/dt is influenced by x_5. In Fig. 28, arcs marked with a letter i indicate an integration step and link a derivative to its variable. Causal ordering follows this time step. Both variables x_3 and x_4 are directly influenced, whereas variable x_5 is exogenous. In a first step, the procedure assumes the left-hand side variables of the differential equations as being constant for the further causal ordering. This assumption can be justified by the fact that the integration of differential equations, e.g. the calculation of new values, involves time, whereas algebraic equations react instantaneously. Therefore, the first type of equations can be treated as being constant during the treatment of the others. This first step transforms the above system into the following form, which is also called equilibrated:

1 $f_1(x_1,x_2,x_4) = c_1$
2 $f_2(x_2,x_3,x_4) = c_2$
3 $x_3 = c_3$
4 $x_4 = c_4$
5 $x_5 = c_5$

The matrix of the new equations looks like this:

	x1	x2	x3	x4	x5
1	x	x		x	
2		x	x	x	
3			x		
4				x	
5					x

Causal ordering can now draw the following dependency graph of the system:

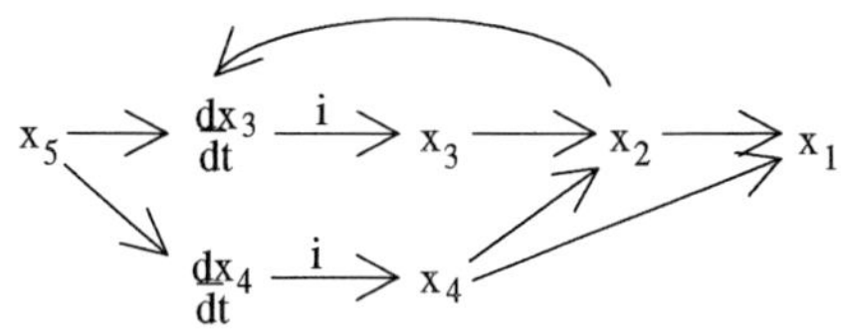

Fig. 28: Causal ordering in a dynamic system

We can identify a further feature of this system: the contact of the system with its environment is only established by the derivatives of the two variables x_3 and x_4, the exogenous variable x_5 acts only on these two. Thus, it could also be stated - as demonstrated by the form of the previous matrix - that variables x_3 and x_4 are also exogenous and independent. This view of the causal ordering procedure uncovers - to some extent - a similarity between causal ordering and the concept of the process-centered ontology. The system can be both well partitioned and encapsulated. The remaining endogenous variables can be analyzed without considering the respective external influences. In the terminology of the process-centered ontology it can be stated that the environment only influences the system by means of external processes.

Neither causal interpretation nor causal direction create difficulties, as long as dynamic systems and their time-ordered state transitions are involved. Both ontologies, the process-centered and the constraint-based approach, provide the necessary operational primitives, either I or DERIV. The device-centered ontology uses the supplementary, implementation-oriented concept of mythical causality based on heuristics to justify its value propagation mechanism in a set of algebraic equations within a state.

2. The Problem of Ambiguity - Improvements in the Representation of Structure and the Generation of Behavior

Qualitative models generate ambiguous results. This is an obvious consequence of the circumstance that qualitative reasoning forms coarser models of reality than it is done when using a classical quantitative technique. Due to undecidable intermediate situations, i.e. locally missing information, during the reasoning process, qualitative simulation produces an entire set of different solutions. Since a qualitative model may represent an entire class of "numerical" models, the different solutions corresponding to these models substantially enlarge the solution set. Additionally, spurious solutions may be generated. Thus, it is crucial to reduce the set of solutions by identifying wrong ones. This chapter provides an overview about several improvements in value representation as well as behavior generation. They are based on the previously discussed main approaches and can also be called second generation systems. The main aim is to develop a more adequate representation of knowledge, especially in cases where more quantitative information is available. Values are still represented as intervals, but their ranges and relationships are reviewed. However, since interval-based reasoning unavoidably leads to undecidable situations, the problem of ambiguity remains in principle.

Before presenting the mentioned improvements, we will discuss the problem of ambiguity in some detail. Fig. 29 shows the relationship between quantitative and qualitative descriptions and solutions (see also [Struss 87]):

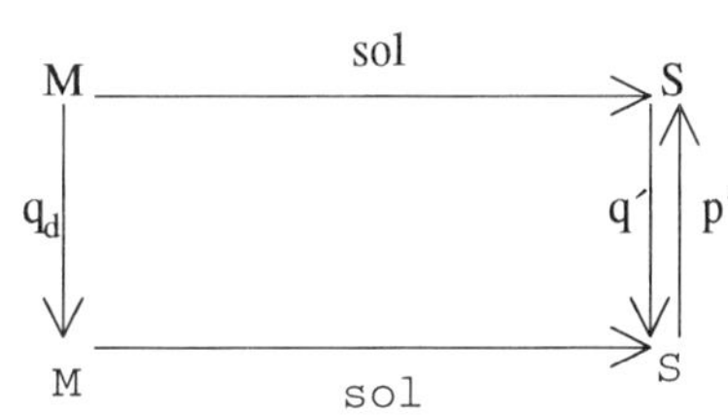

Fig. 29: Quantitative and qualitative models and solutions

In this figure M represents a space of quantitative models in terms of real valued variables and algebraic and differential equations, sol being the respective quantitative solution method producing the set of solution S (tuples of real numbers or functions, respectively). `M`, `sol` and `S` are the respective qualitative counterparts. q_d is a mapping between the two descriptions, for example the method of [Kuipers 86], which maps both values of variables and relationsships between variables (operators and functions). The qualitative solution method can be written - in the case of n qualitative variables with the respective qualitative quantity spaces - as `sol`: `M` $\rightarrow$ `S`, where `S` $= P(Q_1 \times Q_2 \times ... \times Q_n)$, the power set of qualitative states. The power set is used since the set of qualitative solutions may contain all combinations of qualitative states. The quantitative solution mechanism is defined similarly as sol: M $\rightarrow$ S with S = $P(\mathbf{R}^n)$. Finally, we have the two mappings between the qualitative and quantitative solutions p' - producing an interpretation of qualitative solutions - and q' - establishing a coverage of the quantitative solutions. They are defined as q': $P(\mathbf{R}^n) \rightarrow P(Q_1 \times Q_2 \times ... \times Q_n)$ and p': $P(Q_1 \times Q_2 \times ... \times Q_n) \rightarrow P(\mathbf{R}^n)$.[40] We can now state two desired properties of

[40] In the definition of q' and p' the corresponding definitions of chapter II.3 to define the various mappings q_i: $\mathbf{R} \rightarrow Q_i$ and p_i: $Q_i \rightarrow P(\mathbf{R})$ are used. The q_i induce the mapping q": $\mathbf{R}^n \rightarrow (Q_1 \times .. \times Q_n)$ where q"$(x_1, .., x_n)$ =

qualitative reasoning methods: completeness and soundness [Struss 87].[41] A method is complete if the qualitative values of each solution to a quantitative model form a solution of the respective qualitative model, i.e.
$\forall$ m $\in$ M
q'(sol(m)) $\subseteq$ sol(q_d(m)).

A method is sound if each solution of the qualitative model, generated from the quantitative model, covers at least one of the quantitative solutions, i.e.
$\forall$ m $\in$ M
$\forall$ s $\in$ sol(q_d(m))
p'(s) $\cap$ sol(m) $\neq$ 0.

It has been shown by [Struss 87] that qualitative reasoning methods such as the constraint-based approach are complete, i.e. their solution set contains all possible solutions. However, they are not sound, they produce solutions which do not refer to any underlying model. As an example we refer to the system of a frictionless spring, as it is presented in chapter II.2. The following set of constraints defines the system, using the notion of the constraint-based approach:

DERIV(x,v)
DERIV(v,a)
M^-(a,x)

The only possible solution should be, starting with x_0 (location) = 0, v_0 (velocity) = v_{init} and a_0 (acceleration) = 0, that after one cycle all three quantities should again reach their initial values at the same time point. QSIM correctly predicts that a and x will reach the value of 0 at the same time. However, QSIM produces three possibilities for v: variable v reaches its landmark value v_{init} before, after or exactly when the other two variables reach the value 0. The first two trajectories correspond to an increasing or a decreasing oscillation. These behaviors do not correspond to any of the quantitative model that are the basis of the previous qualitative equations. In this case, these behaviors are caused by the fact that variable v behaves independently, whereas the other two variables are related through the monotonic relationship M^-(a,x). Thus, at the end of the first cycle the simulation tree necessarily branches. On a local level, the available information is not sufficient to exactly determine the next calculation step. However, since the set of solutions produced by qualitative simulation contains at least all possible behaviors, it can be followed, that if this set has only one member, i.e. only one trajectory, then this solution represents the correct behavior of the modeled system.

However, we want to add that the statements about completeness and soundness with respect to QSIM can also be made as follows: QSIM proves theorems of the form
QDE & state(t_0) $\rightarrow \vee$ (B_1, ..., B_n). A set QDE of qualitative differential equations and an initial state produce as set of behaviors B_i, where each behavior is an alternating sequence of (state(t_0), state(t_0, t_1),...., state(t_n)). The set of resulting behaviors is represented as a

($q_1(x_1)$, .., $q_n(x_n)$)). Furthermore, q'(H_R) := {v | $\exists$ x $\in$ $H_R \subset \mathbf{R}^n$ and q"(x) = v} for each $H_R \subset \mathbf{R}^n$. Symbol := means equal by definition. Similarly, we can - based on the mappings p_i - define p": ($Q_1 \times .. \times Q_n$) $\rightarrow$ P($\mathbf{R}^n$) where p"(v_1, .., v_n) = $p_1(v_1) \times .. \times p_n(v_n)$). And p'($H_Q$) := $\bigcup_{v \in H_Q} p''(v)$ for each $H_Q \subseteq (Q_1 \times .. \times Q_n)$.

[41] For other properties such as stability, weak completeness and weak soundness see also [Struss 87].

disjunction, since QDE and state(t_0) are incomplete descriptions of an underlying quantitative model and the initial state; B_i are incomplete descriptions of solutions of this model. Considered as a local constraint satisfaction mechanism, QSIM creates two kinds of relations: successor ($S_i(t_i)$, $S_j(t_i, t_{i+1})$) and successor ($S_i(t_i, t_{i+1})$, $S_j(t_{i+1})$). These correspond to transitions from points to intervals and vice versa. Since the description is based on incomplete knowledge, a state may have several successors.

It can now be stated that QSIM is locally complete but not sound, i.e. the constraint satisfaction mechanisms finds all successors of a state, but spurious ones may survive the filtering process. However, globally - QSIM viewed as a simulator - QSIM is sound but incomplete. It generates a tree of qualitative states and successor relations (S_i, S_j), each branch of the tree, starting with state(t_0), represents a possible solution. Since each branch represents just an alternative sequence of states, as already stated previously, the disjunction of behaviors, i.e. QDE & state(t_0) $\rightarrow \vee (B_1, ..., B_n)$, is proven. This is a sound inference. Each real behavior is included, but the disjunction may include spurious solutions. If, for example, B_n represents such a spurious behavior, then the stronger disjunction
QDE & state(t_0) $\rightarrow \vee (B_1, ..., B_{n-1})$ is not proven, thus QSIM is not complete.

Ambiguous situations descend from the limitations of interval-based arithmetic and the fact that in specific situations - due to missing local information - a correct choice is not possible. This source of ambiguity is called the selection problem by [Struss 87]: The constraint $x_1 \oplus x_1 \equiv x_2 \oplus x_1$, for example, is solved by the assignments $x_1 = (0,1)$ and $x_2 = (1,2)$ because $(0,1) \oplus (0,1) = (0,2)$ and $(1,2) \oplus (0,1) = (1,3)$. In this case we use the concept of qualitative equality as the non-empty intersection of two sets, therefore, the following non-empty intersection $(0,2) \cap (1,3) \neq 0$ satisfies the constraint. In the solution of the corresponding quantitative equation $a + b = c + d$, the distinct numbers a, b, c and d have to be chosen from the respective intervals, i.e. $a, b, d \in (0,1)$ and $c \in (1,2)$. An assignment of $a = b = 0.6$, $c = 1.1$ and $d = 0.1$, for example, would solve the equation. However, there is no choice of an identical real number for variable x_1 on both sides to solve the equation. From the fact that $c > b$ it can be followed that $d = (a - c + b) < a$, i.e. $d < a$, as a consequence we have the contradiction $x_1 \neq x_1$. The fundamental problem is that the choices of values for the quantities a and d cannot be done independently. This circumstance could be avoided, if each variable would appear just once in the set of constraints, i.e. every variable in only one of the constraints. However, this would not correspond with the applied approaches in building qualitative models. For example, in the device-centered approach, the single components communicate with each other by means of shared variables, thus they have to appear more than once. However, it should be noted that soundness is defined with respect to an underlying quantitative model. Once arrived at a qualitative level, or if only a qualitative description is available, it cannot be decided whether a solution is wrong or not. It can just be proven that the available inference steps were applied correctly. Qualitative reasoning based on intervals cannot exclude that spurious behaviors are produced and some extraordinary sources of information are needed to overcome this limitation.

As a further example to demonstrate causes of ambiguity, we use the predicate M^+ of [Kuipers 84], which is similar to the concept of qualitative proportionality of [Forbus 84]:

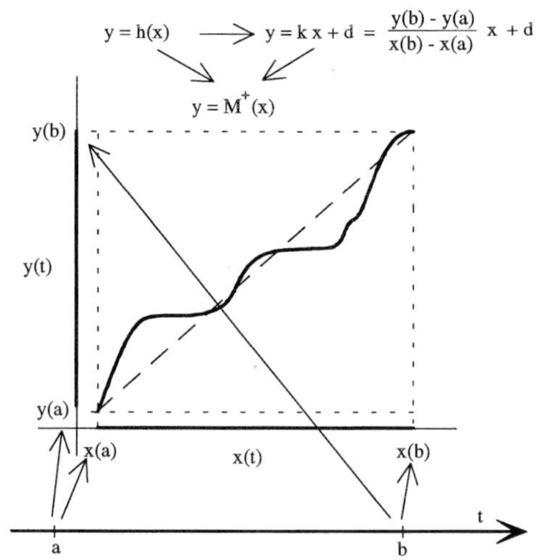

Fig. 30: Graphical representation of $M^+(y,x)$[42]

$M^+(y,x)$ represents the entire set of functions which satisfy the condition $h'(x) > 0$. The specific function $y = kx + d$ (with $k > 0$) can only be seen as its most prominent member. Taking a constructive point of view, i.e. the values of state variables are calculated and not generated by applying the continuity rule and constraint-based filtering, the linear function could be chosen as an approximation of the entire set of M(y,x). This can also be based on the consideration that continuous and differentiable functions can locally be approximated by linear functions. However, the information about the concrete form of the underlying function h is lost. If variable y is used in a further constraint, for example to build the difference between y and another variable, this information about the form of function h might be critical to obtain a result equal to, greater or smaller than zero. In order to include every valid solution, all alternatives have to be maintained, consequently also those which do not correspond to the function h. This, of course, enlarges the solution space.

In order to reduce ambiguity, additional sources of information or knowledge are necessary. They focus on both the method of model representation and the reasoning techniques applied thereafter. However, it should be noted that they are mainly oriented toward a more detailed description of M, thus bringing closer the quantitative and the qualitative description. In the literature several approaches to introduce and to use such a knowledge - leading to second generation systems - can be identified:

- information on a global level by formalizing and using general laws,
- knowledge about the purpose of a specific device,
- identification and usage of local information when available,
- insertion of quantitative information,
- usage of sound reasoning methods which combine both quantitative and qualitative information,
- usage of other, finer grain size representation methods,

---

[42] In this figure it is assumed that there exist no corresponding landmark values, i.e. there is no $t \in (a,b)$ such that $x(t) = p$ and $y(t) = q$ and p a landmark value of x and q of y.

- usage of magnitude or similar quantitative information about time to generate a behavior where time durations of states can be estimated,
- usage of another representation of time, based on supplementary information, and
- introduction of probabilistic and possibilistic methods as fundamentally different approaches to qualitative reasoning.

a. Global Rules about the Behavior of Dynamic Systems

Further information about the behavior of trajectories for systems described by first order differential equations can be gained. This may be provided by rules which are similar to and based on results in system theory and mathematical analysis (see also [Ishida 89], [Aubin 92]). Such a general rule is, for example, that a trajectory cannot cross itself in the phase portrait representation, except if it denotes a closed curve or a critical point, where a closed curve represents a periodic solution. [Lee and Kuipers 88] derive the so-called non-intersection constraint which examines whether any of the solution, i.e. the next possible states as a result of the filtering mechanism, violates this rule. A trajectory from point a to point c spans the rectangle abcd, the rectangle thus being partitioned into two sets {ab,bc} and {ad,dc}. If the trajectory, some time steps later, enters through the edge set {ab,bc} and leaves through {ad,dc}, the rule is violated.

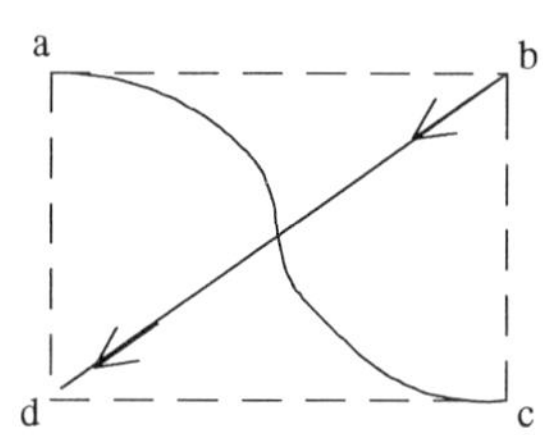

Fig. 31: The non-intersection constraint

A similar observation is made by [Struss 88] with respect to the merging of two different behaviors. The two trajectories $traj_1$and $traj_2$ introduce local pieces of admissible state trajectories: (S_0, S_1), (S_1, S_2), (S_2, S_3), (S_3, S_4) and (S_4, S_5). When the sequence of states b_1 = (S_0, S_1, S_2) is created, two possible continuations exist, i.e. b_2 = (S_0,S_1,S_2,S_3) and b_3 = (S_0,S_1,S_2,S_4). Both are valid, though only b_2 represents the correct behavior. b_3 merges two different solutions of the system, each one starting from different initial values. Thus, a qualitative solution may jump between different quantitative solutions, merge or split them. This fact is also due to the interval-based representation, which leads to a discretisized representation of the state space as shown in the following figure. Constraints similar to the non-intersection rule can be formulated which may discover crossing behavior and filter spurious states.

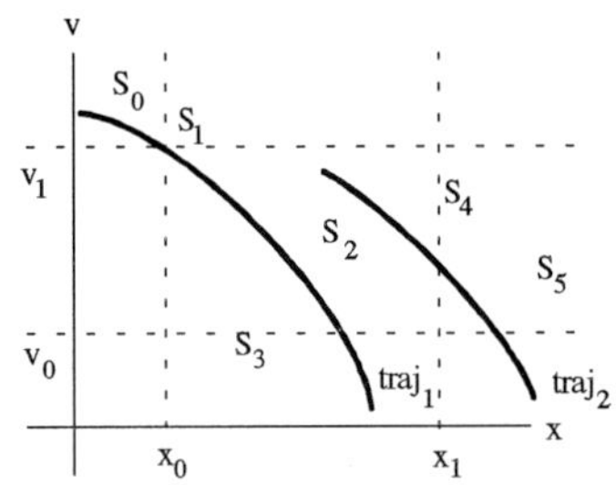

Fig. 32: Two trajectories may merge when a qualitative description is used

The states of the previous figure are described as follows:

	x	v
S_0	$(0,x_0)$	(v_1,v_2)
S_1	x_0	v_1
S_2	(x_0,x_1)	(v_0,v_1)
S_3	(x_0,x_1)	v_0
S_4	x_1	(v_0,v_1)
S_5	(x_1,x_2)	(v_0,v_1)

A further, although at the first glance paradoxical, method to exclude spurious behaviors is presented by [Kuipers and Chiu 87]. Intractable branching of behavior may be due to the fact that in the next possible state the derivative of a variable may take any of the three values of `qdir`, i.e. `qdir` ∈ {*inc, std, dec*}. All three values are admissible. However, in a specific case only the sign of the variable, i.e. the coarse value of `qval`, may be of interest. The following figure - in which the possible changes of the qualitative values are indicated by transition arrows - shows how the set of possible states shrinks. A value of *ign* for `qdir` denotes that this value may be ignored. Both the sign and the derivative of a variable are shown. The figure illustrates the obvious result, that a lumped description may exclude ambiguities on a more detailed level. It should be, however, examined whether the resulting behavior still has any significance.

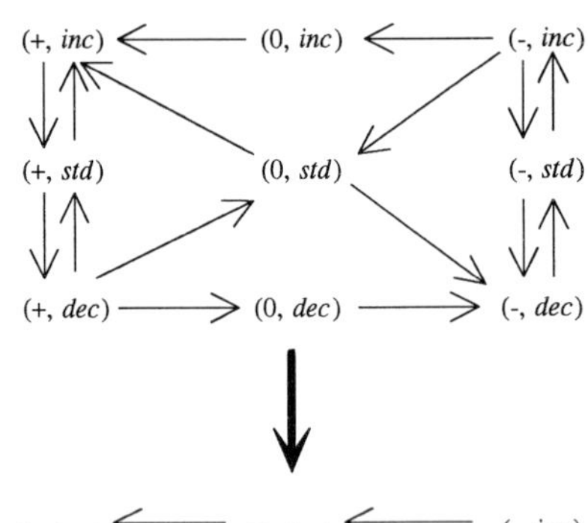

Fig. 33: Detailed state descriptions mapped to more general ones

The introduction of variables and constraints which denote potential and kinetic energy represents another way of introducing global information or global laws [Fouché and Kuipers 91]. The consideration of both forms of energy allows for the formulation of a general law which states that the sum of potential and kinetic energy has to remain constant. Oscillation can be described, for example, as a permanent exchange between kinetic and potential energy. A further example is that friction causes the loss of energy (taking the spring example) and, therefore, the spring cannot reach the same position anymore, whereas in the frictionless case the sum of energy remains constant. Such global constraints could automatically be added to a modeled system to filter admissible states which do not satisfy the principle of energy conservation and, for that reason, do not represent correct solutions.

b. Information about Functionality

Since mainly man-made artifacts constitute the objects of qualitative reasoning, information about their functionality and usage is available and can be incorporated. Man-made devices are designed to fulfill a specific purpose.[43] They incorporate and represent knowledge on a higher level. This part of knowledge should be separated from information about structure and behavior in order to obey - at least to some extent - the no-function-in-structure principle of [de Kleer and Brown 84]. This is recognized in the works of [Bradshaw 91], [Bradshaw and Young 91], [Franke 91] or [Keuneke 91] (see also [Sticklen and Bond 91]).[44] They introduce functionality as a separate concept into the reasoning process. Operational primitives are defined to represent functional tasks such as
- *ToMake:* a partial state has to be achieved,
- *ToMaintain:* a specific situation has to be achieved and maintained,
- *ToPrevent:* to prevent a system from entering an undesirable situation, and
- *ToControl:* to control the relation between an action and a desired effect.

These primitives are designed to guide the reasoning process and to introduce specific goals into the value propagation algorithm. Such primitives are useful to determine the direction of state transitions or to strengthen the filtering process of invalid states. The defined purposes can be seen close to an optimization goal in optimization tasks, where the feasible solution space is defined by constraints on the decision variables. However, such an optimality criterium determines just one point in the feasible space, whereas the above operators or the primitives of a purpose language such as Ted [Franke 91] only define a smaller range of feasible solutions. Such approaches are typically used in design and diagnosis tasks to examine, in an efficient manner, whether a device fulfills its purpose or not.

A further step into the direction of modeling functionality is represented by the works of [Bonarini and Sassaroli 92], [Brajnik et al. 91] and [Chittaro et al. 92]. They distinguish between different parts of knowledge and organize these pieces in a hierarchical manner. Knowledge is differentiated with respect to structure, behavior, function, and teleology.

These pieces of knowledge represent different sources of information as well. They are related to the same real artifact and kept in separate modules. Furthermore, they can be combined during the reasoning process. Teleology is defined as the ultimate goal - it can also be seen as the space of the model's usage [Abu-Hanna et al. 91] - and the functional description is interpreted as a mapping from behavior to teleology. A general scheduler in a kind of opportunistic reasoning guides the reasoning process, depending on its actual state. It controls and manages the work of several local schedulers. The latter are used to reason

[43] At least it is assumed to be so.

[44] In [Sembugamoorthy and Chandresekaran 86] a first distinction between several primitives in terms of functionality is given.

within the respective parts of knowledge. They, in turn, pass their intermediate results to the overall scheduler.

c. Locally Available Information

When, at some time point t, a variable, constrained by a qualitative equation, may take any qualitative value for its direction of change (`qdir` using the notation of [Kuipers 84]) at the next time step, and all of these values are consistent with the constraining equation, this variable is said to "chatter". Chattering introduces branching into the simulation tree. Due to the continuity rule, chattering can only occur when the derivative is zero in the immediately preceding state. To predict the exact future behavior, local information in the form of values of higher order derivatives can be used. When dx/dt is zero, the first derivative which differs from zero is used ([de Kleer and Bobrow 84], [Kuipers and Chiu 87] and [Kuipers et al. 91]). The usage of the so-called highest-order derivative constraint will be explained by the following two cascaded tank system [Kuipers and Chiu 87].

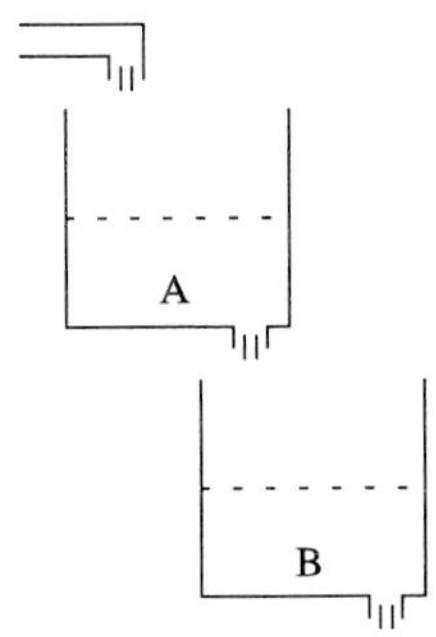

Fig. 34: Two cascaded tanks

The system is described by the following constraints:[45]

inflowA = in   constant input
pressureA = M^+(amountA)
pressureB = M^+(amountB)
outflowA = M^+(pressureA)
outflowB = M^+(pressureB)
netflowA = inflowA - outflowA
netflowB = outflowA - outflowB
d/dt (amountA) = netflowA
d/dt (amountB) = netflowB

In this example it can be shown that netflowB, i.e. the difference of the amount that flows into and out of tank B, has a critical value at a specific time point t, where `qdir`(netflowB, t) = *std.* This happens after a sequence of increasing values and represents a feasible intermediate situation, since water is permanently filled into the upper tank A. Unfortunately, netflowB chatters at this critical point, the variable is not sufficiently constrained by the set of constraints. After this situation, all possible continuations are feasible. None of the possible successor states can be excluded. In the present case this happens, because no exact information about the shape of a function such as outflowB = M^+(pressureB) is available.

[45] In this example the predicates of [Kuipers 84] are written in a different way, e.g. instead of M(a,b) a = M(b) is used.

Consequently, netflowB, as a difference between two quantities, cannot be sufficiently constrained either. In the following we use the notation:

$$\texttt{qdir}(x,t)=\texttt{sd}(x,t)=\left[\frac{dx}{dt}(t)\right],\ \texttt{sd2}(x,t)=\left[\frac{d^2x}{dt^2}(t)\right] \text{ and } \texttt{sd3}(x,t)=\left[\frac{d^3x}{dt^3}(t)\right].$$

Figure 35 illustrates those state transitions consistent with the knowledge of the respective highest-order derivative (HOD) when the first derivative $\texttt{qdir}(x,t_i) = std$. Two filters may be applied: in the cases shown by the sign of the HOD, the prefilter indicates that the respective behavior before the distinguished time point is inconsistent; the postfilter states which behavior is not consistent as a continuation. These statements are based on a Taylor series expansion at a time point t_i:

$$x(t) \approx x(t_i) + (t-t_i)x'(t_i) + \frac{(t-t_i)^2}{2!}x''(t_i) + \frac{(t-t_i)^3}{3!}x'''(t_i)$$

If $x'(t_i)$ = zero, then the behavior is determined by the quadratic term (either a maximum or a minimum); if furthermore $x''(t_i) = 0$, the last term determines the correct behavior:

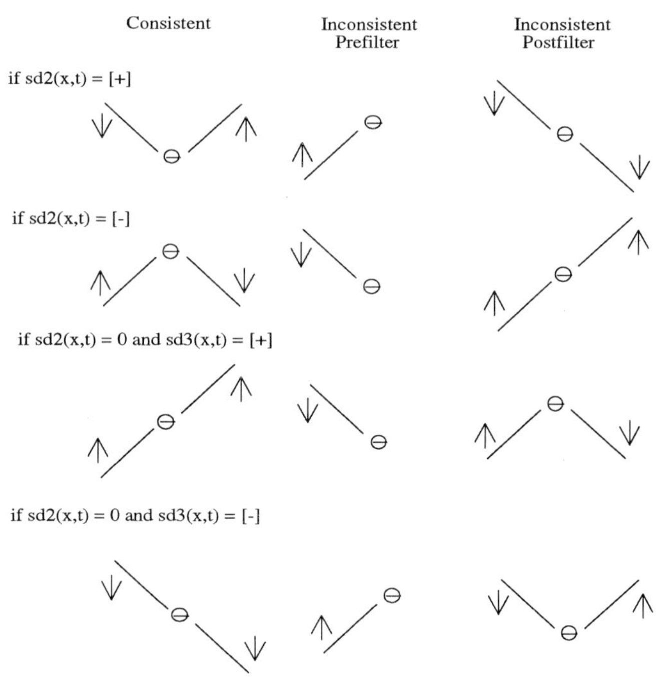

Fig. 35: The highest-order derivative constraint

The following transformation rules, based on differential calculus, can be used to derive an explicit expression for the second derivative at a point t_i where $\texttt{qdir}(x,t_i) = std$, i.e. until all terms on the right-hand side of ":=" can be substituted by explicitly available information. The sign algebra of [de Kleer and Brown 84] with its concept of qualitative equality is critical for these rules.

$M^+(x,y)$ → sd2(x,t_i) := sd2(y,t_i)[46]
x = y + z → sd2(x,t_i) := sd2(y,t_i) + sd2(z,t_i)[47]
constant(x) → sd2(x,t_i) := 0
y = dx/dt → sd2(x,t_i) := qdir(y,t_i)

These rules can now be applied to the cascaded tanks example and the case where qdir(netflowB) = *std* and netflowB chatters afterwards. Spurious behavior can be excluded, netflowB should decrease after having reached a maximum which was indicated by qdir(netflowB) = *std*:

sd2(netflowB) = sd2(outflowA) - sd2(outflowB)
sd2(outflowA) = sd2(pressureA)
= sd2(amountA)
= sd(netflowA) = qdir (netflowA)
sd2(outflowB) = sd2(pressureB)
= sd2(amountB)
= sd(netflowB) = qdir (netflowB)
= 0
and therefore,
sd2(netflowB) = qdir (netflowA).

Since at this time point qdir(netflowA) = *dec*, netflowB has to decrease as well.[48] In the example of two cascaded tanks it can be deduced that, applying a constant input to the upper tank, the netflow of the second tank B first reaches a maximum and afterwards approaches the value of zero. The second-order derivative constraint, based on differential calculus, takes into consideration locally available information which was not used previously.

d. Improvements by the Insertion of Quantitative Information

In many cases, quantitative knowledge is available and also used. [Hegarty et al. 88] show, that in specific situations, even a person reasoning qualitatively uses quantitative knowledge, for example to delimit specific ranges or to confront values. On the other hand, for answering questions like 'Will this happen ?' - in contrast to questions 'May this happen ?' -, quantitative information is necessary as well. If we take our example of water in a container above a heat source, the question 'Will the water start to boil ?' can only be answered when, for example, information about the temperature of the heat source is available. Quantitative information may, therefore, play a prominent role in the main tasks of qualitative reasoning.

Interval-based reasoning provides a framework for the integration of both types of knowledge. Initially inserted quantitative information can be used throughout the propagation process and may also support the filtering of admissible, but spurious behaviors. Furthermore, the use of numbers permits to narrow the intervals which denote qualitative values. The constraint-based approach, for example, allows for the dynamic insertion of new landmark

---

46 This is based on the so-called smoothness assumption, i.e. the monotonic function constraint M behaves "well" in the local neighborhood of t_i, i.e. it can be approximated by a linear function x(t) = f(y(t)). Thus, $x''(t) = f''(y(t)) * (y'(t))^2 + f'(y(t)) * y''(t)$. Since $f'' = 0$ and $f' > 0$, sd2(x,t_i) = sd2(y,t_i).

47 In the sign algebra, a transformation [a + b] := [a] ⊕ [b] preserves validity, but may yield a weaker description when [a] = -[b]. In this case [a + b] has a definite sign, while [a] ⊕ [b] = ?.

48 In this example we do not show the simulation output and its trajectories, we concentrate on the appropriateness of using local information in the form of higher-order derivatives.

values. This feature iteratively refines the qualitative quantity space. Quantitatively bounded intervals can be propagated across the different primitives used in the approach of [Kuipers 86] and the further developments of QSIM, called Q3 and Q4 (see also [Kuipers and Berleant 88], [Berleant 89] and [Berleant & Kuipers 90]).

- *Propagation across the arithmetic constraints* $\otimes$, $\oplus$ *and* $\ominus$:
  Numeric information may also strengthen the laws of interval-based arithmetic. For example, the constraint $a = b \oplus c$ can be reformulated as $c = b \ominus a$, if both the intervals a and b are known, and the interval length of c can be further reduced.[49]

- *Propagation across monotonic functions:*
  Quantitative information may be used by functional relationships as M or α_Q. It can define envelopes which limit the available set of functions which are represented by the monotonic constraint:

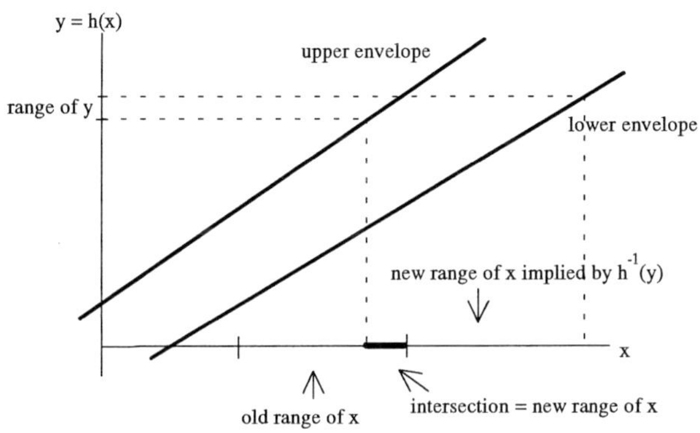

Fig. 36: Envelope of $M^+(y,x)$

The new interval of variable x can be effectively reduced by means of quantitative knowledge about function h.

- *Propagation across the derivative operator:*
  The propagation of values to variables at adjacent states can be simplified by the following transformation:

$$y(t) = \frac{dx(t)}{dt} \approx \frac{x(t_2) - x(t_1)}{t_2 - t_1}$$

Quantitative information may constrain any of the above values, i.e. $y(t)$, $x(t_1)$, $x(t_2)$, t_1 or t_2, depending on the values already propagated. This approach also allows for the calculation of quantitative information about duration of states and their transitions. For example, we can rewrite the above as

$x(t_2) \approx x(t_1) + (t_2 - t_1) * y(t_1)$, where $x(t_1)$ and $x(t_2)$ are two successive values of a continuous differentiable function x in time. It follows that $\Delta t = (x_2 - x_1) / y_1$, where $x_2 = x(t_2)$ and so on.

---

[49] In [Kuipers and Berleant 88] the rule for subtraction is applied erroneously, instead of *(a,b) - (c,d)*, which is correctly defined as *(a-d, c-b)*, *(a-c, b-d)* is used instead, producing wrong results. However, this technical error limits in no way the basic insights of this work.

Taking the approach of [Kuipers 84] two consecutive values are either a landmark followed by an interval bounded by two landmarks or vice versa. We assume that $x_2 = [a,a]$, $x_1 = (b,a)$ and $y_1 = (c,d)$. It follows that the interval of
$\Delta t = (\Delta t_1, \Delta t_2) = (a',b') \,/\, (c,d)$, where $0 < a' < a - b$ and $0 < b' < a - b$ and $a' < b'$; a' is very small and close to zero, whereas b' is close to the width of the interval x_1, i.e. $b' \approx a - b$.
Now $(\Delta t_1, \Delta t_2) = (a',b') * (1/d, 1/c)$ which results in
$(\Delta t_1, \Delta t_2) = (\min\langle a'/d, a'/c, b'/c, b'/d\rangle, \max\langle a'/d, a'/c, b'/c, b'/d\rangle)$ if $0 \notin (c,d)$.
Thus, $\Delta t_1 = \min\langle a'/d, a'/c\rangle$ and $\Delta t_2 = \max\langle b'/c, b'/d\rangle$, since $a' < b'$.

This kind of information may be used, for example, to provide a more detailed description of the behavior and/or to improve the filter mechanism of the propagation algorithm. Two state variables x and y might change their state, but when the state durations are ordered in a form where $\Delta t_x < \Delta t_y$ - the respective durations of state transitions of variable x and y - the transition due to variable y can be ignored.

- *Propagation across quantity spaces:*

Furthermore, also relational operators may be used to propagate quantitative information. The approach is in principle based on the work of [Allen 83], who describes the relationship between intervals of time in the form of a time-ordered graph. Numbers as well as intervals of real numbers may be represented as nodes in a quantity lattice, the arcs of this lattice denote the ordering relationships between these quantities [Simmons 86]. The following graph is used to derive the ordering relationship between the quantities x and y. The relationships between two variables each are given, written in the form of relational symbols above the arcs. The respective numbers and relationship operators in parenthesis indicate the visiting order of the nodes, beginning with x, and the intermediate result. At step 6 it follows, for example, from both $x \leq w$ and $x \geq w$ that $x = w$. Hence, the result is $x = y$.

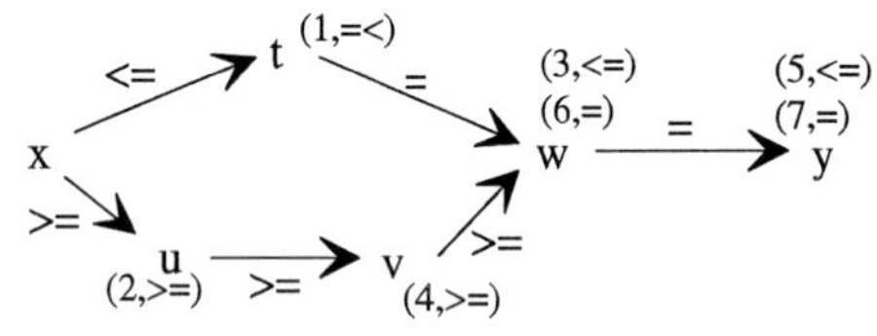

Fig. 37: Quantity lattice of [Simmons 86]

The quantity lattice allows for the integration of reasoning about ordinal relationships with the reasoning about arithmetic expressions. An expression of the form x + 1 can be placed as a node in the lattice, and the representation of a constraining relationship such as y = x + 1 directly follows. Rules for applying relational and constant elimination arithmetics are developed similar to interval arithmetic. In the following we present some of these rules:

relational arithmetic

for rel $\in \{<, \leq, >, \geq, =, \neq\}$, $x = [a,b]$ with $a \leq b$ and $y = [c,d]$ with $c \leq d$

x rel 0 $\Rightarrow$ (x + y) rel y

y rel 0 $\Rightarrow$ (x + y) rel x

x rel y $\Rightarrow$ (x - y) rel 0

constant elimination arithmetic

for rel $\in$ {<,≤, >, ≥, =, ≠}, x = [a,b] with a ≤ b, y = [c,d] with c ≤ d and z $\in$ **R**

x rel y $\Rightarrow$ (x + z) rel (y + z)

x rel y $\Rightarrow$ (x - z) rel (y - z)

x rel y $\Rightarrow$ (z - y) rel (z - x)

Such rules form the basis for constraint propagation algorithms using interval labels, such as the following one, based on [Waltz 75] (see also [Davis 87]). Similar to the quantity lattice approach, the labels are refined iteratively. Each node is labelled with the set of its possible values (i.e. intervals), and these labels are refined iteratively until no refinement is possible anymore. In the following procedures we denote with C a constraint on the nodes {x} and with L_i the label of a specific node $x_i \in \{x\}$. REFINE(C, x_j) represents the set of values for x_j, which are consistent both with constraint C and with all labels L_i of the other constraint's nodes $x_i \in \{x\}$. As an input to the algorithm, an initial value assignment is given, which has to be refined then. If this initial assignment is not consistent with the constraints, the empty set is returned.

Set L_i is the current label of x_i; REVISE refines all $x_1,...,x_k$ of a given constraint C and returns the set of all variables whose value set was changed.

```
procedure REVISE(C(x1,...,xk))
    begin CHANGED ← { }
        for each argument xi ∈ {x} do
            begin L ← REFINE(C,xi)
            if L = { } then stop /* given constraints and parameters are inconsistent */
            else if L ≠ Li then
                begin Li ← L;
                 add xi to CHANGED
                end
            end
    return CHANGED
    end

procedure CONSTRAINT PROPAGATION
    begin K ← queue of all constraints
        while K ≠ {} do
            begin remove constraint C from K;
             CHANGED ← REVISE(C)
             for each Xi in CHANGED do
                for each constraint C'≠ C which has Xi in its domain do
                 add C' to K
            end
    end
```

We will explain the work of the algorithm by means of the following example. The two constraints a + b = c (called CON1) and b ≤ a (CON2) together with the bounds of a $\in$ [2,8], b $\in$ [3,9] and c $\in$ [1,10] are given. The constraint queue K consists of CON1 and CON2. Constraint CON1 is examined first:

- since a ≥ 2 and b ≥ 3, CON1 gives c ≥ 5, the bounds of c are set to [5,10],
- since c ≤ 10 and b ≥ 3, CON1 gives a ≤ 7, a is set to [2,7],

- as the labels of a and c have been changed, and a is an argument of CON2, constraint CON2 is added to the queue,
- CON2 ($b \leq a$) is taken from the queue,
- $a \leq 7$, CON2 gives $b \leq 7$, b is set to [3,7],
- $b \geq 3$, CON2 gives $a \geq 3$, a is set to [3,7],
- a and b have changed, add CON1 to the queue,
- CON1 is popped from the queue,
- $a \geq 3$ and $b \geq 3$, CON1 gives $c \geq 6$, c is set to [6,10],
- since only c has been changed and no other constraint (besides CON1) has variable c as parameter, nothing is added to the queue. Moreover, queue K is now empty, the final labels of $a \in [3,7]$, $b \in [3,7]$ and $c \in [6,10]$ represent the result of the constraint propagation algorithm.

It has been shown that this algorithm halts, when the set of labels is finite. But the halting result does not apply, when the set of possible labels is infinite, which is often the case when quantitative information is available. However, the interval propagation checks the consistency of constraints as well. It is interesting to note that under-constrained situations cannot arise in such interval-based constraint networks represented in the form of quantity lattices. It is implicitly assumed that all variables in the network have default initial values of $(-\infty,\infty)$. However, in such cases special care has to be taken to avoid operations not defined on such value sets. The division operation, for example, has to be eliminated to prevent undefined results. In such cases the respective intervals can be further decomposed to exclude the value of zero (see also [Hyvönen 89]).

Quantitative knowledge improves the value propagation algorithm of qualitative simulation, originally only built on constraint-based filtering, by the use of constructive elements. It brings qualitative reasoning closer to classical simulation algorithms, based on the previously described discretization with its Euler-based integration method. Qualitative and quantitative steps may work in an interwoven manner. In a first step, new states are generated based on continuity rules, then the qualitative filtering methods can be applied on the basis of constraints and other qualitative rules as already discussed. Afterwards, in a supplementary step, the quantitative information can be used to exclude spurious states and, this represents the pure constructive part, to narrow the intervals of qualitative variables. In this way intervals, as the terms used in constraints, are updated and shrunk in an iterative refinement process. Quantitative information is not only used to exclude impossible behaviors but also to improve the quantitative content of a model - described also in a practical example by [Eisenberg 90].

e. Use of Hybrid Reasoning Methods

The improvements as discussed in this chapter, above all the introduction of quantitative information, need more elaborated reasoning methods. QSIM and its subsequent developments, based on the introduction of quantitative knowledge, as presented by [Berleant and Kuipers 90], represent an important step toward a more detailed behavior generation. A further approach to combine quantitative with qualitative information, both in structure representation and value propagation, is described by [Karp and Friedland 89]. Their propagation mechanism integrates quantitative, interval, relational and qualitative calculus. All these methods represent important pieces in the qualitative reasoning puzzle. The hybrid algebra of ([Williams 88] and [Williams 91]) represents another approach to integrate qualitative with quantitative information. Algebraic operations are defined on qualitative values as well as on quantitative numbers, variables may be represented both quantitatively and qualitatively. Consequently, two value sets are defined, the real numbers **R** and the set Q = {+, 0, -,?}, with its interpretation of the intervals (0,∞), [0,0], (-∞,0) and (∞,∞). The operator [] performs the mapping from elements of the set **R** to elements of set Q. Expressions can be composed by the elements of **R** and its operators {+, -, /, *} as well as by members of Q with the analog qualitative operators and the mapping []. The following two tables define the qualitative operations of ⊖ and ∅, where U denotes an undefined result:[50]

⊖	
-	+
0	0
+	-
?	?

∅	-	0	+	?
-	+	U	-	U
0	0	U	0	U
+	-	U	+	U
?	?	U	?	U

In this algebra, equality is defined in such a way that both values must have the same sign, hence transitivity is supplied. The algebra is defined by the tuple ⟨**R** ∪ Q, +, -,⊕ ,⊗⟩, division and negation are defined by means of the two operations addition and multiplication, both quantitative and qualitative. ⟨Q, ⊕ ,⊗⟩ corresponds to the case i') of chapter II.3. The algebra integrates signs with the reals and allows for a substitution and abstraction process from **R** to Q on quantities as well as on operators. In the following figure, the abstraction of the expressions increases when moving the hierarchy upward.

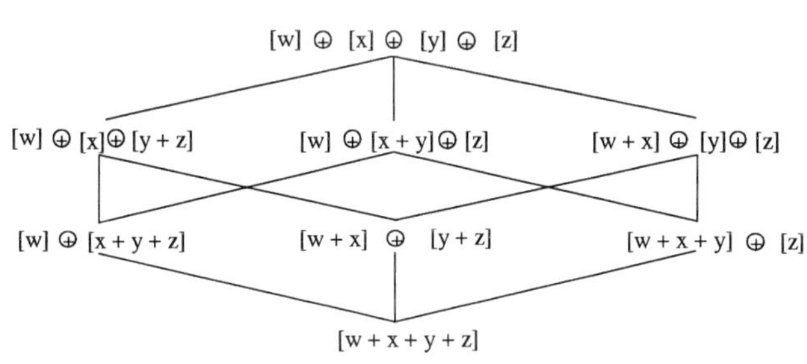

Fig. 38: Abstraction hierarchy of qualitative values and operators

The properties of the algebra are stated as follows, with s, t, u ∈ Q and a,b,c ∈ **R**:

---

[50] The qualitative operations ⊗ and ⊕ have been defined in chapter II.3.

	$\langle Q, \oplus, \otimes \rangle$	$\langle \mathbf{R}, +, \times \rangle$
Commutativity:		
	$s \oplus t = t \oplus s$	$a + b = b + a$
	$s \otimes t = t \otimes s$	$a \times b = b \times a$
Identity:		
	$s \oplus [0] = s$	$a + 0 = s$
	$s \otimes [+] = s$	$a \times 1 = s$
Inverse:		
	None	$a - a = 0$
	$s \oslash s = [+]$ if $s \neq [0]$ or $[?]$	$a / a = 1$ if $a \neq 0$
Associativity:		
	$(s \oplus t) \oplus u = s \oplus (t \oplus u)$	$(a + b) + c = a + (b + c)$
	$(s \otimes t) \otimes u = s \otimes (t \otimes u)$	$(a \times b) \times c = a \times (b \times c)$
Distributivity:		
	$s \otimes (t \oplus u) = s \otimes t \oplus s \otimes u$	$a \times (b + c) = a \times b + a \times c$

The main deficiency of Q is its lack of an additive inverse. The constraint $s \oplus u = 0$ is only solved by $s = 0$ and $u = 0$. As a consequence, no cancellation law exists for $(Q,\oplus)$, so it cannot be followed from $s \oplus u = t \oplus u$ that $s = t$. Additionally, from $s \oplus t = u$ it does not necessarily follow that $s = u \ominus t$.

However, Q also possesses properties additional to **R**:
- the operator $\otimes$ is its own multiplicative inverse: $s \oslash t = s \otimes t$ if $t \neq 0$ and ?, i.e. $+ \otimes + = +$ and $- \otimes - = +$. All occurrences of $\oslash$ can be replaced by $\otimes$ as long as the denominator does not contain the value of 0.
- since $\oslash$ can be replaced by $\otimes$, $s \otimes t = u \Leftrightarrow s = u \otimes t$ for $t \neq 0$.
- since for $s \in \{+,-\}$ $s \oslash s = s \otimes s = +$ and $+ \otimes s = s$, the following can be stated: if s^n denotes $s \otimes s \dots \otimes s$ (n times), then $s^n = s^i$, where either $i = 0$ if $n = 0$ or $i = 1$ if n is odd or $i = 2$ if n is even, regardless of whether the number n is positive or negative.

This approach takes into consideration that signs are too vague to represent values in a case where more information is available. It has several advantages: it combines both qualitative and quantitative knowledge, it supplies a function to map values onto each other and it supports reasoning with both types of representation methods. The following example from [Williams 91] shows the reasoning capabilities as well as the substitution and abstraction features. It represents a nice combination of the quantitative and qualitative worlds.

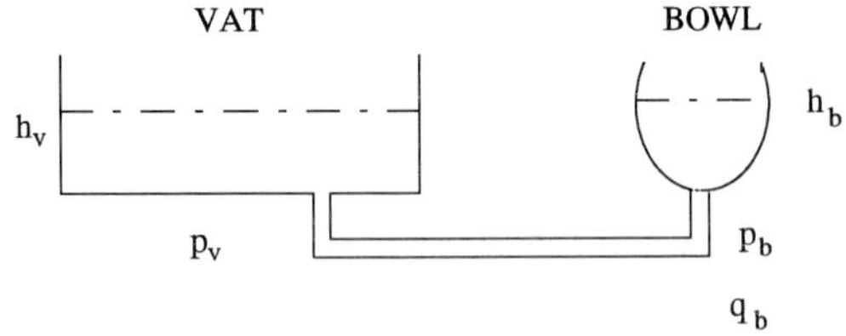

Fig. 39: A bunch bowl has to be filled automatically from a vat

The figure shows that a bunch bowl has to be automatically filled from a vat, keeping the level of the bowl at that of the vat. Initially, the goal is to let liquid flow from the vat to the

bowl whenever there exists a difference in height, i.e. $d(h_b)/dt = (h_v - h_b)$, the height of the bowl should change in the direction of the height difference. The final and inferred solution indicates to attach a pipe and to connect it to both containers. The last line shows this solution by setting the quantity q (indicating flow) equal to the difference of the respective pressures (denoted by p). q will automatically be greater than 0 (indicating an automatic filling) if the pressure difference is greater than 0. This implicitly refers to a construction, for example a pipe which fulfills this task. The letters in the first column have the following meaning:
D .. desired relation, F .. given facts and C .. consequences.

D1	$[h_v - h_b] = [d(h_b)/dt]$	original desired relation
F2	$h_b \times a_b = v_b$	container model (v .. Volume, a .. Area)
C3	$h_b = v_b / a_b$	resolve line F2 for h_b
D4	$[h_v - h_b] = [d(v_b / a_b)/dt]$	substitute line C3 in line D1
D5	$[h_v - h_b] = [d(v_b)/dt] \varnothing [a_b]$	simplify line D4 (area is a constant)
F6	$[a_b] = +$	container model, area is greater zero
D7	$[h_v - h_b] = [d(v_b)/dt]$	substitute F6 in D5
F8	$q_b = d(v_b)/dt$	container model (flow is difference in volume)
D9	$[h_v - h_b] = [q_b]$	substitute F8 in D7
F10	$p_v = d \times g \times h_v$	container model of vat (d .. density, g .. gravity)
C11	$h_v = p_v / d \times g$	resolve F10 for h_v
D12	$[p_v / d \times g - h_b] = [q_b]$	substitute C11 in D9
F13	$p_b = d \times g \times h_b$	container model of bowl
C14	$h_b = p_b / d \times g$	resolve F13 for h_b
D15	$[p_v / d \times g - p_b / d \times g] = [q_b]$	substitute C14 in D12
D16	$[p_v - p_b] \varnothing ([d] \otimes [g]) = [q_b]$	simplify line D15
F17	$[d] = +$	property of density of fluid
F18	$[g] = +$	property of gravity
D19	$[p_v - p_b] \varnothing (+ \otimes +) = [q_b]$	substitute F17 and F18 into D16
D20	$[p_v - p_b] = [q_b]$	simplify D19

f. Usage of Other Quantity Representation Methods

In the approaches discussed so far, intervals denoting qualitative values have more or less the same width (excluding the representation of zero). All intervals are treated in the same way. The order-of-magnitude reasoning approach works differently: values of variables may differ by some order-of-magnitudes. This may lead to the fact that perhaps some variables are neglected with respect to other ones. Consider two balls colliding, one 10.000 times the mass of the other. When the direction and speed of the bigger ball has to be deduced, the influence of the smaller ball can be neglected. This approach states that infinite small, infinite large, and "normal" numbers cannot be treated similarly. Regions located far away on the real number line behave differently. If we take a range which denotes the infinitesimals close to zero, then this range can be added to any other range without changing the value of the latter. On the other hand, a multiplication with this range will map all numbers to this range close to zero without being zero. Such a form of knowledge about variables may be available about given numbers without constituting concrete quantitative information.

The order-of-magnitude method defines relationships between variables which are similar to those of the quantity lattice of [Simmons 86], whereas its operators are different. Three fundamental relationships between quantities are developed between two quantities in [Raiman 88]:

- x Ne y denotes that quantity x is negligible in relation to y.
- x Vo y denotes that x is close to y, i.e. (x - y) Ne y.
- x Co y denotes that x has the same sign and order-of-magnitude as y. If, in this case, y Ne z is valid, so is x Ne z.

Operator Co is less restrictive than operator Vo. The fact that (x + y) Vo x leads to the conclusion that y Ne x, by using an extensive list of rules. In contrast, the relationship (x + y) Co x does not allow to deduce the same. Rules such as x Vo y → [x] = [y] and x Co y → [x] = [y] map numbers to the respective qualitative representation. These rules allow to create homogeneous regions, where qualitative operations are uniquely defined. However, this formalism only deals with symbolic representations and it is not clear how to integrate concrete quantitative information as the most important means to improve qualitative reasoning techniques.[51]

The O[M] formalism described by [Mavrovouniotis and Stephanopoulos 87] and [Mavrovouniotis and Stephanopoulos 88] represents a further step into this direction. Quantities are represented by a sign and a magnitude, both variables and landmarks are treated as quantities. The following relationships are defined:

x << y	x is much smaller than y
x -< y	x is moderately smaller than y
x ~< y	x is slightly smaller than y
x == y	x is exactly y
x >~ y	x is slightly larger than y
x >- y	x is moderately larger than y
x >> y	x is much larger than y

If x rel y then (x/y) rel 1, where rel is one of the mentioned relational operators. Two quantities x and y can be ordered (in the form of x/y) on the number axis, where e_1 to e_4 indicate the borders between the respective intervals of magnitudes. To satisfy the relationships x >~ y ⇔ y ~< x and x >> y ⇔ y << x, as indicated in Fig. 40, the following is imposed: $e_3 = 1/e_2$ and $e_1 = 1/e_4$. To satisfy that, for x > y > 0, the relation x - y << y ⇔ x >~ y is valid, e_3 is set to $1 + e_1$. If we substitute e for e_1, the other values and the interval lengths are direct functions of e: $e_3 = 1 + e$, $e_2 = (1+e)^{-1}$ and $e_4 = e^{-1}$. The accuracy parameter e depends on the application domain.

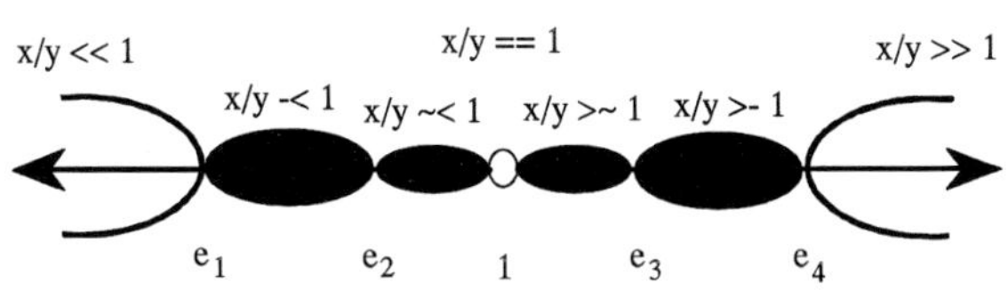

Fig. 40: Subdivision of the number line by order-of-magnitude relationships

Ordering of quantities is a straightforward procedure best interpreted through a graph where arcs indicate the known magnitude relationships. Such arcs also denote constraints between variables. A solved constraint results in a value assignment for the respective variable. The symmetry and transitivity properties of O[M] relationships permit the creation of new

[51] Furthermore, the set of rules is very large and their choice seems to be somehow arbitrary. Additionally, the distinction between Vo and Co turns out to be very artificial.

magnitude relationships between variables. Therefore, given some initial constraining equations about a device and its variables and magnitude relationships between its variables, O[M] produces final ordinal relationships between the variables. Since it is also possible to insert quantitative information (in the form of landmarks), both qualitative and quantitative information can be well combined.

g. Other Forms to Represent Time

The process-centered approach of [Forbus 84] with its concept of histories may be related also to another representation of time. A history describes the life of an individual and its variables. If histories overlap in time, individuals influence each other by means of processes. Histories are composed by a sequence of elementary episodes. Each episode describes a fixed process and view structure. Episodes have a temporal extension, i.e. intervals. These temporal intervals and their qualitative relationships may be described by means of a language which allows for the further inferencing from these temporal primitives [Allen 83]. The possible qualitative relationships between two intervals are described in the following figure.

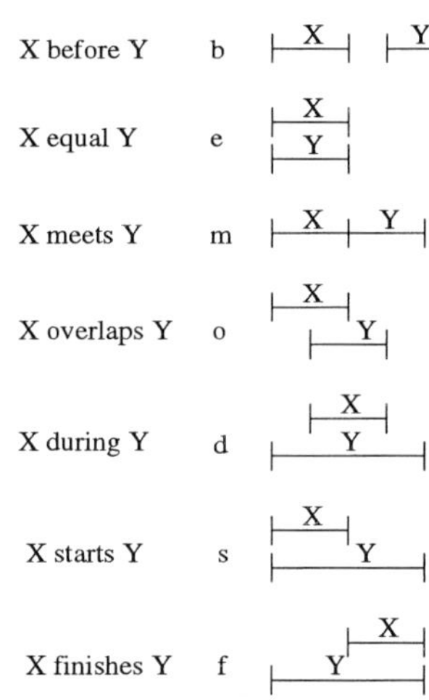

Fig. 41: Temporal relationships between two intervals

Intervals can be organized in the form of a graph, where arcs represent the respective relationships. In addition, this graph can be used to derive further relationships between nodes. In the following example the symbol *{?}* resolves to *b*, i.e. interval A will occur before interval C.[52]

[52] In general, the proof of the consistency of a set of temporal assertions is NP-hard as shown by [Vilain et al. 86].

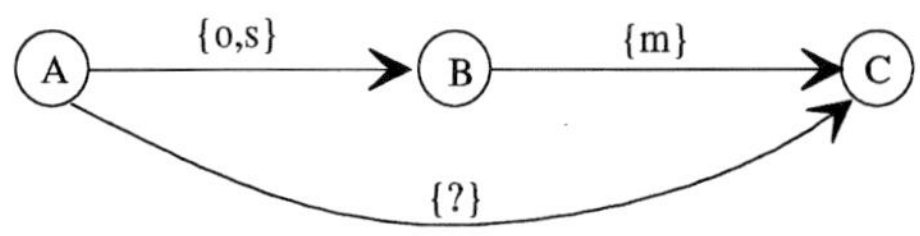

Fig. 42: The temporal node A is before node C

Such time-ordered intervals may form the base for an improvement of the limited possibilities to reason about time [Williams 86]. The behavior of a variable - as mentioned previously - is described by a history, which in turn is a sequence of single episodes. An episode is represented by the pair of the variable's value and the time duration of this assignment. The episodes are assumed to be maximal, i.e. they embody the largest time span during which the assignment does not change. Such episodes form a concise history, interesting events are now those time points where the variables' values change.

In this approach, the constraint propagation mechanism needs to know, in addition to information about the value, the duration of time intervals. For example, given the constraint a + b = c, a value of 5 for variable a, an extent of [30,200] for the episode of a, a value of 3 for b and its extent of [100,300], then it can be derived that c = 8 for the interval [100,200]. The value propagation proceeds along the time sequence of an input episode and applies the respective constraining rules. This may result in new episodes. These steps are repeated until the input history is exhausted.

The following figure explains the procedure to satisfy the constraint c = a ∨ b. The justification histories (R1, R2, R3) both overlap and contain gaps. Together, however, they cover the episodes of c. c = a ∨ b may be defined by the rules:
R1: if a = 1 then c = 1
R2: if b = 1 then c = 1
R3: if a = 0 and b = 0 then c = 0

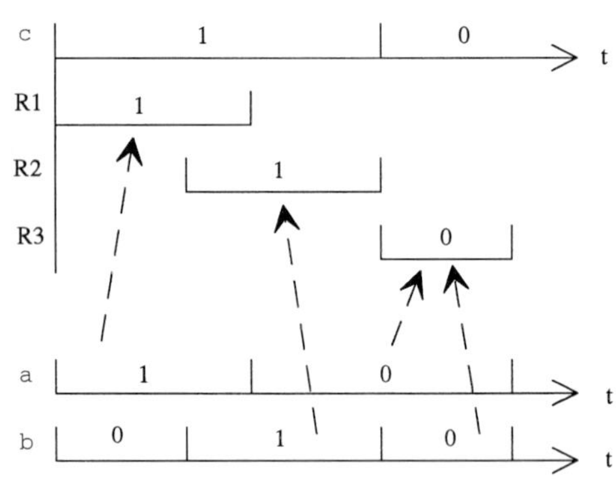

Fig. 43: History of A ∨ B = C

The extents of the episodes have to be defined properly to determine the time point when the value of c changes from 1 to 0. This approach results in additional ordering information between time points and intervals of states. The available knowledge about both qualitative and quantitative relationships may be used to infer further relationships as well as to exclude impossible transitions.

h. Restricting the Behavior in Time

If more quantitative information is given in the form of finer grain size intervals or order of magnitudes, then this knowledge can be used to determine the duration of states and the amount of time necessary to change to a subsequent state. Based on the knowledge (either in an exact or an approximate form) about single quantities, a Taylor series expansion can be used to gain this information. Another example is presented by [Weld 88]. With his HR-QSIM, he provides an enhancement of QSIM of [Kuipers 86] by introducing so-called hyperreal numbers of non-standard analysis, expressing infinitesimal and infinite values [Robinson 66]. If the landmark value of p_i is given, then HR-QSIM assigns one of the following qualitative values to a variable f at time t:

inf or *minf*	if f(t) is infinite and > 0 or < 0, respectively.
p_i	if f(t) = p_i.
(*halo* p_i +)	if (f(t) - p_i) is infinitesimal and > 0.
(*halo* p_i -)	if (f(t) - p_i) is infinitesimal and < 0.
(p_i,p_{i+1})	if both differences (f(t) - p_i) and (p_{i+1} - f(t)) are non-infinitesimal and > 0.
(p_i,*inf*)	if f(t) is finite and (f(t) - p_i) is non-infinitesimal > 0.

It follows that every landmark value p_i has a *halo* of numbers which are infinitesimal close to it. Positive infinitesimals are represented by (*halo* 0 +). Thus, a distinct representation for infinitesimal numbers is introduced. The derivative of a variable has, in addition to its direction of change (*dec*, *std*, *inc*), one of the four possible indications of magnitude:

inf	if $|z|$ > every finite number.
fin	if $|z| = a, a \in R$.
negl	if $|z|$ is a positive infinitesimal.
0	if z = 0.

A typical qualitative description of a variable is [x(t)] = ⟨(*halo* x_0 +) ⟨*inc*,*fin*⟩⟩. It indicates, that at time t, variable x has a value around the landmark value x_0 and changes positively with a finite magnitude. This information about magnitudes of numbers, e.g. infinitesimally close to some landmark or somewhere between landmarks, can be used to infer additional information about time: how long a state will last (called persistence time) or how much time it will take to change its value (called arrival time). A so-called distance rate table defines the time which is necessary to reach a new value. The entries of this table are the time distances between two points and the rate of change. The definition of a distance between two values is given as follows: the distance between a *halo* and its landmark value is *negl*, the distance between *inf* and any other value is *inf*, the distance between a *halo* and its neighboring interval is *fin*. If we have, for example, a finite rate of change and an infinite distance between two points, the arrival time is infinite, i.e. the successor state can never be reached:

		Distance			
		inf	*fin*	*negl*	0
	inf	?	*negl*	*negl*	0
Rate	*fin*	*inf*	*fin*	*negl*	0
	negl	*inf*	*inf*	?	0

Let us now consider the case where we denote with x = ⟨0,⟨*inc*,*fin*⟩⟩ and y = ⟨(*halo*, 0, -), ⟨*inc*,*fin*⟩⟩ two variables in some state S. This means that x has a value of zero and steadily increases with magnitude *fin*, variable y is infinitesimally close to and smaller than zero and increases with the same speed as x. In this moment, three possibilities exist: x may change from zero before, after or at the very moment when y changes to zero. This constitutes an ambiguous situation. The distance-rate table tells us that the time for x - having distance 0 and speed *fin* - is 0, whereas the time for y is *negl* - having distance *negl* and rate *fin*. Variable x changes before variable y, therefore only the first transitions is valid. The successor arrival time can be calculated in a similar way. Such information about time can also be used to exclude inconsistent behavior.

Reviewing the presented methods of this chapter to improve qualitative reasoning, which reduce the space of possible solutions, we can conclude that they cannot entirely exclude ambiguity, initially lacking information cannot be regained. These features are inherent to qualitative reasoning.

3. The Representation of Uncertainty

Qualitative reasoning provides a formalism to describe situations and their features, when information to give an exact description is missing. The information about objects of reality is vague. If, for example, the exact value of a quantity cannot be determined, then nothing more can be derived than a wider range of an interval which is supposed to include the searched number. Qualitative abstraction widens the set of possibilities. As knowledge only exists in a vague and hesitating form, several different solutions, i.e. behaviors, are feasible in qualitatively described situations, and all of these results are equally likely. The methods of qualitative abstraction discussed so far only specify a value to be within or outside a specific range. Intervals representing qualitative values have a crisp form. However, sometimes even this knowledge may not be available. In ecological problems, for example, it may not be easy to exactly define a value of some substance, it may fall into, at least two, qualitative regions. Therefore, intervals representing qualitative values also may overlap. This kind of knowledge can often be found in modeling, when experts in the respective field of application use simulation and modeling methods with new phenomena [Guariso et al. 92]. Such form of knowledge has to do with beliefs as well as assumptions regarding the modeled reality. It is different from probability. Fuzzy sets are a means to implement and compile such knowledge. This concept states that the possibility of some element to be in two set at the same moment may be higher than one, which is impossible from a probabilistic point of view. Randomness has to do with uncertainty concerning membership or nonmembership of an object in a nonfuzzy set. Fuzziness, on the other hand, has to do with classes in which there may be grades of memberships intermediate between full membership and nonmembership. For example, "The grade of membership of Jim in the class of small men is 0.3", is a nonprobabilistic statement concerning the membership of Jim in the fuzzy class of small men, whereas "The probability that Jim will get married is 0.3", is a probabilistic statement concerning the uncertainty of the occurrence of a nonfuzzy event [Bellman and Zadeh 70].

Furthermore, fuzzy sets may also form the base of an inference mechanism [Yager et al. 87]. This approach supports facilities to model available knowledge along the dimension of qualitative abstraction as well as that of uncertainty. From this point of view it represents a progress in qualitative reasoning research. This approach shows a double relationship with interval-based methods: fuzzy sets deal with situations where the range of a qualitative number is not exactly known; however, results of fuzzy reasoning procedures indicate priorities among different possible behaviors, i.e. which of the resulting behaviors is most possible. This fact somehow constitutes a paradox: with less information better results may be obtained. But it should be noted that these better results are in general a consequence of the introduction of quantitative information in order to define fuzzy subsets and consequently the set Q of qualitative values.

3.1 Fuzzy Sets Used in Qualitative Reasoning

The universe of discourse U defines the set of all available objects, in the case of discrete numbers it is based on a discretization of the underlying numeric range. $A \subseteq U$ is called a fuzzy subset of U, when A has an associated membership function $\mu_A(x) \rightarrow [0,1]$. This function defines for every $x \in U$ its degree of belief of being a member of the subset A. It may be written in the form $A = \{(x, \mu_A(x)) \mid \mu_A(x) \in [0,1], x \in U\}$ or $A = \{\mu_1/x_1, ..., \mu_n/x_n\}$. The closer the value of $\mu_A(x)$ is to 1, the more x belongs to A. Fuzzy sets may also have a linguistic interpretation such as low, medium, or large. These sets - or their linguistic counterparts - in turn may constitute the value range of a qualitative variable, i.e. Q = {*low, medium, large*}. If we assume, for example, a universe of {1, 2, 3, 4, 5}, then *low* may now be defined by {1/1, 0.8/2, 0.2/3, 0/4, 0/5}, *medium* by {0.2/1, 0.9/2, 1/3, 0.9/4, 0.2/5} and *large* by {0/1, 0/2, 0.2/3, 0.8/4, 1/5}. If we take the case of low it is stated that the number 1 is in this subset with a certainty of 1, the number 2 with a certainty of 0.8, and so on. Different to probability distributions, the sum over $\mu_A(x)$ for each x and all $A \in Q$ normally exceeds 1. Therefore, the concepts of possibility and probability differ. While the former indicates the ease of assigning some value to an object, without excluding that other objects may also have this value, the latter defines crisp borders.[53]

The representation method based on fuzzy sets which is used in qualitative reasoning operates with finite sets, i.e. the number of qualitative values is finite. The following definition of qualitative values uses the concept of convex fuzzy numbers. In this approach the membership function is expressed by a tuple $\langle a,b,\alpha,\beta \rangle$ (see also [Shen and Leitch 90], [Shen and Leitch 91], their approach will be used as an example in the following):

$$\mu_A(x) = \begin{cases} 0 & x < a-\alpha \\ \dfrac{x-a+\alpha}{\alpha} & x \in [a-\alpha, a) \\ 1 & x \in [a,b] \\ \dfrac{b+\beta-x}{\beta} & x \in (b, b+\beta] \\ 0 & x > b+\beta \end{cases}$$

In the qualitative fuzzy quantity space Q = {*small, medium, large*} of the following example, the number 39 belongs to the value of *medium* with a possibility of 0.9, and to the value of *small* with a degree of 0.05. Figure 44 illustrates that this method to describe qualitative quantities represents a further development of the interval representation methods used by the other approaches.

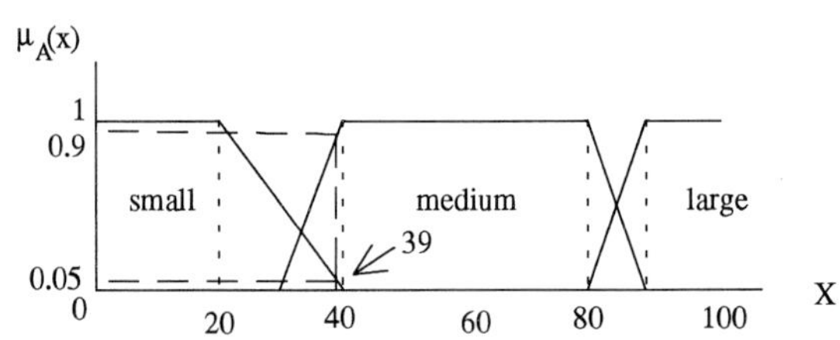

Fig. 44: Qualitative values represented by fuzzy sets

Fuzzy sets also allow for the formulation of algebraic constraints and functional relationships between variables [d'Ambrosio 89]. Constraint propagation may in principle proceed in the same way as in the non-fuzzy case: if an algebraic constraint between three variables is given, then the constraint may be satisfied, whenever two of them are known. The operations of addition, subtraction and multiplication are defined as follows, where $m, n \in Q$ are $m = \langle a, b, \alpha, \beta \rangle$ and $n = \langle c,d,\chi,\delta \rangle$:

[53] A detailed discussion is beyond both the scope of this publication and the intention of the author; for more information see [Yager et al. 87].

m ⊕ n = $\langle a + c, b + d, \alpha + \chi, \beta + \delta\rangle$,
m ⊖ n = $\langle a - d, b - c, \alpha + \delta, \beta + \chi\rangle$,
m ⊗ n = $\langle \min(ac, ad, bc, bd), \max(ac, ad, bc, bd), \Phi, \Gamma\rangle$, where Φ and Γ take into consideration the respective combinations of values of α, β, χ, and δ, depending on the signs of a, b, c and d.

Unlike the constraint-based approach of [Kuipers 86], which can generate new intervals, the resulting qualitative quantities have to be reprojected onto the original members of the fuzzy set. If we have, for example, the following constraint: z = small + small, and we use the definition of the fuzzy numbers as in Fig. 44, it can be calculated that z = ⟨0,20,0,20⟩ + ⟨0,20,0,20⟩ = ⟨0,40,0,40⟩. This result does not exactly correspond to a given range, it intersects with the values of small and medium. A distance measure between intervals is defined, which calculates that the most adequate candidate again is the qualitative value of small. This ensures that the resulting qualitative value is again a member of Q. This representation of qualitative values has properties similar to the case iii) of chapter II.3, operations are commutative, but not associative, neutral elements may be defined and, similar to the other qualitative algebras, no inverse elements exist. Furthermore, it is not exclusive anymore, since qualitative values may overlap.

In this approach, functional relationships between variables - represented by fuzzy sets - may be described as well. This is done by means of fuzzy relations $\mu_R(x,y)$ with variable $x \in U$ and $y \in V$ and can be written in the form of a two-dimensional matrix, i.e. $[0,1] \times [0,1] \rightarrow [0,1]$. If $A \subseteq U$ and $B \subseteq V$, then $\mu_R(x,y) = \min(\mu_A(x),\mu_B(y))$, $(x,y) \in U \times V$. This relationship is more expressive than that defined by the function M of [Kuipers 84] and corresponds to an implication $A \rightarrow B$. The so-called compositional rule of inference and the interpretation of the fuzzy relation as an implication enable the max-min composition of a fuzzy variable with a fuzzy relation, i.e. $D = C \circ R$ with $C \subseteq U$ and $D \subseteq V$ and R a fuzzy relation from U to V. We obtain $\mu_D(y) = \max_x(\min(\mu_C(x),\mu_R(x,y))$. The max-min composition works in the same way as a multiplication of a matrix by a vector. Multiplication is substituted by the min and addition by the max operator. Therefore, if a qualitative variable C is represented as a fuzzy subset of U, we are able to calculate the qualitative variable, i.e. fuzzy subset, D.

[Shen and Leitch 91] describe a qualitative variable x and its state by $\langle A, B, \Delta T_p\rangle$, where A, B $\in$ Q, A is the fuzzy magnitude (corresponding to qval of [Kuipers 86]), B the fuzzy rate of change (corresponding to qdir) and ΔT_p the persistence time of the state. If B = 0, then the persistence time obviously is ∞, otherwise it is calculated based on the width of A and the relative magnitude of B, i.e. if A = $\langle p_1,p_2,p_3,p_4\rangle$ and B = $\langle q_1,q_2,q_3,q_4\rangle$, then

$$\Delta T_p \in \frac{W(A)}{|B|_\alpha} = \frac{[p_2 - p_1 + (1-\alpha)(p_3 + p_4)]}{[(q_1 + q_3(\alpha - 1)), (q_2 - q_4(1-\alpha))]}$$

This formula produces a time interval.[54] The constant α defines the so-called α - cut. It represents a method to transform fuzzy ranges into crisp intervals and constitutes a threshold value for belonging to an interval or not, i.e. the α-cut of a set A is defined as $A_\alpha = \{x \in U \mid$

[54] The result is calculated according to $\frac{[a]}{[c,d]} = [a/d, a/c]$ (if c and $d > 0$).

$\mu_A(x) \geq \alpha\}$. Therefore, intervals have a crisp form again. An α - cut has the supplementary property of dividing the underlying number range into adjacent intervals which, depending on the choice of α, may overlap, touch each other or be distant from each other. Therefore, this form of representation can no longer guarantee the property of coverage. Similar to the state persistence time, an arrival time may be calculated, which also depends on the value of α. A small α results in long persistence and short arrival times, a large α in short persistence and long arrival times. In this way, the choice of a constant α, independent from the modeled system, strongly determines the dynamic behavior of the system. The information about time may be used to exclude impossible behaviors, for example, from the set of available next states that with the smallest arrival time is taken. This improvement, however, owes to the incorporation of numerical information and not to the fuzzy representation. Indeed, the method of fuzzy representation is abandoned when calculating both time intervals.

The simulation procedure works in a similar way as QSIM [Kuipers 86]. All possible state transitions are generated in a first pass, the impossible ones are filtered out in the subsequent step. In principle, the following state transitions - based on the rule of continuity - between two adjacent states $\langle A_1, B_1 \rangle$ and $\langle A_2, B_2 \rangle$ are possible ($A_1, B_1, A_2, B_2 \in Q$):

Null transition:	$A_1 = A_2$, $B_1 = B_2$
M - transition:	$A_1 \neq A_2$, $B_1 = B_2$
R - transition:	$A_1 = A_2$, $B_1 \neq B_2$
MR - transition:	$A_1 \neq A_2$, $B_1 \neq B_2$

Furthermore, based on the fact that variables vary continuously, the following state transition rules are defined:

- if $B_1 > 0$ ($B_1 < 0$), then
    - if $A_1 \in \mathbf{R}$[55], then $A_2 > A_1$ ($A_2 < A_1$)
    - else $A_2 \geq A_1$ ($A_2 \leq A_1$)
- if $B_1 = 0$ then
    - if $A_1 \in \mathbf{R}$ then
        - if $A_2 > A_1$ ($A_2 < A_1$, $A_2 = A_1$), then $B_2 > 0$ ($B_2 < 0$, $B_2 = 0$)
    - else
        - if $A_2 \geq A_1$ ($A_2 \leq A_1$), then $B_2 > 0$ ($B_2 < 0$)
        - if $A_2 = A_1$, then $B_2 \in \{0, x, y\}$ where x and y are the adjacent qualitative values of 0

These transition rules determine the set of all possible values for variables at the next state. In addition to the steps of constraint-consistency-based filtering, pairwise constraint-based and of global filtering, the filtering mechanism of this approach uses the knowledge about the persistence and the arrival time. In the calculation of these time intervals, the knowledge about the type of transition, i.e. either Null-, M-, R- or MR-transition, is used. This results in a more powerful technique in order to exclude spurious states. This approach, however, introduces a constructive element as well. In the case of a pure algebraic constraint, for example, the result of the straightforward application of the algebraic operation is compared with the value of the respective variable obtained by uisng of the described transition rules. If the intervals of these two qualitative variables do not intersect, then this variable value for the next state can be eliminated. In such a way, the available quantitative knowledge is also used in behavior generation.

---

[55] If A is a real number, then the value of A immediately has to change due to the transition rules discussed in the previous chapters.

The fuzzy representation of quantities and the use of fuzzy value propagation methods reduce ambiguous situations. However, this approach is not able to completely eliminate ambiguous situations either, and one state still may have several successor states. The algorithm has to proceed for all different possibilities. In contrast to [Kuipers 86], no new elements of the quantity space Q are generated during simulation. After each step, each value is reprojected to the closest qualitative value, i.e. interval. [Leitch and Shen 92] make a further step toward classical simulation and the straightforward application of constraints as rules for calculating new values. They introduce additional information to restrict the number of states and to prioritize these states by examining which of them is the most probable continuation of the current situation. This procedure works as follows: first all possible successor states with respect to continuity and value propagation are created. If there are more than one candidate, then the values of the variables in the last state and the set of constraints are used to directly calculate the values of the variables in the next state. These latter results - denoting only one possible next state - are compared with all members out of the set of successor states which have been generated in the first step. The state with the smallest distance to the calculated state, resulting from the straightforward calculation, is selected as the most likely one to continue the simulation. If at a later moment - because of some inconsistency - the propagated behavior has to be interrupted, then these points of ambiguity can be used for backtracking. At such re-entry points the respective state with the next best ranking - if the best one already failed - can be selected. This approach is similar to a best first or most likely method to explore the simulation tree, in contrast to a depth or breadth first strategy otherwise. The information about the likelihood of states is obtained by the direct propagation of fuzzy numbers through the constraints. This approach works both in an interpretative and constructive manner and is very close to "classical" simulation algorithms. This direction of research expands the traditional concept by several notions: it integrates uncertainty; it enables the representation of quantitative information; it provides information about time durations; and it introduces constructive approaches into the simulation techniques.

3.2 QUALSIM

A similar approach is represented by the program QUALSIM of ([Guariso et al. 89b] and [Guariso et al. 92]) which - besides using fuzzy representation methods - is based on influence diagrams. Its modeling perspective is close to system theory, based on the identification of input, state and output variables and the respective influences between these variables. Thus, causality is already identified in the modeling process and compiled into the model. The main motivation of QUALSIM is to provide an highly interactive tool in the complicated phase of model building, in which the structure of a model has to be identified.[56] Its scope is to support fast model building and to provide an estimation of possible qualitative behaviors. In a further step, the qualitative model could be transformed into a quantitative one in order to proceed with the analysis of a real system by means of quantitative methods.

The algorithm can be seen as a constructive one, dedicated to the straightforward generation of a system's qualitative behavior. In close relationship to numerical simulation, time is considered as an integer counter, i.e. a unit increment corresponding to one step of computation. This may or may not constitute a change of the system state. This is different to the other approaches where at every step of calculation a state transition occurs. QUALSIM

[56] For further discussion of the important software engineering aspects we refer to [Guariso et al. 89b] and [Guariso et al. 92].

may thus also provide an indication how long a system remains inside a state. Each qualitative variable is represented by its magnitude. The value of a state variable may take one of the following labels from the set Q of qualitative values:

+/- *extralarge*
+/- *large*
+/- *medium*
+/- *small*
+/- *extrasmall*
zero

QUALSIM assumes that the entire range of possible values of a variable can be defined in advance. All intervals have the same width - excluding zero - and they are, differently to the order-of-magnitude approaches, treated the same way. This value representation covers the whole range of interest, it is finite, ordered; addition is associative, excluding the extreme intervals on both sides. However, it is assumed that both the maximum and minimum value of a variable can be given or estimated.[57] Thus, each variable x is identified by a numeric range R_x, defined as a subrange of the real number space. Each qualitative value is, similar to the approach of [Shen and Leitch 90], represented by the following fuzzy membership function $\mu_A(x)$, based on a tuple $\langle v_k, a, b \rangle$. The characteristic values v_k with k= 1,...,12 are evenly spaced in the positive and negative ranges of **R**:

$$\mu_A(x)=\begin{cases} 0 & x < v_k - a \\ \dfrac{x - v_k + a}{d+a} & x \in [v_k - a, v_k + d) \\ 1 & x \in [v_k + d, v_{k+1} - d] \\ \dfrac{v_{k+1} + b - x}{d+b} & x \in (v_{k+1} - d, v_{k+1} + b] \\ 0 & x > v_{k+1} + b \end{cases}$$

for each k and the corresponding $A \in Q$. In the case of the delimiting points v_1 (*-extralarge*) and v_{12} (*extralarge*), the membership function $\mu_A(x)$ remains at a value of 1. The constant *d* is defined global and determines, together with the variable-dependent values *a* and *b*, the fuzziness of the qualitative values.

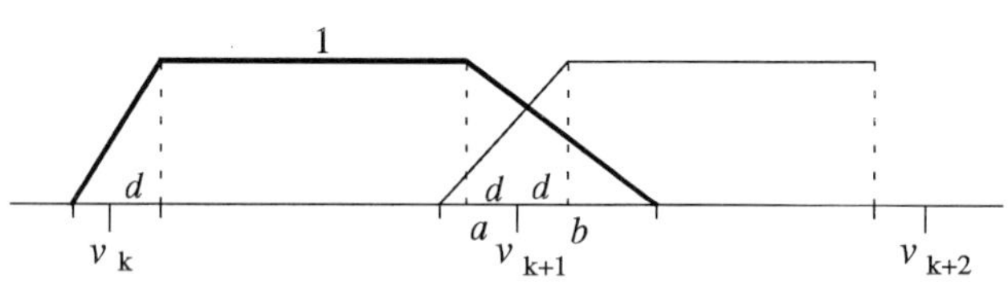

Fig. 45: Qualitative value representation in QUALSIM

Connections between two variables may possess one of the following labels:

[57] But this does not seem to be a hard restriction, in ecological modeling, as the main application area of this approach, this assumption could always be satisfied.

+/- *extrastrong*
+/- *strong*
+/- *medium*
+/- *weak*
+/- *extraweak*

These labels are assumed to correspond to numeric subranges of the unit interval [-1, 1]. They are instantiated to specific numeric values c_{ij} randomly distributed in the respective subrange. The probability distribution of these values is normal and centered on the center of the subrange. Its standard deviation is chosen by the user in order to reflect his/her subjective perception of the uncertainty of the connection. For instance, if the user selects a standard deviation $\sigma_{ij}=0$ (the default value), then the distribution shrinks to an impulse and represents a high confidence in the appropriateness of the selected value. Thus a kind of an influence graph is constructed ([Glymoure at al 87], [Scheines et al. 91]). However, the influences indicate the strength of a connection and not its probability (as in [Wellman 88], [Pearl 86] and [Peot and Shachter 91]).

The algorithm is fundamentally based on the conversion of qualitative values to quantitative ones and vice versa. The propagation of uncertainty during the simulation is represented by the bifurcation of the simulation tree. The algorithm works as follows:

- At the beginning of the simulation, the initial qualitative value x for the state variable is transformed into its numeric equivalent x, being the characteristic point at the center of the relative fuzzy set.

- Given a qualitative value $x_i(t)$ and numeric value $x_i(t)$ for the state variable at time t, and assuming that $I_i = \{x_j \mid x_j$ is connected to x_i, $j \in 1..n\}$ is the set of variables that exert an influence on the variable x_i, the new numeric value is computed as

$$x_i(t+1)=x_i(t)+\sum_{j\in I_i}\Delta x_j(t) \quad \text{where } \Delta x_j(t)=c_{ji}\frac{x_j(t)}{R_{x_j}}R_{x_i}$$

and c_{ji} is the normal distributed connection with standard deviation σ_{ji} between x_j and x_i, recalculated at each iteration, and R is the range of the respective variable.

- QUALSIM distinguishes - as already mentioned - between state and output variables.[58] The calculation of the latter proceeds similarly to that of state variables. The influencing arcs of QUALSIM may therefore represent either an integration step (when state variables are influenced) or, in the case of output variables, only a simple influence. Given a qualitative value $y_i(t)$ and its numeric value $y_i(t)$ for the output variable at time t, assuming that $K_i = \{x_j \mid x_j$ is connected to y_i, $j \in 1..n\}$ is the set of variables that exert an influence on y_i, the new numeric value is computed as follows.

$$y_i(t)=\sum_{j\in K_i}\Delta x_j(t) \quad \text{where } \Delta x_j \text{ is calculated as before.}$$

- The numeric value of a variable is transformed again into its qualitative counterpart:

[58] QUALSIM has also input variables which are defined either as constant, oscillating or in-/decreasing. The user may define parameters which determine the respective qualitative properties of these variables.

+ If the membership grade of $x_i(t+1)$ exceeds a predefined threshold $\alpha(x)$ at least in one of the sets (i.e. if $x_i(t+1)$ belongs to the α-cut of at least one of the sets), then the new qualitative value assigned to x_i is the label of the set where $x_i(t+1)$ has the highest membership grade. This is similar to the previously discussed α-cut of [Shen and Leitch 91].
+ If all the membership grades are lower than α, ambiguity occurs and either the user is asked to assign the qualitative value by choosing between the one at time t and the higher (lower) value depending on the sign of $\Sigma_j \Delta x_j$ or a fixed strategy like depth, breadth first or a random choice is applied.

- If the qualitative value of a state variable computed with the above procedure is different from that at time t, then the corresponding numeric value $x_i(t+1)$ is set to the characteristic value at the center of the relative set. Otherwise, the new value of $x_i(t+1)$ is set to

$$x_i(t+1)=\frac{(1+p)v_{k+1}[x_i(t)]+(1+m)v_{k-1}[x_i(t)]}{p+m+2}$$

Thus, the approach takes into account the direction of change, i.e. the derivative, and the number how often a variable moves into the respective directions. *p* denotes the number of time steps with the variable in the same qualitative state with positive increments, and *m* is the number of time steps with negative increments. This leads to different results than in the case of order-of-magnitude methods, where a qualitative operation of the form *extralarge - extrasmall* will forever produce the result *extralarge*. In QUALSIM a frequently repeated application of this operation will force the variable to change value. This is also different to the other approaches where a system cannot remain in the same qualitative state for two or more consecutive time steps.

These operations are repeated till the time counter reaches a predefined value. This procedure takes into account that variations may lead to a state transition with time and allows to distinguish two different levels of time-granularity during inter- and intrastate behavior. The simulator marks every point of ambiguity and provides the possibility of backtracking to those points. Thus, the entire simulation tree may be traversed. An important feature of QUALSIM is, that in order to avoid the generation of the entire simulation tree, the user may define, in an ambiguous situation, with which branch to proceed (this may also be automatically defined as depth or breadth first, or randomly). This is consistent with the view that the user also defines the level of uncertainty in the modeling phase. Uncertainty enters in two different ways: by the definition of the standard deviation σ_{ij} of each influence c_{ij} and by the fuzzy representation of qualitative values.

QUALSIM describes a system of the form $x' = Ax$ with x the state vector and A the system matrix. Due to the uncertainty which the user assigns to the influences, matrix A also represents the random influences. QUALSIM's mode of calculation leads to discontinuities, when the range of a qualitative variable is passed. The new value is set to the center of the next qualitative variable. Thus, QUALSIM follows in a piecewise manner the trajectory of the described system. However, as output only the sequence of qualitative variables is shown. In the following figure with two state variables the arrows indicate such jumps to the respective new center, just one of the set of the qualitative solutions with a fixed c_{ij} is displayed. A standard deviation $\neq 0$ on the influences would generate trajectories which fluctuate within a cone around the trajectory with $\sigma_{ij} = 0$. The qualitative trajectory is ⟨(*small,*

small), (*small, medium*), (*small, large*), ...,(*medium, large*)⟩, reflecting the discretization of the state space.

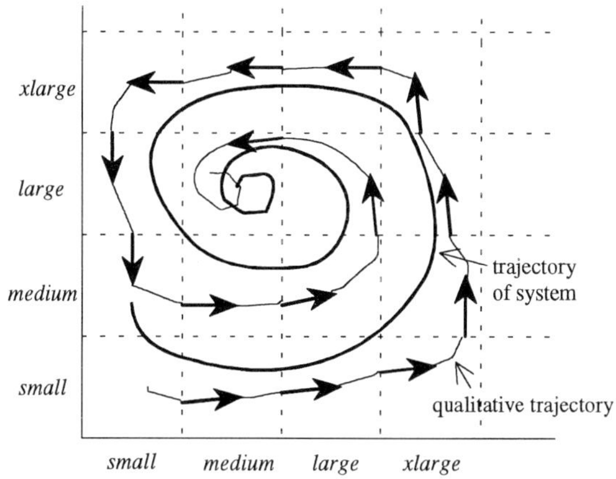

Fig. 46: Qualitative trajectory of QUALSIM

The following example shows a typical application of QUALSIM by studying the structure of an eutrophication model which describes the seasonal evolution of water quality in a reservoir. This example also makes clear the basic - already mentioned - motivation of QUALSIM. The modeler has no exact information about magnitudes of variables, functional relationships and parameters. However, he can identify causal influences and looks for a model to explain a certain phenomenon. If the user can identify such a structure by using an iterative modeling approach as described in the following, he might continue with more elaborate, quantitative methods. Eutrophication is a complex phenomenon due to the increase of nutrients concentration in the water, which leads to an increase in phytoplankton population, a decrease of fishes and a general lowering of water quality which may prevent its normal use. All the elements of the chain (nutrients, phytoplankton, decomposers, zooplankton, fish and so on) are, to different degrees, involved in the process ([Odum 71]), but the most evident effect is the periodic algal bloom which occurs in many reservoirs of temperate countries. A typical pattern of the phytoplankton population, which is frequently observed in reality and usually measured in terms of chlorophyll concentration, is shown in the following figure. It indicates a peak at the beginning of summer and then a reduction to very small values for the rest of the year. Sometimes the decline is followed by a series of smaller oscillations.

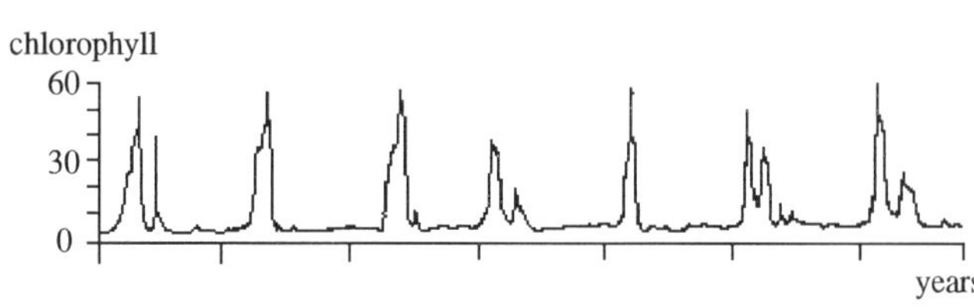

Fig. 47: Trajectory of the phytoplankton population

At least two components are required to describe this behavior, nutrients (NUR) and phytoplankton population (FITO); see Fig. 48. Since nutrient inflow (INFLOW) is due to industrial and urban discharges, it may be assumed to be constant. The negative influence of phytoplankton on itself represents mortality as a function of population. Moreover, sunlight (SUNLIGHT) is incorporated as an input, since algal photosynthesis is strongly affected by light intensity, which varies during the year with a periodic (usually assumed sinusoidal) shape. These considerations lead to the first qualitative model of Fig. 48. The simulation results on the right side show the expected summer peaks of chlorophyll content, i.e. FITO, but no other oscillation of higher frequency.

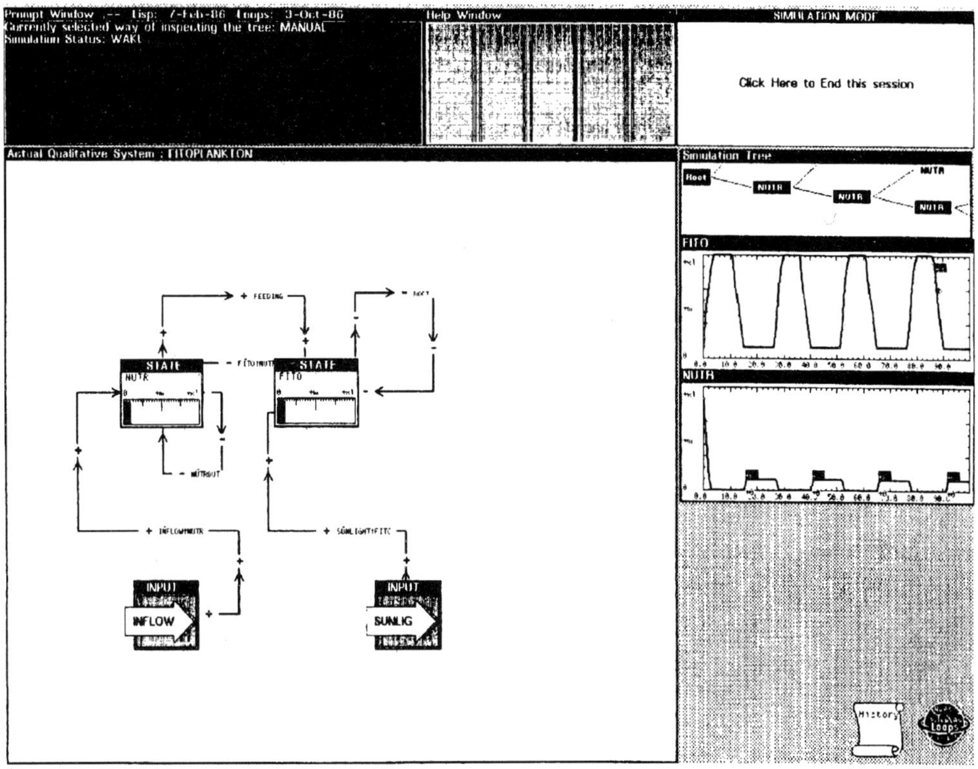

Fig. 48: First qualitative model of the eutrophication process

In a further step, the state variable ZOO, denoting zooplankton, is introduced. Zooplankton population lives from phytoplankton and, thus, has a negative influence on the latter. Figure 49 shows the final model structure. The result of the simulation is similar to the measured data of Fig. 47 as it qualitatively reproduces the periodic blooms (qualitative trajectory of FITO) - the typical phenomenon observed in developed countries. The simulation tree on the right upper side shows that there will be a branching with according to the ambiguity of zooplankton. Time proceeds from 0 to 90. It is an important and explicitly stated assumption of this approach that the user has an idea about the real phenomenon as well as some indications about the magnitudes of and the relationships among the variables.

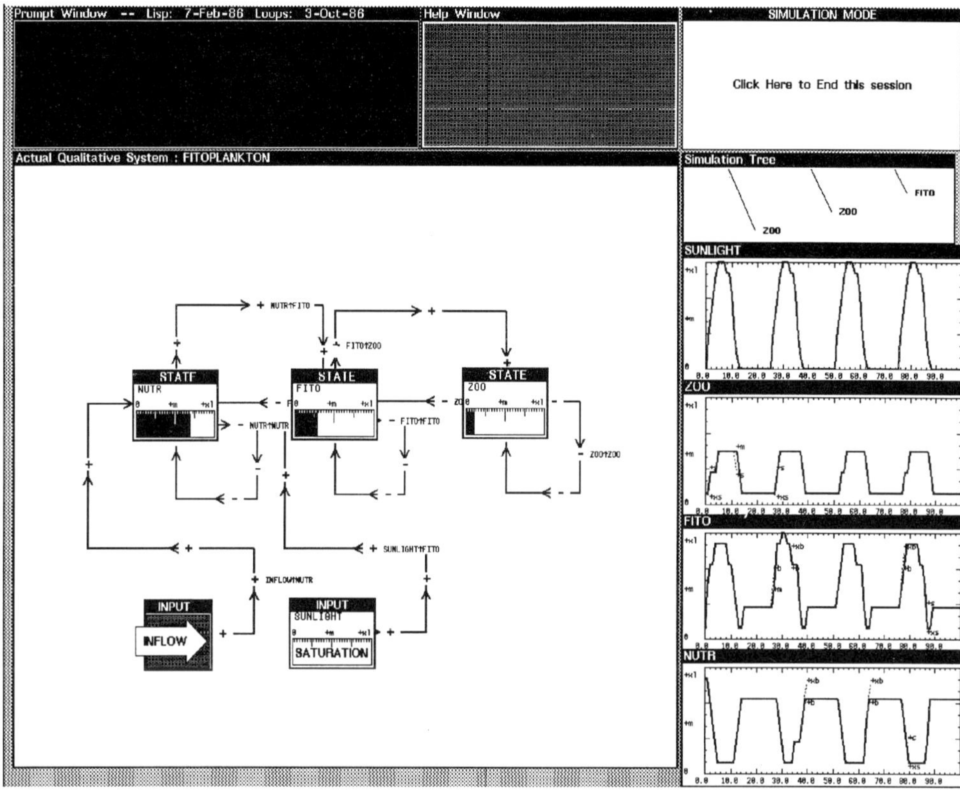

Fig. 49: Final qualitative model of the eutrophication process

QUALSIM proceeds - similar to the other approaches - on two time scales. Its interstate behavior is represented by discontinuous jumps to one or more neighboring cells, depending on the fuzzy value representation and the randomly distributed influences. The intrastate behavior inside one cell follows nearly exactly the underlying quantitative model. Thus, QUALSIM takes into consideration processes which act on two very different time scales. The interstate behavior with its jump to the center of a neighboring cell considers the possibility of long term changes of the system's environment (e.g. models in the field of climate change).

It may be argued that the underlying model could be simulated directly by means of quantitative methods. But this would pretend a precise solution which cannot exist because of the inaccuracy of the available information. Therefore, QUALSIM tries to cover the entire space of solutions which is consistent with the available information. A purely quantitative solution technique would miss such other solutions. Ambiguity, which may only occur during interstate behavior, also serves for identifying all possible continuations of the simulation.

A further important feature of QUALSIM is the way of interaction with the user. Given that he has some idea about the behavior of the real system, he has the possibility to concentrate on some of the branches of the simulation tree, or to backtrack to specific points of ambiguity. Thus, QUALSIM represents - as already mentioned - a modeling support tool to identify the qualitative structure of a model which may be further elaborated by quantitative methods. It should be noted, however, that for decision making in practice it is very often sufficient to know whether a system may enter a specific qualitative state or whether it remains in a specific range of the state space.

The constructive approach of QUALSIM largely corresponds with the approach of QSIM [Kuipers 86]. This refers to the two predicates M(y,x) and DERIV(y,x) of QSIM and the way how state and output variables are calculated in QUALSIM.

The basic operation of QUALSIM is a directed influence which can be written as $y(t+1)=y(t)+\sum_{x_{t_i}} c_{x_iy}\frac{x_i(t)}{R_{x_i}}R_y$. This can directly be transformed into $DERIV(y,\sum c_{x_iy}\frac{x_i(t)}{R_{x_i}}R_y)$. Rewriting $c_{x_iy}\frac{x_i(t)}{R_{x_i}}R_y$ as $M(z_i, x_i)$ we obtain $DERIV(y,\sum M(z_i,x_i))$.

A sequence of ADD operations may substitute the operator Σ in a constructive interpretation of QSIM.

On the other hand, DERIV(y,x) of QSIM denotes y′ = x, in a discrete form written as $\frac{y_{t+1}-y_t}{\Delta t}=x_t \rightarrow y_{t+1}=y_t+\Delta t * x_t$. Thus, if we set $\Delta t = 1$, both forms of representing a differential relationship can be mapped onto each other.

However, there are differences in the notion of an output variable. In QSIM - different to QUALSIM - no explicit concept of an output variable exists. We may interpret variable y of a constraint M(y,x) as an output variable, since no explicit time step is involved and y can be expressed as a direct function of x. However, QSIM's constraints permit that such a variable y may reappear in a constraint DERIV as an "influencing" variable. Thus, this QSIM form of an "output variable" may reinfluence a state variable as well. Since in QUALSIM the different sets of variables (input, state and output) are strictly separated, QUALSIM would need a modification to support this view, enabling a "feedback" from an output to a state variable (via an input variable). However, there is a further difference between the predicate M of QSIM and QUALSIM's way of calculating an output variable. M(y,x) relates the variables x and y by $y(t) = h(x(t))$ for $t \in [a,b]$. Function h denotes a whole class of continuous and differentiable functions. As already discussed, M(y,x) can be approximated by a the function of the form $y = kx + d$. In QUALSIM the influence of a variable x upon an output variable y can be written in a linear form as well, i.e. $y = c_{xy}\, x * (R_y/R_x)$. But this assumes that functions relating state to output variables pass through the origin. The term R_y/R_x corresponds to the factor $k = (y(b)-y(a))/(x(b)-x(a))$ of QSIM. The additional term $c_{xy} \in [-1,1]$ determines whether the influence is negative or positive, similar to the sign of M^+ or M^-. But since $|c_{xy}| \leq 1$, the output function of QUALSIM will just at the respective boundaries of c_{xy} correspond to the linear approximation of M. Consequently, in the case of "output functions" there is only a restricted correspondence between QSIM and QUALSIM.

This discussion demonstrates the closeness of qualitative reasoning to classical simulation, where the basic ideas of QUALSIM are derived from. However, the fundamental difference in their way of representing qualitative values has to be mentioned: QUALSIM has a predetermined number of values with fixed ranges, no new intervals being generated, all intermediate results being reprojected to existing values. Moreover, Fig. 46 shows that trajectories of QUALSIM, different to QSIM, can only pass through extreme points which differ at least by one qualitative value; intermediate critical points cannot be discovered. This deficiency could only be avoided if all critical values of a function denoting a variable are known in advance and the set Q of qualitative values is appropriately defined.

3.3 A Representation Based on Markov Chains

In a further step we will show that the approach of QUALSIM can also be mapped onto a representation which is based on Markov chains (see [Freedman 71] or [Pflug 86]).[59] Given the set of random difference equations of QUALSIM describing a system, a matrix of transition probabilities between the system states can be created. In contrast to the "classical" qualitative state space description, where each of the described behaviors is equally likely, a description in the form of Markov chains additionally defines priorities between transitions [Grossmann and Werthner 93].

The Markov property of a system says that the state of a system only depends on its predecessor state. X_1, .., X_n being random variables and S the finite set of states, a Markov chain is a sequence of the random numbers where $P[X_n = S_j \mid X_1,...,X_{n-1}] = P[X_n = S_j \mid X_{n-1}]$. Homogeneous Markov chains do not depend on n, i.e. $p_{ij} = P[X_n = S_j \mid X_{n-1} = S_i]$ with S_i, $S_j \in$ S and p_{ij} being independent from time. p_{ij} denotes the probability that the system changes from state S_i to state S_j. All these probabilities p_{ij} can be written in the form of a quadratic matrix P indicating the state transition probabilities between each two of the states. The rows of this matrix add up to 1, i.e. a state has to change to its successors. The initial situation can be described by a row vector v, i.e. v is a probability distribution describing the probability of each state to be an initial state. Multiplying v with matrix P gives a vector w, i.e. w = v * P. Vector w describes the probabilities of the system to be in a specific state after the first transition, at the second time point. In a stationary case we have v = w, the probabilities are not changed by applying P. Matrix P describes the transition probabilities in one step. If we multiply P with P, then a transition table for two steps is generated. Thus, P^n describes the transition probabilities of applying n transitions.

This transition matrix P has some nice properties. For example, it partitions the states into equivalence classes. If there exists a number n with n > 0 and $p_{ij}^n > 0$, then it can be said that state S_j may be reached from S_i, which can be written as $S_i \rightarrow S_j$. In the other case, S_j cannot be reached from S_i. If both properties $S_i \rightarrow S_j$ and $S_j \rightarrow S_i$ are valid, then S_i and S_j are called equivalent, i.e. $S_i \leftrightarrow S_j$. Those states which are equivalent form an equivalence class. Once the system has left an equivalence class, then it can never return. Such classes are partially ordered by means of the following definition: G_1 is before G_2 if $\exists\, S_i \in G_1$ and $\exists\, S_j \in G_2$ and $S_i \rightarrow S_j$. Therefore, a transition matrix not only defines probabilities of specific behaviors, but also indicates the sequence of visited states or the existence of cycles.

The application of a Markov process requires several problems to be considered:
- the given fuzzy number representation of QUALSIM has to be transformed into a probabilistic form to guarantee the discussed Markov properties,
- QUALSIM only denotes the strength of an influence between variables, no state description is given in advance,

[59] In this work we use the concept of finite, in contrast to infinite, Markov chains. Moreover, we do not discuss the case of possibilistic automata, which can also be described by means of Markov processes.

- the entire set of possible system states is not known.

The solution of the first problem requires a "normalized" representation of qualitative values, i.e. $\Sigma_{A \in Q} \mu_A(x) = 1$ for every $x \in R_x$, i.e. fuzzy numbers are modified in order to represent probabilities.

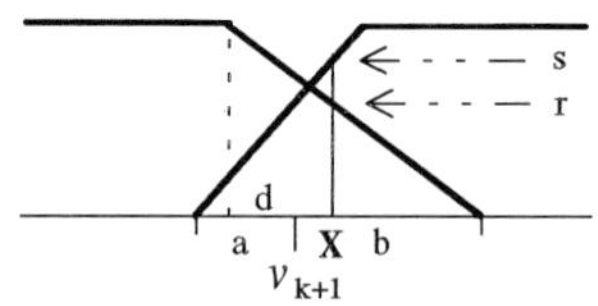

Fig. 50: Relationship between two qualitative (fuzzy) values

Such transformation has to maintain the relationship between the two fuzzy numbers, i.e. if x is the current value of the respective state variable the following has to be satisfied: $r{:}s = \frac{b-x}{d+b} : \frac{a+x}{d+a}$ and $r + s = 1$. The important feature is the relationship between both values and not their magnitudes.[60]

The second and the third of the above mentioned problems can be discussed together: the set S of system states can be constructed in advance based on the limited value set of the qualitative quantity space. If $w = \#(X)$ denotes the number of state variables - X being the set of state variables - and $u = \#(Q)$ the number of qualitative values, then the number of all possible states is u^w. Therefore, the set S can be generated by enumerating all possible value combinations of each element of X. Each element of S represents a vector, the first element of the vector denotes the qualitative value of the first variable, the second element denotes the value of the second state variable, and so on. Every value combination represents a state and for every combination of values the respective state can be identified. Thus, a finite state space can be constructed in advance and the dimension of the transition matrix P is $u^w \times u^w$.

In the following we denote with succ($m \mid m \in Q$) the neighbor which follows a member of Q, and with pred($m \mid m \in Q$) the neighbor which precedes a member of Q. *large* is succ(*medium*) and *small* is pred(*medium*). succ(*extralarge*) is defined to be *extralarge*, pred(-*extralarge*) is -*extralarge* again. The transition probabilities $p_{S_iS_j}$, i.e. going from state S_i to state S_j, can now be derived (S_{ik} denotes the kth component of vector S_i - with $S_{ik} \in Q$ - and G denotes the distribution of the numerical correspondents R_{ik} of a qualitative value S_{ik}):

$$p_{S_iS_jk} = \begin{cases} 0 & \text{if } S_{jk} \notin \{\text{pred}(S_{ik}), S_{ik}, \text{succ}(S_{ik})\} \\ \int \mu_{(S_{jk})}(\sum_q R_{iq} \times c_{qk} + R_{ik})dG & \text{otherwise} \end{cases}$$

The probability to change from S_i to S_j - the system is in S_i at time t and in S_j at time t+1 - is zero, when the law of continuity is violated. R_{iq} correspond to those components q, i.e. state variables, that influence the state variable k of X. The second case represents the original formula to calculate the new value of a state variable, where the quantitative correspondent of

---

[60] The discussed transformation is necessary in order to guarantee the Makov property of P, i.e. the sum of the values in one row of the matrix has to be 1. However, the arguments presented herein would also work without satisfying this condition.

a qualitative value is weighted by the respective probability distribution. G can be obtained in the following way: for each numeric value within a qualitative state, the probability of whether the new numeric value will remain within the state, will fall into the ambiguous range, or will pass to the next qualitative neighbor, depends on the independent, normal distributed c_{ij}. In the case that the new value falls into the ambiguous range, the "normalized" membership functions $\mu_A(x)$ and $\mu_B(x)$ of the two adjacent qualitative values A and B are taken into consideration. In this case, they define the probability of change. Thus, each of the numeric values has a well-defined probability of occurrence.

Based on the fact that variables vary continuously, it follows that P is very sparse. Every state S_i may just have 3^w successors, since only three possibilities of change for each state variable exist in each transition, i.e. in each row of P a small number of elements is $\neq 0$.

Although the joint probability of the states depends on the structure of the system, one can obtain ranges for the joint probabilities $p_{S_iS_j}$ by using different methods of combining the respective $p_{S_iS_jk}$ (which represent the kth component of a vector). These different methods lead to different Markov chains, each one representing different assumptions about the structure of the QUALSIM model and the dependencies among its variables.

a) Since the decisions of choosing a specific range for each component of a state variable are independent, in cases where the state variables are only loosely coupled, the multiplication of the single components of the probability vector is a reasonable operation, i.e. $p_{S_iS_j} = \Pi_k p_{ijk}$. Multiplication is a reasonable operation, since it eliminates those transitions where one or more components of the probability vector are zero, i.e. the values of these components of S_j cannot be reached. Rewriting $p_{S_iS_j}$ as p_{ij}, the Markov property of $\Sigma_{j \in succ(Si)} p_{ij} = 1$ can be demonstrated as described in the following.

The Markov property can be shown by means of the following formula, where the k components of all vectors for all transitions from state i to state j are included: $\sum_{j=1}^{3^w}\prod_{k=1}^{w} p_{ijk} = 1$. The single elements can be written as a matrix with dimension w x 3^w, w being the number of state variables - each value can have only three neighboring values. The left side denotes the w state variables, the upper side the 3^w possible successors of S_i:

				S_j		
		S_1	S_2	S_3		S_{3^w}
	k = 1	p_{i11}	p_{i21}	p_{i31}	:	p_{i3^w1}
S_i	k = 2	p_{i12}	:	:	:	:
		:	:	:	:	:
	k = w	p_{i1w}	p_{i2w}	:	:	p_{i3^ww}

The formula $\sum_{j=1}^{3^w}\prod_{k=1}^{w} p_{ijk} = 1$ can be shown by induction:

If w = 1, then S_i only has 3 successors S_j. The values of these successors are either pred(S_i) or S_i or succ(S_i). Since the membership functions have been normalized at the beginning, these three probabilities add up to 1.

Now, assuming that the above formula is true for the number of state variables being n, it can be shown that the formula is also true when the number is n+1. For that we construct the respective matrix: we add one row for the probabilities of state variable n+1, which triples the number of columns:

$$\left|\begin{array}{cccc|cccc|cccc} p_{ir_1n+1} & p_{ir_1n+1} & p_{ir_1n+1} & p_{ir_1n+1} & p_{ir_2n+1} & p_{ir_2n+1} & p_{ir_2n+1} & p_{ir_2n+1} & p_{ir_3n+1} & p_{ir_3n+1} & p_{ir_3n+1} & p_{ir_3n+1} \\ p_{i11} & p_{i21} & : & p_{i3^n1} & p_{i11} & p_{i21} & : & p_{i3^w1} & p_{i11} & p_{i21} & : & p_{i3^n1} \\ p_{i12} & : & : & : & p_{i12} & : & : & : & p_{i12} & : & : & : \\ : & : & : & : & : & : & : & : & : & : & : & : \\ p_{i1n} & p_{i2n} & : & p_{i3^nn} & p_{i1n} & p_{i2n} & : & p_{i3^nn} & p_{i1n} & p_{i2w} & : & p_{i3^nn} \end{array}\right|$$

p_{ir_1n+1} denotes probability that variable n+1 does not change its value at the next state, p_{ir_2n+1} that the next value is $succ(S_{in+1})$, p_{ir_3n+1} that the next value is $pred(S_{in+1})$. The sum of these three probabilities necessarily add up to 1. Furthermore, we have assumed that the matrix describing n state variables also results in a value of 1. Therefore

$$1 = p_{ir_1n+1} \times 1 + p_{ir_2n+1} \times 1 + p_{ir_3n+1} \times 1 =$$

$$= p_{ir_1n+1} \times \sum_{j=1}^{3^n} \prod_{k=1}^{n} p_{ijk} + p_{ir_2n+1} \times \sum_{j=1}^{3^n} \prod_{k=1}^{n} p_{ijk} + p_{ir_3n+1} \times \sum_{j=1}^{3^n} \prod_{k=1}^{n} p_{ijk} =$$

and, by modifying the indices, for example $p_{ir_1n+1} = p_{ijn+1}$, and by changing the order of summation and multiplication

$$= 3 \times \sum_{j=1}^{3^n} \prod_{k=1}^{n+1} p_{ijk} = \sum_{j=1}^{3^{n+1}} \prod_{k=1}^{n+1} p_{ijk}$$

, i.e. the formula is also true for w = n+1. Therefore the Markov property is satisfied.

b) Instead of multiplying the components of the probability vector, the minimum of the components could be chosen. This would mean that the most unlikely case inside each column determines the overall probability of this specific transition or that the most inert variable determines the behavior of the system. In this case a strong dependence between the state variables is assumed. To obtain the Markov property, every single value has to be weighted by the row sum of all minima, i.e.

$$p_{ij} = \frac{\min_k (p_{ijk} \mid k \in 1..w)}{\sum_j \min_k (p_{ijk} \mid k \in 1..w)}.$$ The Markov property directly follows $\sum_j p_{ij} = 1$.

c) As a final approach, the single components of each vector could be added. Also in this case we assume a strong dependence between the model's variables. A possible interpretation would be some kind of averaging of the transition probabilities, which makes sense only if no component has a probability of zero. A further interpretation, adapting an opportunistic point of view, would be some kind of "OR" operation. If the single components of each vector are added, this value can be calculated according to the following formula

$p_{S_iS_j} = \frac{1}{F_w} \sum_k p_{ijk}$. The factor F_w represents the sum over all components of $p_{S_iS_j}$ for all successor states S_j of S_i, i.e. $F_w = \Sigma_{j \in succ(S_i)} \Sigma_k p_{ijk}$. F_w can be calculated in a recursive way: $F_0 = 0$ and $F_i = 3 * F_{i-1} + 3^{i-1}$, $\forall\, i > 0$.

Similar to point a), this can be proved by induction:

For w = 1 the formula obviously holds. S_i can only have three successors. Since the probabilities are properly defined by the initial transformation, these have to add up to 1, i.e. $F_1 = 1$.

Now we assume that the result holds for a number of state variables i = n, i.e. $F_n = 3*F_{n-1} + 3^{n-1}$. If now one state variable is added, i.e. i = n+1, then we can show that $F_{n+1} = 3*F_n + 3^n$. We can assume, without loss of generality, that this state variable has a probability of 1 to change to just one of the members of {pred(V(S_{ik})), V(S_{ik}), succ(V(S_{ik}))}. The two other probabilities are set to 0. Similar to point a), the new probability vectors for all successors can now be grouped in a matrix, which again has one row more and three times the number of columns of the original matrix where i = n. The first two thirds of the columns are created by adding, as first row, the probabilities that the new state variable changes to impossible values, i.e. all probabilities in the first row are 0. Thus, these first two thirds of the matrix add up to $2*F_n$. The last third of the columns of the matrix has the probability of 1 in the first row, i.e. state variable n+1 has to change to the respective successor value. The sum of the elements in the first row of this last third of the matrix is 3^n, since the number of these rows in the last third of the matrix is 3^n as well. This is due to the specific form of the matrix. The other rows of this last part of the matrix again add up to the old value F_n. Thus we obtain $F_{n+1} = 3*F_n + 3^n$, and the recursive formula is correct.

It follows directly that for each S_i the transition probabilities add up to 1, thus the Markov property of the sums of the rows of P is fulfilled, i.e. $\Sigma_{j \in succ(S_i)} p_{ij} = 1$.

However, the method of computing the overall probability of a state transition has to be explored further. It depends on the knowledge about the dependencies between the state variables and it can be assumed that this method will determine whether and how fast specific states can be reached, which, in addition, has to be compared with the simulation results of the original QUALSIM approach.

The simulation of a system could now be performed by multiplications of matrices and vectors, the latter describing the probability of each state to be an initial state of the system. These are simple operations. However, in realistic cases the dimension of the matrix - even if it is very sparse - will be enormous. An advantage is that it can be built in advance and that it provides a richer description of the state space, indicating privileged behaviors as well. Furthermore, this approach can be used to subdivide the state space into equivalence classes, providing a qualitative interpretation of the whole state space. A finite and previously advance known set of qualitative values is a necessary prerequisite of this approach. Therefore, approaches such as QSIM [Kuipers 86] cannot be transformed in this way.

Finite Markov chains have an initial stationary probability such that $v^* \times P = v^*$. In our case, the elements of vector v^* denote the initial stationary probability of each state. If the number of transitions tends to infinity, the probability of states equals the stationary initial probability, independent from the choice of the initial situation. As a consequence, a repeated application of QUALSIM provides an approximation of the plausibilities of the different states of the system to be in the final solution, assumed that the choice of continuing the simulation at ambiguous points is randomized with respect to the membership functions of the qualitative variables. Thus, assuming that the qualitative model represents the real system, QUALSIM generates real solutions with a higher rating then spurious ones. This statement cannot be made for the other approaches.

QUALSIM has a discrete and finite representation of the state space, thus infinite positive / negative numbers are included in the qualitative values of +/- *extralarge*. A trajectory which tends to infinity will therefore remain in the respective cell of QUALSIM, it cannot distinguish between just extralarge and infinitely large. This is a shortcoming of the approach. However, in practical applications - as in our case of ecological phenomena - it might be sufficient to know whether the system tends to such extreme values or not. For example, to satisfy the "risk-aversion" in areas such as water reservoir management, it is sufficient to show that a system will never meet such critical situations. These types of answers QUALSIM can provide. However, this discussion shows one of the central problems of qualitative reasoning: similar to all other methods discussed to determine state transitions Markov chains proceed on a local level - since each state just depends on its immediate predecessor states - and do not support global views and information.

4. A Graph-based Interpretation of Qualitative Models

This chapter provides an additional framework for integrating the discussed techniques and for identifying their similarities and differences. This is done by means of graphs, which can also be interpreted as a qualitative representation of a model. However, this chapter does not pretend to be a survey of graph-based modeling techniques. No references to techniques such as bond graphs or petri nets will be made, we restrict our notion of a graph to a simple structure consisting of nodes and directed / undirected arcs. We can distinguish several types or levels of graphs which correspond to the different approaches in qualitative reasoning. Each level adds further knowledge to the previous layer. The lowest level of description constitutes the layer with the smallest knowledge on which the following graph denoting so-called Boolean models can be placed:

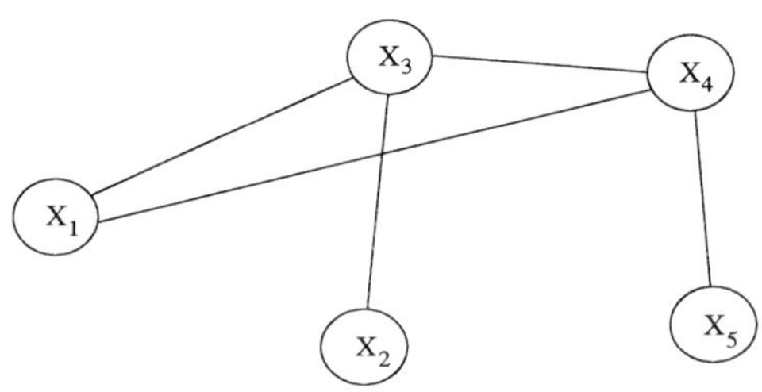

Fig. 51: A graph providing a Boolean description of a model

This graph illustrates how variables are mutually related, i.e. (x_1, x_3, x_4), (x_2,x_3), (x_4,x_5). This information can be used to infer further relationships between variables. Additionally, if we know which variable may serve as input, then we can also deduce causal influences, for example through the concept of mythical causality [de Kleer and Brown 84] or causal ordering [Iwasaki and Simon 86a]. Nodes denote either state variables or their derivatives, arcs algebraic relationships. This representation corresponds to the device-centered ontology (see also Fig. 5 of chapter II.1.1), however, the approach of [de Kleer and Brown 84] would need an additional arc between a variable and its derivative. This relationship is not explicitly represented in the original description, although it is used in the identification step of state transitions. This is different from the other approaches, which mark all necessary relationships between variables by means of some operators. The representation on the next level contains information about the direction of influences as well:

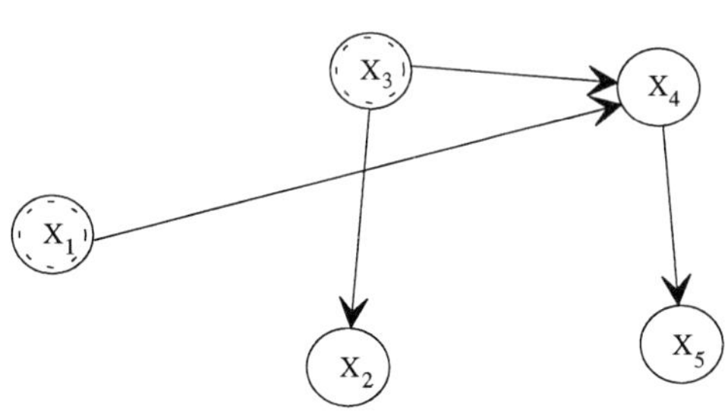

Fig. 52: A graph also providing direction of influence

In this representation, arcs indicate the flow of calculation, causality is compiled into the model. Nodes still denote variables. In addition, specific variables may be marked, in Fig. 52, for example, x_1 and x_3 are shown as exogenous variables. In the QUALSIM approach of [Guariso et al. 92], which corresponds to this type of graph, arcs may have a further interpretation, i.e. they represent a time step as well. They also denote an integration method of differential equations. Influences on one variable are added, hence a node implicitly and additionally denotes an operation.

These considerations lead to the next type of graph to represent a qualitative model, with an explicit representation of operators. Operators may be of different types, and these in turn may have a different number of arguments, similar to variables which may be connected to several operators. Therefore, we may represent both operators and variables as nodes. The arcs may or may not indicate a direction of influence, they explicitly / implicitly possess such information, for example in the approaches of [Forbus 84] or [Kuipers 84] and [Shen and Leitch 91] (we use M and d/dt to denote α_Q and I of [Forbus 84] as well):

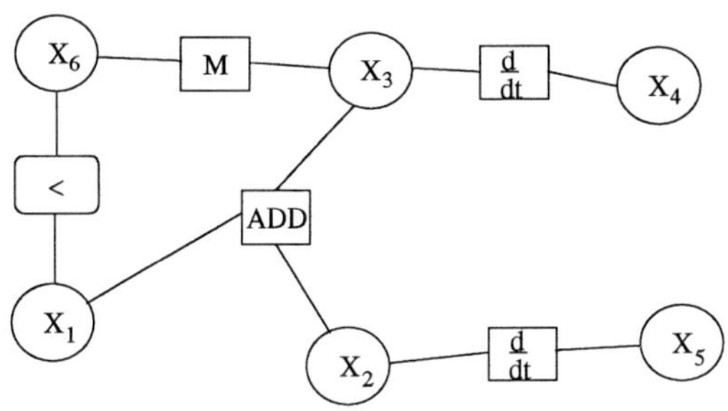

Fig. 53: A graph where both variables and operators are represented by means of nodes

At this level, time is explicitly introduced by the operator d/dt. Two different types of operators are indicated: relational operators, i.e. the symbol < between x_1 and x_6, are checked as to whether they are satisfied or not, the other operators have an interpretation based on the propagation of values. The relational type of operator to some extent denotes rules that have to be obeyed, the other type also possesses a constructive interpretation (the constraint-based approach, however, has no relational operators). Every path in this graph must have interchanging node types, variables must succeed operators and vice versa. This mode of representation shows some similarity with the quantity lattice of [Simmons 86]. Relational operators could in fact also be used to deduce new relationships between variables not related so far. Furthermore, this representation permits the integration of quantitative information and its usage in the value propagation process [Waltz 75]. Enhancements of QSIM such as [Kuipers and Berleant 88] and [Berleant and Kuipers 90] may also be represented.

On the last level of our graph-based classification we can position a description which may serve for classical numerical models as well. The following example is taken from [Guariso et al. 89a], however, other approaches, such as the well-known of [Ören 84], work in a similar way. Arcs denote the direction of calculation.

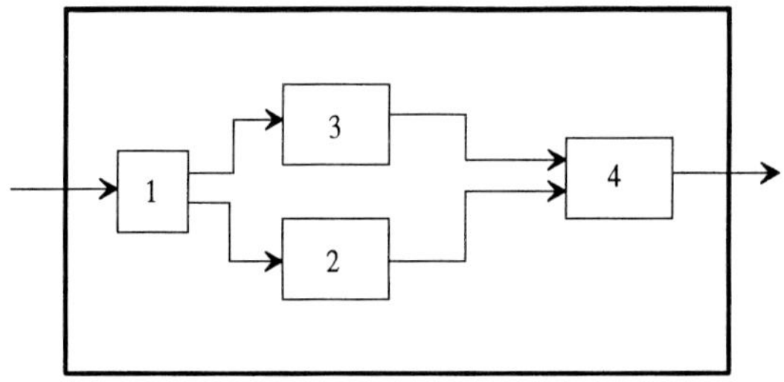

Fig. 54: Numerical model described by a graph, indicating connected submodels

Each variable has its calculation function stored, i.e. how its value is calculated based on its predecessors. This representation has the disadvantage that time is not explicitly expressed. The boxes, i.e. nodes, may denote both variables and entire models. Due to the integration of entire models, this representation also allows the description of an iterative and hierarchic approach to building models. Arcs denote the flow of data in its direction. Thus, Fig. 54 illustrates the causal sequence of variables and / or model pieces in the flow of calculation. This discussion shows that the four presented layers of graphs can be assigned to the different approaches in qualitative reasoning: the first layer to the device-centered ontology, the second layer to the approach of [Guariso et al. 92], the third layer to both the process-centered and the constraint-based ontology. The last level corresponds to the classical description of numerical simulation models.

The graphs presented so far only describe relationship between variables. However, approaches such as the process-centered ontology depict a mixture of representing both the relationship between variables and between different states. The structure of Fig. 53 is valid just for one state with a fixed structure of participating views and processes. After the occurrence of an event which forces one of the state variables to pass a threshold value or to modify its relationships to other variables, the state and its view and process structure changes. New relationships between variables become effective. A possible means of representation is shown in the following figure, integrating both the relationships between variables and between states:

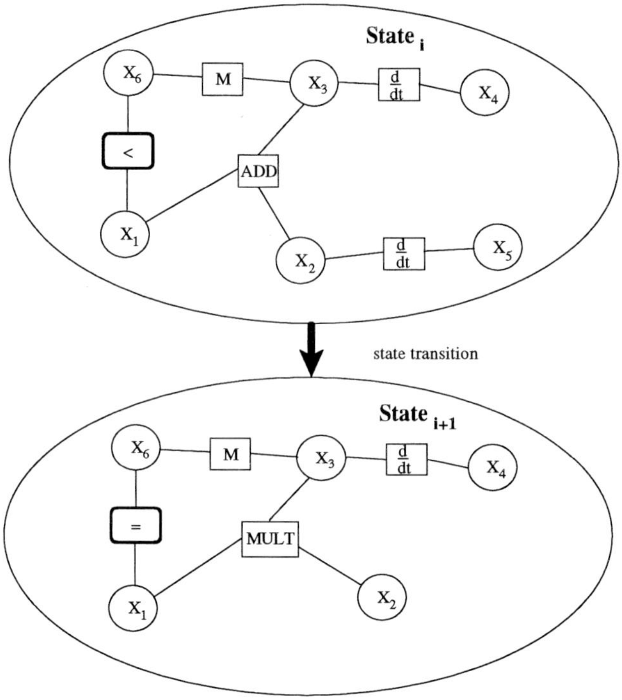

Fig. 55: Graph describing both the relationship between variables and states

Due to a changed relation between variables x_1 and x_6, a state change happens which leads to a new structure. Variable x_5, for example, does not appear anymore. The thick arrow represents the transfer of all values from $state_i$ to $state_{i+1}$. Therefore Fig. 55 also denotes a state transition diagram. Furthermore, this transition restricts, based on the law of continuity, the possible values of variables in adjacent states. Thus, the state transition arrow also denotes an operation. For example, in the constraint-based approach the I- and P-transition rules are applied. Different types of nodes within a state are used denoting either variables or operators. Moreover, different operators can be identified, i.e. relational operators, algebraic and functional operators which link variables at the same time step and operators which are responsible for the time advancement. Nodes for quantities can be further differentiated with respect to variables and known landmark values.

This form of representation uncovers the similarity and differences between the different primitives used. For example, as an important difference between [Forbus 84] and other authors it can be noted that the process-centered approach has the ability of changing its structure from state to state, whereas the other approaches do not possess this capability. In fact, in this case the thick arrow would be better indicated by a loop back to $state_j$, where index j enumerates the states. Thus, the process-centered approach offers the possibility of representing discontinuities. However, this would need a modified version of its limit analysis, which would violate the law of continuity. The mode of operation of the device-centered approach could be added as a further enhancement. These modes represent something like general states, which in turn can be subdivided into several more detailed states. However, adding to the respective states the conditions which identify these general modes would again supply a flat state structure.

This graph-based representation of a qualitative model may now illustrate the value propagation mechanism in qualitative reasoning. At the beginning, values are assigned to the input variables and initial values to the model's state variables. In addition, such initial values of state variables are sometimes already well-defined by the choice of a specific structure of states and/or variables. In the process of propagation these "given" values are passed from one node to another in the form of a wave by taking only admissible paths. Transition arcs, from a constructive point of view, based on the law of continuity, "carry" values from one state to the next. Each node is visited just once. The algorithm stops when all nodes are visited and all variables have been assigned new values. In this process, relational operators can be used to examine the conditions for a state change and to infer new values for variables as well as new relationships between variables. Ambiguity can now be interpreted as not having enough information at a specific node to assign only one value. In such a case, assumptions have to be made and a next state has to be created for each possible and admissible value. The process continues as described, but the set of all states which has to be visited may be extremely enlarged. Each alternative may be represented by a respective subgraph. The entire graph can be visited either by a depth, a breadth or a most likely first strategy. The ATMS of [de Kleer 86a] can now be interpreted as being just a mechanism to record the choices and to guarantee the visit of all nodes. In the case that quantitative information is added in order to iteratively refine the intervals, this special process may be viewed as a permanent visiting of nodes within one state until no refinement is anymore possible.

The representation in the form of graphs may also serve to illustrate the filtering mechanism of qualitative reasoning. Filters exploit locally available information on the one hand and use knowledge about global behavior on the other. Both the constraint consistency and the pairwise consistency filtering of [Kuipers 86], for example, belong to the first case. In the first step, all neighboring variable nodes to an operational node - taking the representation of Fig. 55 - are visited and their sets of variable values examined with regard to the respective operational node. Pairwise consistency filtering, in contrast, starts from a variable node. If such a node has more than one operational neighbor, its set of values consists of different subsets - each of them is the result of the application of the different neighboring operational nodes. Only those values which figure within the intersection of all subsets remain consistent. Global behavioral rules, e.g. the global filters of no change or cycles of [Kuipers 86], leave the state internal relationships of the graph in Fig. 55 and look at its overall structure. The introduction of quantitative knowledge can now be seen as a further restriction of nodes of both the variable and the operator type. In addition, further available global knowledge could be represented by a supplementary node, something like a hyper node, connected to the respective influenced nodes. The interpretation based on graphs could provide a framework for the introduction of this hyper node. The mentioned filtering procedures could - on a technical level - remain the same.

Qualitative constraints define the value range of a qualitative variable. Available additional knowledge, as for example knowledge about functionality of a device, would further reduce this value range, but some degree of freedom may still exist. Such knowledge would require some more nodes with distinct numerical values as well as nodes for functionality operators such as ToMaintain or ToPrevent (see also chapter III.2.). This approach could be extended to the integration of an optimality criterion, which could be interpreted as the optimal use of a device and would represent a super node guiding the value propagation mechanism. Assuming that such a criterion can be fulfilled within the range defined by the constraining equations, it would definitely reduce ambiguities. However, the definition of such a qualitative optimality criterion and its related operators is a pending problem. Furthermore, the propagation algorithm would need some changes to guarantee the optimal result even in the case of several local suboptima.

Part IV

Qualitative Reasoning and Related Fields

In the following we will relate qualitative reasoning to other fields of research such as the area of simulation in system theory or expert systems. Moreover, we will also take a short look at cognitive science. This comparison will uncover several correspondences with these fields and support further distinction between the different approaches in qualitative reasoning. Since we are concentrating on dynamic systems, we will not discuss other related fields such as spatial reasoning.[61]

1. Simulation in System Theory

In this chapter we attempt to confront the different approaches of qualitative reasoning with several concepts developed in the field of system theory, which represents a large area of research. It may serve two important tasks: as a common theory of modeling which can be applied to very different systems in different areas of science and as an instrument to simulate the behavior of such systems in order to derive statements about them. In the following we will concentrate on simulation theory with its representation of dynamic systems and its respective simulation methods. These are well developed and highly sophisticated (see for example [Klir 85], [Ören et al. 84], [Pichler 75], [Zeigler 76], [Zeigler 79] and [Zeigler et al. 79]). Thus, they may serve as a very suitable reference. Furthermore, qualitative reasoning and simulation theory both deal with dynamic systems; also, they coincide in their principle task of predicting the future of a system on the basis of its structural description. However, they differ in both the mode of representation and the mode of reasoning. In the second part of this chapter we will additionally present several applications of AI methods to investigate dynamic systems which are somehow outside the pure qualitative reasoning approach.

a) Concepts and Methods of Qualitative Reasoning and Simulation Theory

One can interpret system theory as the theoretical background of the "art" of modeling. Two relations can be identified: the modeling relation, which maps from the real world onto a model, and the simulation relation, which connects the model to the simulation motor and the respective results. In principle, modeling can be described as the process of deducing structure from observed behavior, simulation is in some sense the inverse operation, i.e. the generation of behavior given the structure of a system [Fishwick and Zeigler 91].

We use the following figure to show correspondences between the two fields in dealing with dynamic systems:

[61] We refer to [Forbus 80], [Forbus et al. 87], [Faltings 87], [Gardin and Meltzer 89], [Nielsen 88] and [Hodges 92] for a description of different approaches in this area.

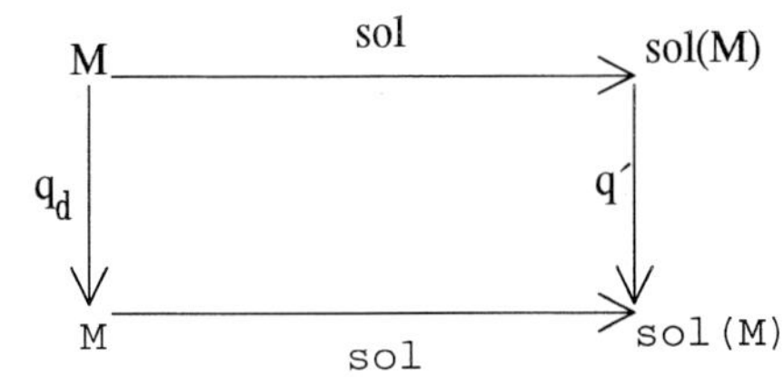

Fig. 56: The mapping between quantitative (M) and qualitative models (`M`)

The letter M denotes dynamic systems which will be defined in the following, `M` the corresponding qualitative models. sol and `sol` are the applied behavior generation methods, sol(M) and `sol(M)` the respective solutions. Whereas in chapters II.3 and III.2 we concentrated on the power as well as the limitations of `M` and `sol(M)`, in this chapter we will discuss the description mapping q_d, i.e. mapping both variable values and relationships between variables, and show that similar semantic concepts are related to the two solution mechanisms sol and `sol`. In general, a dynamic system M can be described by the following tuple (see [Zeigler 76] and [Spriet and Vansteenkiste 82]):

$M = \langle T, U, X, Y, \delta, \lambda, P\rangle$ where
T: time base,
U: input value set,
X: state set,
Y: output value set,
P: parameter set,
δ: state transition function, and
λ: the output function.[62]
δ: $U \times X \times P \times T \rightarrow X$
λ: $U \times X \times P \times T \rightarrow Y$.

Every state variable x_i has a range X_i, X denotes the cross product $X_1 \times X_2 \times .... \times X_n$ and defines the state value space, for example $\mathbf{R}^n$. The set of state variables is $\underline{X} = \{x_1, x_2, .. x_n\}$ and $x \in X$ denotes the vector $(x_{v1}, x_{v2}, ..., x_{vn})$, where x_{vi} is the value of state variable x_i. The same notation is valid for the other value sets. The time base may be either continuous or discrete, the range sets continuous or discrete as well. This is different to qualitative reasoning with its very limited set Q of possible values for qualitative quantities. It is also valid for the approach of [Kuipers 86] and all further interval-based approaches which allow for an iterative refinement, although these methods may produce a very fine grain size interval set. Given the general structure of a dynamic system M, it can be examined which of its sets and functions can be mapped onto a qualitative counterpart. Different levels can be distinguished. If just a qualitative input `U` and a qualitative output set `Y` are available i.e. the value sets of the variables in $\underline{\mathtt{U}}$ and $\underline{\mathtt{Y}}$ are limited (we use again `A` to denote the qualitative equivalent of A), but the model itself is quantitative. The mappings p_u: `U` $\rightarrow$ U and q_y: Y $\rightarrow$ `Y` have to be defined which are mappings from the qualitative to the quantitative input value space and from the quantitative to the qualitative output space (see also part V and [Beck and

[62] In the "classical" definition also the set of all input segments $\Omega \subseteq (U,T)$ is included, it describes the pattern of inputs over some time period, i.e. a map ω: $\langle t_0, t_1\rangle \rightarrow U$. $\langle t_0, t_1\rangle$ denotes the open/closed interval between t_0 and t_1. For example, in the continuous case of n input variables $T = \mathbf{R}$ and $U = \mathbf{R}^n$. Ω may also be related to the concept of an experiment, defining the environment of a specific simulation run.

Fishwick 89]). These mappings are based on the respective mappings q: $\mathbf{R} \rightarrow Q$ and p: $Q \rightarrow P(\mathbf{R})$ between a quantitative and qualitative value space (see chapter II.3). The simulation algorithm itself - sol, or respectively, the two functions δ and λ - does not change and works in strictly quantitative terms. The definition of the "quasi-inverse" mappings p_u and q_y are of great importance (see also [Fishwick 89]). In the general case, all sets and functions are mapped to their qualitative counterparts, the parameter set P disappears completely and the other elements of M express slightly different meanings. The qualitative counterpart of M can be written as

$$M = \langle T,\ U,\ X,\ Y,\ \delta_Q,\ \lambda_Q \rangle.$$

One qualitative model may describe several distinct quantitative models. The elements of M have to be reinterpreted. Time base T is an alternating sequence $[t_0, (t_0, t_1), ...(t_{n-1}, t_n), t_n, ..)$, i.e. $T = T_I \cup T_P$, where $T_P = \{[t_i, t_i]\}$ and $T_I = \{(t_i, t_{i+1}) \mid t_i < t_{i+1}\}$, but no information about the distinct values may be available. Since each variable has the set Q of qualitative values as value range, in the case of n state variables the state set can be written as $X = Q_1 \times Q_2 \times ... Q_n$. Q is defined by the set of landmark values and open interval between any two such adjacent landmarks. The same is valid for the other sets U and Y. Furthermore, set X can be partitioned into two non-overlapping sets, i.e. those states with a duration of an interval and those with a duration of zero: $X = X_I \cup X_P$, where $X_I = \{x \in X \mid x = (x_{v1}, ..., x_{vn})$ and $\forall x_i\ (x_{vi} \neq [l_j, l_j]$ or $x_{vi} = [l_j, l_j]$ and $\partial x_i = 0)\}$ and $X_P = \{x \in X \mid x = (x_{v1}, ..., x_{vn})$ and $\exists\, x_i$ with $x_{vi} = [l_j, l_j]$ and $\partial x_i \neq 0\}$. l_j is a landmark value from the set of landmarks.

The distinction between the sets $\underline{U}$, $\underline{X}$ and $\underline{Y}$ is not straightforward. An "input" may be applied in different ways, either by some input variable or just by some initial state. In the normal case, either $\underline{U}$ does not exist at all or consists of just one variable. Initial values of members of $\underline{X}$ are represented by a known value x_v at time t_0, normally these are implicitly assumed default values. The distinction between the sets $\underline{X}$ and $\underline{Y}$ depends on whether the variables are directly influenced - by means of operators such as I or d/dt - or not. These are the only primitives which allow for the identification of state variables. All other variables are members of the output variable set $\underline{Y}$, however, these variables may also participate in the calculation of the members of $\underline{X}$, i.e. they may serve as arguments of the qualitative functions δ_Q and λ_Q as well. In the device-centered approach, taking an inverse point of view, state variables are those variables which appear in mixed confluences in a non-derivative form, i.e. in the confluence $[x_i] = \partial y_j$ x_i denotes the state variable.

The two functions can now be stated as follows:
λ_Q represents the intrastate behavior: it is responsible for calculating the values of all variables within one state, i.e. completing a state, once this state is reached by a state transition.
δ_Q is responsible for the interstate behavior, it forces variables to change from known values to new ones at the next time step and also checks whether some state variables may pass some threshold value and make the system pass to a new state.

The two qualitative functions may be written with different arguments as
$\delta_Q\colon U \times X \times Y \times T \rightarrow X$
$\lambda_Q\colon U \times X \times T \rightarrow Y$

Set P is eliminated due to qualitative abstraction. Different transition rules are applied depending on the value type of T, either a point or an interval. Furthermore, qualitative reasoning puts some important limits on the functions δ_Q and λ_Q. Both have to be local and may not incorporate knowledge about the entire system. They should obey the no-function-in-structure principle. The envisionment of [de Kleer and Brown 84] and [Forbus 84] produce the entire state space, similar to a global system analysis approach. The constraint-based approach of [Kuipers 84] produces a distinct set of trajectories depending on qualitatively given values of the members of $\underline{U}$ and x at time t_0.

In the following we will look at the correspondences between the two behavior generation techniques sol and sol, as shown in Fig. 56. In particular, we will examine discrete event simulation, difference-equations-based simulation and the concept of a finite state automaton. These different modeling formalisms are more specific, but they all describe dynamic systems. Moreover, they show nice similarities with the main techniques used in qualitative reasoning, at least on a semantic level. Thus, when interpreting the respective qualitative reasoning approaches, we conceive them as constructive algorithms and abstract from their specific reasoning techniques. Although we distinguish between model representation and simulation techniques, they determine each other. In such a way the mentioned formalisms can be interpreted as further specializations of formalism M to describe dynamic systems.[63] Thus, also the mapping q_d from the respective representations of M onto the approaches in qualitative reasoning will be discussed.

A discrete event system changes state when a well-identified event changes the value of a variable. This variable is part of the vector which describes the state of a system. Therefore, such event "touches" only one or a few variables, and it may or may not generate a new event. Events are the basic primitives which change states; only events can change things and create new or destroy existing objects. Events may occur at inequidistant time points and they are not always known in advance. For example, in a customer queuing system where the state is described by the number of persons in the system, the state is changed at the inequidistant time points of customer arrivals. In contrast, in continuous system simulation all variables change simultaneously. Difference-equations-based simulation is the discretisized approximation of continuous simulation based on an integration with a fixed time step. The integration method defines time points where all variables change their values.

A discrete event system can be described by the tuple $\langle X, U, Y, E, \delta, \lambda \rangle$:

X: the state set,
U: the input set,
O: the output set,
E: the list of events,
δ: state transition function, and
λ: the output function.

An event $e \in E$ changes state x, i.e. if e is applied on x_{t_i} the state changes to $x_{t_{i+1}}$, where i denotes the sequence of states with respect to time, i.e. $x_{t_i} = x(t_i)$. The time between two consecutive states is not equidistant, i.e. $\exists$ i, that $t_{i+1} - t_i \neq t_i - t_{i-1}$. Each event has an associated time point of its occurrence (e,t_e). Furthermore, an event may either be external, i.e. defined

[63] For a detailed classification and theory of mapping between the different formalisms see [Zeigler 76]. Moreover, in [Zeigler 84], [Zeigler et al. 79] and [Zeigler 89] detailed presentations of discrete event simulation and modeling methods as well as their object-oriented implementation are given.

by the environment as a kind of input (e^{ext}), or internal as a result of some previous event (e^{in}). Two consecutive events are partially ordered and
if (e_i,t_{e_i}) generates (e_j,t_{e_j}), then $i < j$ and $t_{e_i} \leq t_{e_j}$.

An event touches just some state variables $x_i \in \underline{X}$, and they may be classified as different event types with respect to these state variables. Additionally, every event type is linked to its specific state transition function $\delta_{type(e)}$. In the following we will not distinguish between an event and its state transition function.

Since we use a list of events containing the sequence of events ordered with respect to their activation time, a state change can be written as
(e_i,t_{e_i}): $(u, x_{t_{e_i}}) \rightarrow (x_{t_j}, E')$
where $x_{t_{e_i}}$ is the state of the system at time t_{e_i} and $t_j \geq t_{e_i}$.
$E' = E \cup E_1 \setminus E_2 \setminus \{(e_i^{\text{in or ext}},t_{e_i})\}$ with
$E_1 = \{(e_{j_k}{}^{in},t_{e_{jk}}) \mid k \geq 0, i < j, t_{e_i} \leq t_{e_{jk}}\}$, i.e. new events which are created by (e_i,t_{e_i}), and
$E_2 = \{(e_{l_m},t_{e_{lm}}) \mid m \geq 0, i < l, t_{e_i} \leq t_{e_{lm}}\}$, i.e. those events which are eliminated from the list due to the activated event.

Furthermore, the output function λ is defined as $\lambda_{type(e)}(u, x) = y$, also depending on the type of the applied event. Each event - external or internal - has as arguments the state variables it acts upon and its input variables. It produces a new state and a probably empty set of new internal events. Furthermore, the activated event and probably some more events are deleted from the set of events. The time base T is given as $[t_0, \infty) \subset \mathbf{R}$. It is important to note that an output function can calculate also only some $y_j \in \underline{Y}$. Thus, both transition and output functions may be classified with respect to their arguments.

A discrete event simulation algorithm, based on a scheduler, works as follows:
1 - at the beginning take the set of external events, place them into a set of events E,
2 - choose the event with the smallest event occurrence time, i.e. $(e^{act},t_{act}) = (e,t_k)$,
  where $t_{act} = \min(t_k)$ for all t_k and $e \in E$,
3 - set the simulation time t equal to t_{act},
4 - apply e^{act} to its defined arguments at the actual time,
5 - apply $\lambda_{type(e)}$ to its arguments,
6 - update E,
7 - if E is not empty or the time limit not reached, then goto 2.

The ordering relation in the list of events determines the advancement of time. The central point of discrete event simulation is the notion of event, its inequidistant occurrence of time points and the fact that not all variables need to be arguments of every type of event.

A system based on difference equations can be written as $\langle X, U, Y, \delta, \lambda\rangle$. T is now a sequence of discrete values $[t_0, t_1, ..t_n, ..)$ with $\forall$ i: $t_{i+1} - t_i = t_i - t_{i-1}$. The set of all state variables is necessary to determine the next state, the functions are the following ones:
$\delta(u, x_t) = x_{t+1}$
$\lambda(u, x_t) = y_t$
where $x_{t_i} = x(t_i)$ describes the system at time t_i. In this approach a permanent iterative cycle calculates all values at equidistant time points, the calculation of the new values is described by the state transition function δ and no extra devoted primitive such as an event is necessary.

Finally, we take the concept of a finite state automaton, specifically a finite automaton recognizer, to conclude our representation of different formalisms.[64] However, in the following we use the term finite state automaton which is described by $\langle X, \Sigma, \delta, q_0, F\rangle$, where

X: the set of states,
Σ: the input alphabet,
δ: a mapping $X \times \Sigma \rightarrow X$, i.e. $\delta(x_r,a) = x_s$ for $x_r, x_s \in X$ and $a \in \Sigma$,
q_0: the initial state, and
F: the set of final states.

Such a finite automaton accepts a string of input symbols if it starts at state q_0, processes all symbols of the string, and its final state is in the set F. T is represented by a permanent clock which defines the clock rate of the state transitions. In this description there is no direct reference to input and output variables. However, Σ denotes the value set of possible input values, which is sufficient for our purpose.

The constraint-based and the process-centered ontology can be distinguished as follows: we claim that the first ontology resembles the difference-equation-based methodology, whereas the latter corresponds to the discrete event simulation approach. QUALSIM, the approach of [Guariso et al. 92], based on influence diagrams and fuzzy sets, obviously corresponds to the difference-equations-based simulation. This follows straightforward from its definition. The device-centered ontology will be considered similar to a finite automaton.

In contrast to [Fishwick and Zeigler 91]and [Travé-Massuyès 92] we classify QSIM [Kuipers 86] and its constraint-based ontology as a difference-equation-based approach. The contrary would be only true if the calculation of a specific value can already be classified as an event. In the following we will not consider the fact that the algorithm of [Kuipers 86] works interpretatively, i.e. from a simulation's point of view inverted and backward. In the actual discussion we will consider it as a constructive algorithm which, given a set of state variables, calculates the sequence of states. This approach bears a resemblance with the discrete event simulation scheme in so far as time points are not equidistant but nearly arbitrarily spaced on the number line.[65] However, QSIM and its successor and relatives generate new states in a fixed sequence and, even more important, in all these calculations all variables are engaged.

Taking a constructive point of view and using the formalism for difference-equations-based simulation, QSIM can be written as $M = \langle U, X, Y, \delta_Q, \lambda_Q\rangle$. More specifically, the set of all state variables $\underline{X} = \{x_i \mid x_i$ appears in DERIV$(x_i,z)\}$, i.e. all those variables which appear as first argument of a predicate DERIV. The set $\underline{Y} = \{y_i \mid y_i$ does not appear in any DERIV$(y_i,z)\}$. It should be noted that a clear distinction between input, state and output variables does not exist, since "output" variables may influence state variables. In the normal case, $\underline{U}$ is empty or has just one member. The sets X, U and Y are defined as in the general case. The time base is represented by an interchanging sequence $[t_0, (t_0, t_1), t_1, \ldots (t_j, t_{j+1}), t_{j+1}, \ldots)$, where for every t_i exists a function denoting a variable z with $z(t_i) = l_k$, with l_k a landmark value. This sequence also determines the sequence of states, i.e. states of a duration zero interchange with states with an interval duration. Qualitatively, these states just differ in

[64] See [Beckman 81] for a classification of different types of automata.

[65] Note that this can also be the case when solving differential equations numerically: "intelligent" algorithms, i.e. integration methods, set the time points as they need, i.e. close to discontinuities the integration step size Δt becomes smaller, in linear ranges larger.

the rules that determine the state transitions, while in all other aspects they can be treated as equidistant.[66] Furthermore, they are always totally ordered, which is not the case in discrete event simulation.

The state transition function includes all DERIV predicates, i.e. $\delta_Q = \cup$ {DERIV in the constraints of the QSIM model} and δ_Q: $U \times X \times Y \times T \rightarrow X$. More detailed, the state transition function can be distinguished with respect to the applicable transition rules, either from point to interval or vice versa, i.e. $X_P \rightarrow X_I$ and $X_I \rightarrow X_P$. Since output values may influence state variables, Y is included as well. Similarly, the output function includes all other predicates, i.e. $\lambda_Q = \cup$ {{MULT, ADD, M} in the constraints of the QSIM model} and λ_Q: $U \times X \times T \rightarrow Y$.

The most important difference between QSIM and the discrete event approach is that there is no dedicated representational primitive such as an event, which is responsible for all state changes. Together with the lack of such an operational and ontological primitive, the algorithm works in a completely different way, at least on a semantic or constructive level. Whereas in discrete event simulation a scheduler has always to check and to look for the event with the smallest occurrence time and to update the event list every time an event has been activated, QSIM permanently "recalculates" the values of all state variables with previously defined equations. The generation of new events contains the idea of unforeseen things. Discrete event simulation may introduce new quantities and change the structure of the model during simulation. The only thing QSIM can change or add is new information about the quantity space, i.e. a refinement of intervals based on a fixed structure.

The approach represented by the qualitative process theory and implemented by the qualitative process engine [Forbus 86] can be classified as a discrete event simulation approach. It can be described by $\langle U, X, Y, E, \delta_Q, \lambda_Q \rangle$. The distinction between $\underline{X}$ and $\underline{Y}$ is similar to the previous discussion, $\underline{X} = \{x_i \mid x_i$ appears in $I(x_i,z)\}$, i.e. all those variables which appear as first argument of the operator I; the set $\underline{Y} = \{y_i \mid y_i$ does not appear in any $I(y_i,z)\}$. The representation is more complex, since it includes - in addition to variables - also processes and views, i.e. these define specific relationships between variables, which lead to a state space description.[67] Given such a specific view structure, one or more processes are active. This leads to an extended value space $X^* = Q_1 \times ... \times Q_n \times Q_{n+1} \times ... \times Q_{n+m}$ of n state variables and m output variables. This is necessary, since the relationship between all variables may define the view and process structure. If we denote with $\gamma_{vj}, \gamma_{pi} \in \{0, 1\}$, depending on whether view j or process i is active or not, the view and process structure can be written as $VP = \gamma_{v1} \times .. \gamma_{vk} \times \gamma_{p1} \times ... \times \gamma_{po}$, where γ_{pi} denotes the process i, γ_{vj} the view j, and there are k views and o processes. The vector $x^* \in X^*$ determines VP. Processes are the only primitives which can change values over time and force the system into a new state. Hence, new views and processes become active. The concept of a process constitutes a dedicated entity which is responsible for changes. But while processes take some time, events happen instantaneously. Processes can be interpreted as an assembling of events which are

[66] The introduction of quantitative information in QSIM as done by [Kuipers and Berleant 88] or [Berleant and Kuipers 90] requires a separate treatment. However, also in this case a correspondence to difference-equations-based simulation exists due to the mode of calculation, i.e. the permanently alternating application of two types of rules on the one hand and the fact that these techniques still lack a representational primitive such as an event to drive the simulation on the other.

[67] This is a further reference to the object-orientation of this approach, very different to the mathematical, "flat" description of systems only by means of variables.

responsible for both the change of values and the detection of such changes. The sequence in time of all processes in the form of events, i.e. the union of the histories of the engaged individuals, corresponds to event list E. This is close to the process-oriented approach in discrete event simulation (see [Dahl et al. 67] and the language SIMULA dedicated to this approach).

Processes and views touch just some individuals with their variables, the remaining ones can be neglected. Thus, the influences of processes correspond to the functions related with different event types, whereas the relation parts of both processes and views denote the different output functions. Therefore, we can write a state transition function related with an event as $\delta_{Q\ \mathrm{type(e)}}\ (u_{[t,t]}, x_{[t,t]}) = x_{(t,t+1)}$ or $\delta_{Q\ \mathrm{type(e)}}\ (u_{(t,t+1)}, x_{(t,t+1)}) = x_{[t+1,t+1]}$, where type(e) depends on VP and just those state variables mentioned in the actual state of VP have to be considered. The state transition function can be distinguished whether or not the topical state has duration zero. Moreover, since the new state produces a new view and process structure, new events are generated. $\delta_{Q\ \mathrm{type(e)}}$ is the union of all direct influences which are mentioned in the processes corresponding to type(e). The output function is $\lambda_{Q\ \mathrm{type(e)}}\ (u_t, x_t) = y_t$, where t denotes either an interval or a point. $\lambda_{Q\ \mathrm{type(e)}}$ is the union of all indirect influences which appear in the processes and views corresponding to type(e). Time is again represented by an interchanging sequence of points and intervals. This sequence also represents the activation times of the respective events and their associated functions. The event list E can be interpreted - as already mentioned - as the union of the events of the respective object histories. The scheduler corresponds to the step-by-step processing of this list and to the limit analysis, responsible for the identification of the appropriate state transitions.

Moreover, the process-centered approach could also enable the representation of discontinuities as it is done by the multi-modeling approach, described among others by [Ören 91] and [Zeigler and Louri 93]. The change of a view and process structure may represent such discontinuity and further indicate the jump to a different model, described by new individuals, views and processes. However, this would require a redefinition of the concept of limit analysis - the law of continuity, for example, would not be valid anymore. A further difference between the constraint-based and process-centered approach can be mentioned: in discrete event simulation as well as in its process-oriented sub-direction events can happen simultaneously, in parallel. Consequently, several processes of the qualitative process engine may also work simultaneously - indeed, in most cases more than one process is active. In the difference-equations-based approach, however, the time advancement also represents a sequentialization of behavior.

It follows that a process-centered approach with its dedicated primitives and encapsulated objects has also a close relationship to object-oriented programming (see for example [Meyer 88]). Both the discrete event simulation method and the process-oriented ontology work with individuals described by variables. QSIM and difference-equations-based simulation deal directly and only with variables. There is no formal and representational concept above variables.[68] The concept of instantiating distinct processes and views from a predefined library, i.e. classes, as well as the fact that its influencing mechanisms can be easily interpreted as message passing, brings this approach close to the object-oriented paradigm. It

[68] This supports our opinion that it was not by accident that the first object-oriented language was SIMULA [Dahl et al. 67], which is both a discrete event (process) simulation and a general-purpose language. For a concept to be modern, it does not have to be recently invented. The OO paradigm also blurs differences in computer science and a distinction between database design and software engineering will vanish as both deal with modeling.

may be followed that also the object-oriented approach represents an ontological approach to represent and to model real world entities.

The classification of the device-centered approach with respect to the above discussed techniques is different and it corresponds well with the concept of a finite state automaton as defined before. Therefore, we rewrite M as $\langle X, U, \delta_Q, \lambda_Q, q_0, F\rangle$ and describe how M is constructed, using the concepts of the device-centered approach. X is the finite set of states defined by the qualitative value combinations of all state variables of $\underline{X}$ and $X_i = Q = \{+,0,-\}$. The number of states is 3^n, if there are n state variables. State variables are those which are contained in mixed confluences in a non-derivative form. Furthermore, X can again be partitioned into two non-overlapping sets of states, i.e. those states with a duration of an interval and those with a duration of zero: $X = X_I \cup X_P$, where $X_I = \{x \in X \mid x = (x_{v1}, ..., x_{vn})$ and $\forall\ x_{vi} \neq 0\}$ and $X_P = \{x \in X \mid x = (x_{v1}, ..., x_{vn})$ and $\exists\ x_{vi} = 0$ and $\partial x_i \neq 0\}$. In the following we denote with Y - there is no direct counterpart in the description definition of a finite state automaton - the value set of all derivatives of all variables excluding the variable of $\underline{U}$. $\underline{Y}$ may be seen as a set of auxiliary variables, each of these variables has the value range Q. In the normal case, the set of input variables $\underline{U}$ has just one element, its value range is $\Sigma = \{+,0,-\}$. λ_Q denotes the value assignment mechanism within a state, i.e. the intrastate behavior, given the values of the input and of the state variables. Thus, λ_Q: $X \times U \rightarrow Y$, that is $\lambda_Q(x,a) = \cup_q\, y_q$ for each $x \in X$, $a \in \Sigma$ and $y_q \in Y$ (a is the value of the input variable). The vectors y_q correspond to the different possible interpretations within one state and the elements of y_q have values from $\{+,0,-\}$. However, y_q has to be consistent with the constraints defining the system, all constraints are used in λ_Q. Function λ_Q has no counterpart in the definition of a finite automaton, it serves for a further characterization of states, determining also the transition function.

The state transition function is partitioned with respect to X_I and X_P: i.e. δ_Q: $X_I \times Y' \rightarrow X_P$ and $X_P \times Y' \rightarrow X_I$. This can be written as $\delta_Q(x_r, y'_q) = x_{s\,q}$ for all $y_q \in Y'$, $x_r \in X_P$ and $x_{s\,q} \in X_I$ or vice versa. $Y' \subseteq Y$ denotes the value set of the derivatives of the state variables. Thus, δ_Q identifies the state transition dependent on the topical state and the derivatives of the state variables. Furthermore, several rules are applied to restrict δ_Q. q_0 can be any state of X, depending on the initial values of the state variables x_i. The set of final states $F = \{x \in X \mid \forall$ state variables $x_i \in \underline{X}$ $\partial x_i = 0$ or if $x_{vi} \neq 0$ then $x_{vi} = \partial x_i\}$. This corresponds to the limited, but compact, state space description of the device-centered approach. If the state is in a cell where the values of the state variables differ from zero and the derivatives point into the same direction, the system will remain in this state. The task of the envisionment process is to identify δ_Q and the sequence of states $(x_{t0}, x_{t1}, .., x_{tm}, ..)$, which is only finite if some $x_{tk} \in F$. This sequence represents the causal interpretation of the system's behavior that is looked for. This constitutes a difference to the finite automaton: a finite automaton recognizer checks whether a system, depending on the provided string of input symbols, reaches a final state; the device-centered approach analyzes possible state transitions and identifies the sequence of states.

On the highest level, an envisionment graph looks like a non-deterministic automaton. However, when the values of the respective derivatives in each state are taken into consideration, their values - corresponding to different interpretations - deterministically define the next transition. While the other methods may be classified to some extent as being constructive algorithms which produce new states and values, and thus explore the state space, this is not valid in the case of [de Kleer and Brown 84]. This approach analyzes and defines possible state transitions, their preconditions and their sequential and causal order.

The modeling view of [de Kleer and Brown 84] also resembles the approach taken by [Cellier 91] and the modeling and simulation tool DYMOLA. It allows for the hierarchical modeling of continuous systems. Submodels may be connected by means of terminal nodes, similar to the device-centered ontology. Coincidentally, DYMOLA also relies on Kirchhoff's current and voltage laws, which resemble the conditions of continuity and compatibility of [de Kleer and Brown 84]. However, while DYMOLA permits a straightforward description of a system's dynamic behavior by stating a set of normalized differential equations, the formalism of the device-centered ontology only supplies an algebraic and logical description.

Based on these considerations, we can draw the following correspondences:

system specifications in simulation theory	approaches in qualitative reasoning
discrete event simulation	process-centered ontology
difference-equations-based simulation	constraint-based ontology
difference-equations-based simulation	influence-diagram-based approach
finite state automaton	device-centered ontology

b) Simulation Support Tools

Qualitative reasoning is not the only field of science which provides qualitative statements about systems such as being at equilibrium or approaching a fixed point. Mathematical analysis provides descriptions of systems in the form of state space diagrams, transition regions or qualitative cells. These descriptions limit the behavior of a system to a specific range and provide a qualitative description of its set of behaviors. Based on these methods, programs have been developed which derive qualitative system properties, for example [Aubin 92]. Furthermore, such methods form the basis of specific AI techniques which may aid and support system scientists in their respective work. In the following we will describe several of such applications. Contrary to the main stream of qualitative reasoning, they do not represent a mapping of engineer's reasoning to formal models nor describe the entire process of model building in qualitative terms. These approaches assume that a quantitative model, which has to be elaborated, is available. They can be seen as intelligent modeling, simulation and analysis support tools for model builders. The methods do not include any qualitative simulation mechanism and are based on other techniques rather, like graph grammars, although they also deal exclusively with dynamic systems. They are focused on the building and analysis of quantitative models, the preparation of input data, the control of experiments, the choice of effective computational methods and the interpretation of results in qualitative terms. The described applications to some extent model the mappings p_u and q_y, taking the notation of dynamic systems with quantitative and qualitative input and output sets. It is assumed that several steps of numerical modeling and simulation can be automated. The following approaches can also be classified as part of qualitative reasoning research, although they have a very close relationship to mathematical analysis and system theory. However, they are based on AI methods, deal with dynamic systems and produce results similar to those of the main approaches discussed in this work.

The first of these examples, described by [Ishida 89] and [Ishida 92], takes as an input a system described by means of differential equations and produces a qualitative description of its possible behaviors. The example deals with the motion of a block on a flat surface. This system is described by the two equations

$dx/dt = v,$

$dv/dt = -kx - fv,$

where k and f are positive constants, the second term, i.e. -fv, denotes frictional force. The variables x and v denote position and velocity.

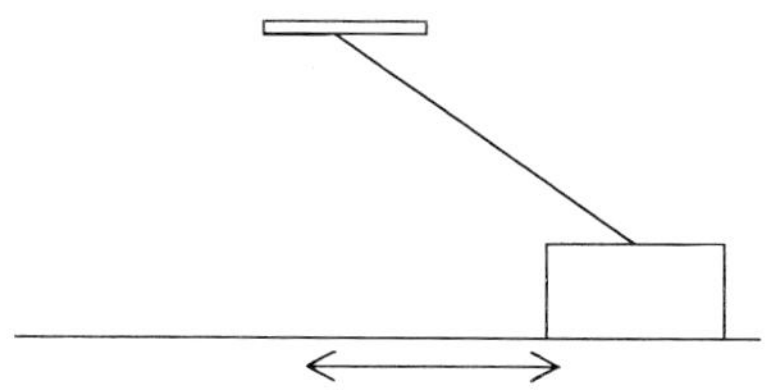

Fig. 57: Motion of a block on a flat surface

The phase diagram of this system shows that it moves asymptotically to the fixed point (0,0). The signs of the coefficients of the matrix dx/dt = Ax may be used to determine whether or not such a system moves to a stable point. This can also be represented by a graph (see Fig. 58), where the nodes denote the variables and the coefficients a_{ij} of A form the arcs, $a_{ij} \in \{+, -, 0\}$, depending on the sign of a_{ij}. This graph has the form of an influence diagram. By inspecting this graph, properties such as sign stability can be deduced. If a system is sign-stable, then it asymptotically approaches a fixed point. A system is called sign-stable, if all loops have a non-positive sign and there exists at least one loop with a negative sign; all circuits of length 2 must have non-positive signs; there exists no circuit larger than 3; the system is sign-observable from those elements with a negative loop.[69] Therefore, just by a simple examination of the graph of Fig. 58, the qualitative property of the system to approach to stable point can be deduced.

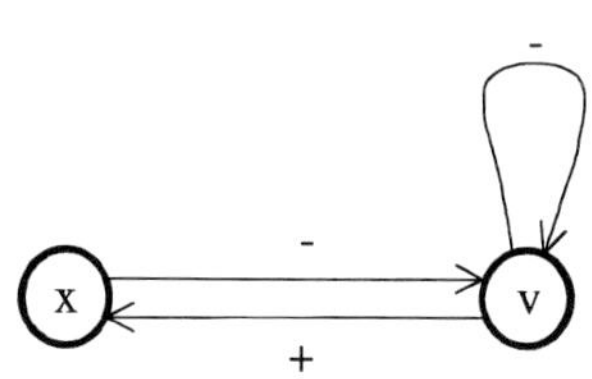

Fig. 58: Graph describing the influences of the moving block example

However, when f is set to zero, the system would permanently oscillate, no negative loop would exist anymore. A very similar approach is discussed by [Sacks 90a] with its fixed point algorithm. Instead of the signs of the original system matrix, it uses the matrix of partial derivatives with $a_{ij} = \partial f_i(x_1, ..., x_n) / \partial x_j$ to describe necessary and sufficient conditions for sign stability. These are similar to the conditions of [Ishida 89].

---

[69] A circuit is a closed path of connected nodes with arcs of the same direction. The length of an arc is the number of arcs and the sign of a circuit that is the product of the arc's signs. A circuit of length 1 is called a loop. A system is defined to be observable by an observer, if it is possible to determine the initial state by observing the output signal from the observer during a finite time. This concept allows to check for the direction of influence and causality.

A similar problem, the generation and interpretation of qualitative results of numerical models described by differential equations, can be exemplified by the works of [Yip 88], [Sacks 90b] and [Sacks 87]. This approach will be demonstrated by the so-called Van der Pol equation based on Kirchhoff's law of current, which describes the electronic circuit of Fig. 61, with k being a scaling factor, x the current, L inductance and C capacitance:

$$x'' + \frac{k}{L}(x^2 - 1)x' + \frac{1}{LC}x = 0$$

[Sacks 87] provides a qualitative behavior description of this nonlinear dynamic system. This is based on a piecewise linear approximation and employs the theory of linear systems. These have well-understood dynamics, either all trajectories are periodic, all approach a fixed point, or all approach infinity.

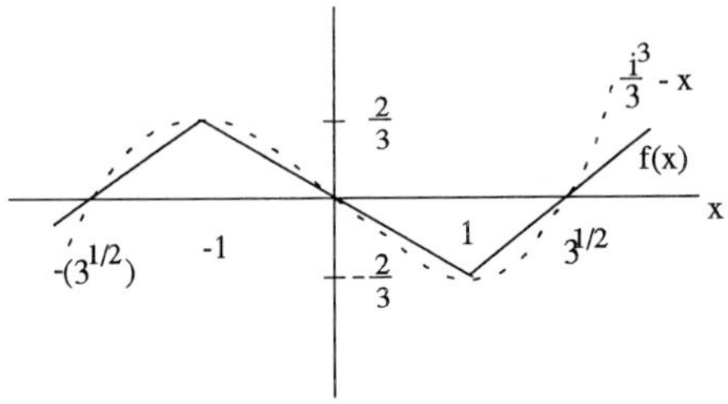

Fig. 59: Linear piecewise approximation

The program PLR (piecewise linear reasoning) transforms the term $(x^2 - 1)\,x'$ to $(1/3\,x^3 - x)'$ and approximates $(1/3\,x^3 - x)$ with a piecewise linear function, linear pieces are chosen with respect to uniform regions

$$f(x) = \begin{cases} \dfrac{\frac{2}{3}(x+\sqrt{3})}{(\sqrt{3}-1)} & \text{for } x < -1 \\ -\frac{2}{3}x & \text{for } -1 \le x \le 1 \\ \dfrac{\frac{2}{3}(x-\sqrt{3})}{(\sqrt{3}-1)} & \text{for } x > 1 \end{cases}$$

The resulting system can be written as
$x' = y$ and
$y' = -(1/LC)\,x - (k/L)\,f'(x)\,y$

In a further step, PLR performs a local analysis of the linear systems based on their eigenvalues. In our case, the characteristic equation of the system matrix A has complex roots for small k and real ones for large k, which corresponds to under- or overdamped systems, respectively. In a next step, it is checked whether local trajectories access adjacent regions in the state space by examining the behavior at the respective boundaries. Trajectories cannot cross boundaries within a linear region denoted by asymptotes. Then the local phases are combined by identifying which sequences of regions trajectories can traverse. The final result is represented by means of a state phase diagram and the possible transitions between regions. This is shown in the following Fig. 60, describing the results for both cases produced by the program PLR. The thick lines denote boundaries at which the piecewise linearization changes, dashed lines denote asymptotes. The inner symbols on the right side denote sources. Trajectories cross boundaries from left to right above the origin and from right to left below. Both parts of Fig. 60 show that the trajectories spiral around the origin. A further global analysis proves that the system converges to a unique limit cycle.[70] The system oscillates, because the nonlinear resistor adds energy to the circuit at low currents and drains energy at high currents.

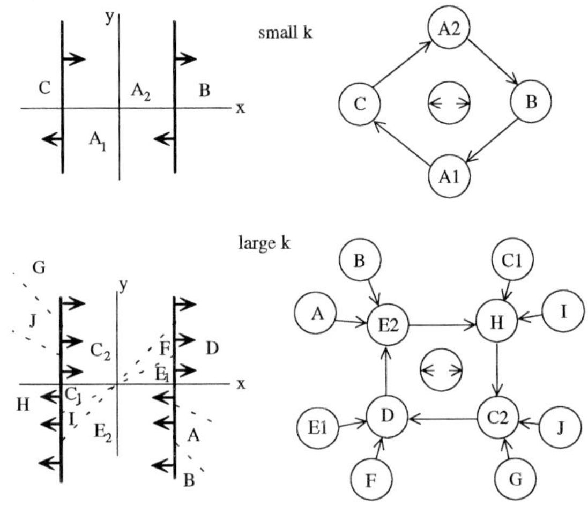

Fig. 60: State space diagram and transition regions

This result looks very much like the envisionment graph of the device-centered ontology, but provides a much better characterization of the state space and classification of trajectories. This is based on an exact description in form of a quantitative model, the applied algorithm takes into account magnitudes of parameters as well. A similar approach, based on mathematical analysis of a system's description is undertaken by [Aubin 92], generating so-called qualitative cells which correspond to homogeneous regions in the state space diagram.

A complementary approach, adapted by ([Abelson and Sussman 87] and [Abelson et al. 89]), is shown in the following electronic circuit of Fig. 61. Starting with a qualitative description of a system, a numerical model is generated, which is further used to calculate the time-dependent behavior. The circuit is described by a sequence of LISP statements, x again denoting the current.

[70] It is not the task of this chapter to provide a detailed description and derivation of the results but to demonstrate the similarity of this approach to qualitative reasoning.

```
(define-network driven-van-der-pol)
        ((a parameter v/x^3)
         (b parameter resistance)
         (d driven voltage)
        (n1 n2 n3)
        (parts
                (n1-res non-linear-resistor (n + n3) (n - gnd)
                        (vic (lambda (v x)
                                (= v (- (* a x x x) (* b x))))))
                (l inductor (n + n1) (n - n3))
                (c capacitor (n + n2) (n - n3))
                (s voltage-source (n + n1) (n - gnd) (strength d))))
```

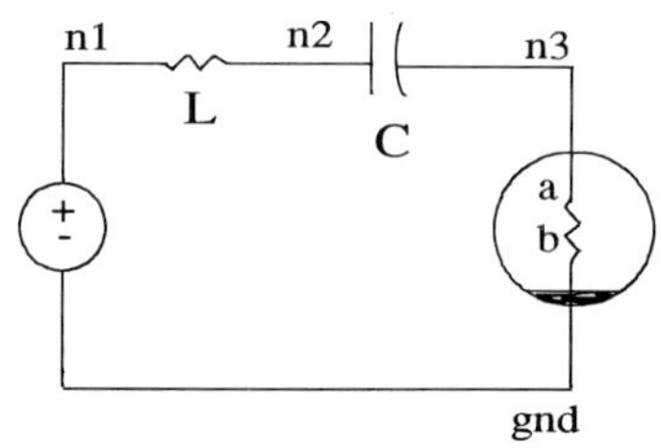

Fig. 61: Non-linear circuit with capacitance (C) and inductance (L)

This approach uses a symbolic description of real situations and produces an internal quantitative model which can be simulated and numerically solved. The potential user is supposed to be a person who understands methods and techniques and just needs an intelligent support.

The work of [Guariso et al. 89a] proceeds, in principle, in the same way. Given a qualitative description, it produces a numerical model which can be simulated numerically. It represents a simulation model generator which is based on a model type and instance tree. Models are constructed graphically, where parts of models or entire models may be taken from the model base or created from scratch. These, in turn, may be connected with other models to form more complex structures. Based on this graphical representation, the respective code is automatically generated. A simulation motor, which mainly processes a set of differential or difference equations, runs the simulation; the results can be postprocessed, stored in a data base and the distinct experiments and their environment memorized in a distinct base. The following picture represents a sequence of interconnected models which form a compound model.

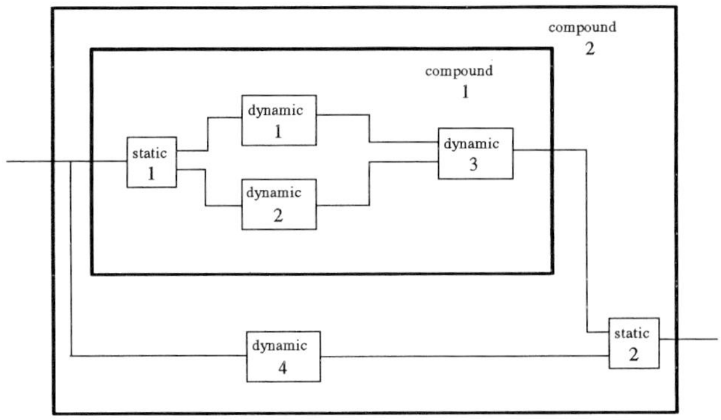

Fig. 62: Compound model built automatically by the approach of [Guariso et al. 89a]

Dynamic models are responsible for the time advancement, as they incorporate differential or difference equations. In contrast, static models directly map input onto output variables. The linking from succeeding output to preceding input variables is performed automatically, dimensions and integration steps are checked and, when necessary and possible, converted automatically.

This approach can easily be expanded to build entire environments for simulation and modeling (see for example [Guariso and Werthner 89a], [Ören 84]). They are also conceived as tools for systems engineers. Thus, they fit into our classification. Such environments are closely related to DSS and they contain well-modularized bases for the different tasks to be fulfilled:

- *Model base:* The specific knowledge about the domain of interest is stored in the form of models and model parts and their types of relationships such as *is-a*, *part-of* or *connected-to*. A model is constructed by assembling these parts - or just by selecting a proper model candidate - and by instantiation, i.e. initializing the respective parameter and initial values.

- *Data base:* It stores the sequences of input and output data, since the models represent dynamic systems. By means of this database, the communication between a connected sequence of models may be established.

- *Experiment base:* The experiment base contains the final instantiated model and links to the respective input value sets. Furthermore, the whole environment for simulation has to be defined, including simulation and / or optimization methods. Experiments are orthogonal to models, they are treated separately.

- *Postprocessing facility:* The results of different simulation runs have to be compared, or the result of a single run to be postprocessed. For example, some variable can be calculated on the basis of the observed output values.

- *Simulation and/or optimization motor:* Both mechanisms are necessary parts of the environment. The first is obvious and defines the way the simulation is performed, similar to the behavior generation of qualitative reasoning. The second may be used in a goal-directed simulation, where a simulation is iteratively repeated until some goal, i.e. optimization criteria, is satisfied. The starting values of a new run are recalculated on the basis of the last run's results and the optimization criteria.

Obvious similarities can be identified between the field of simulation in system theory and the qualitative reasoning approach. Some results of qualitative reasoning research with regard to qualitative features of dynamic systems are not novel. However, we cannot agree with criticisms which state that qualitative reasoning "reinvents" well-known methods and neglects scientific knowledge, which has been incorporated into models to produce "correct" results - as the shortcomings of daily common-sense knowledge were the main motor for scientific development [Fishwick and Zeigler 91].[71] We think that qualitative reasoning provides new reasoning methods as well as novel representations of structure. The former are necessarily new due to the specific form of structural representation. Since both fields deal with the description of dynamic systems, it is obvious that the techniques used by both largely correspond. Nevertheless, while being similar in the semantics of behavior generation, qualitative reasoning provides a profound approach to structure knowledge about the physical world on different levels. Such knowledge may also be used to preselect appropriate quantitative methods or to explain behavior. The approaches discussed at the end of this chapter show that both fields may cooperate in the research of dynamic systems.

[71] According to Mark Twain's famous sentence that "common-sense aims to the common".

2. Qualitative Reasoning and Expert Systems

Expert systems represent a classical method of AI to fulfill tasks similar to qualitative reasoning. However, limitations of these systems, as described in the following, have also motivated the research presented in this work. Expert systems traditionally structure their knowledge about a domain of interest in the form of facts and rules, based on heuristics to solve specific problems. Facts are statements about distinct real entities which are assumed to be true, rules relate generic descriptions and facts. Both are used by an inference engine to derive new facts. Facts and rules are primitives to model the real world. Thus, expert systems also use models to represent real world situations, although in a specific way. Expert systems describe what is stated to be true in the domain of discourse, and solutions are produced "automatically".[72] They describe what has to be solved, not how it has to be done. This is similar to qualitative reasoning, where the problem is stated and a reasoning, i.e. inference, engine automatically produces the respective results. It should be noted that also in simulation environments like InGenOSS of [Guariso et al. 89a] the model building corresponds to a problem formulation and the system automatically solves the problem, i.e. simulates the model.

However, the form how expert systems, especially the so-called first generation expert systems such as Mycin [Shortliffe 76], represent their knowledge differs from qualitative reasoning. Knowledge is available in a compiled form, antecedents are connected to their consequents in a fixed manner. A typical rule connecting two observations about faults in a repair action may look like

```
IF Engine_not_starting
        AND Battery_empty
THEN Replace alternator.
```

If the knowledge changes, e.g. new knowledge has to be incorporated, the rules have to be modified:

```
IF Engine_not_starting
        AND Battery_empty
                AND NOT Headlights_on_during_night
THEN Replace alternator.
```

The premises are assumed to be independent and may not interfere each other. The representation of knowledge is mainly a heuristic one. No formal methods are developed to deduce this knowledge and to implement it. This "shallow" form of representation shows serious limitations as discussed by [Price and Lee 88]:

- it only encodes situations that are previously known;
- the system does not behave gradually, it only can or cannot solve a situation;
- causal chains are fixed to specific situations;
- it is not robust, new situations need an extension of the knowledge;
- thus, reusability constitutes a problem;
- assumptions are not explicitly stated, composability is a problem;
- it has difficulties to represent time and to dynamically change knowledge in time.

Qualitative reasoning constitutes an approach to bypass these limitations using its so-called deep models of reality. It supplies a structural description of a model including the

---

[72] This statement is not totally true. In languages such as Prolog the way how a problem is stated, i.e. the sequence of logical statements, strongly influences the "automatic" solution procedure.

participating individuals, their attributes and complex relationships. The differentiation between structural and compiled knowledge can be represented by the following figure.

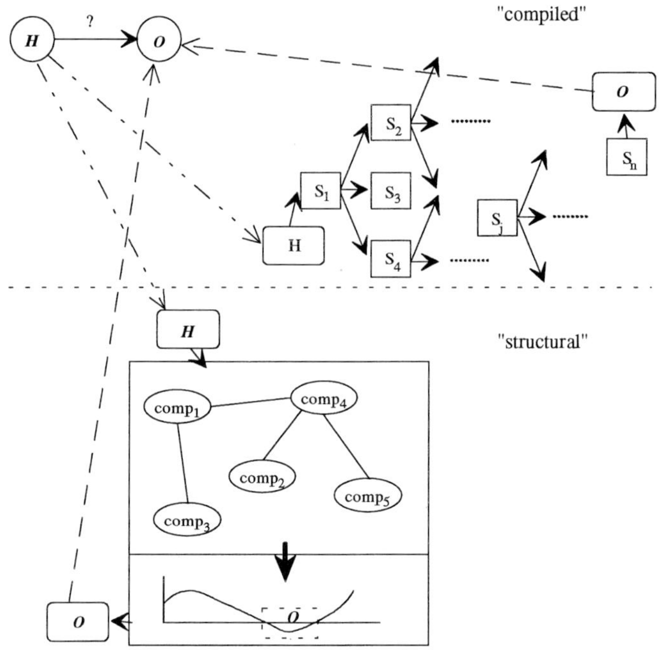

Fig. 63: Distinction between "compiled" and "structural" knowledge representation, *K(H,O)* is derived either from structural or compiled knowledge

The case of diagnosis may explain the difference between the two forms of representing knowledge. A program should test whether an observation *O* can be explained by a malfunction hypothesis *H*, indicated by a piece of knowledge *K*(*H*,*O*). If *K* is directly available, it can be called compiled [Chandrasekaran 91]. If *K* has to be derived from some underlying knowledge, this knowledge is called deep with respect to *K*(*H*,*O*). This knowledge can now be a sequence of rules (upper part of Fig. 63), but also a qualitative model which simulates the malfunctioning device under hypothesis *H*. The model is used to check whether hypothesis *H* may generate observation *O* (lower part of Fig. 63). Both cases can now be called deep with respect to *K*(*H*,*O*). The difference is, that in the second case, a very large number of observations *O* can be tested - in principle all which can be produced by the model under different initial conditions and input values. Moreover, all internal states of the device can be used to explain the malfunction. Once represented in a compiled form, this information is lost forever. To obtain the same powerfulness as in the case of structural knowledge representation, all observations ought to be enumerated and compiled in advance, assuming that they are known. In the qualitative reasoning approach abnormal behavior can be identified as a deviation from normal behavior and the reasoning mechanism can be used to identify the cause, i.e. the part which does not behave correctly. Furthermore, multiple causes may be identified.[73] Only one basic model has to be constructed, not all faulty cases have to be enumerated. Thus, such models are also able to account for unpredicted situations.

But the question structural versus compiled knowledge is not a matter of principle. The structural approach is much slower, since it stands for a large number of cases, just as in classical simulation, where depending on the distinct combinations of parameter and initial values, several different if - then questions can be answered. In cases where the application domain is well-defined and the gain in speed is important, knowledge may be compiled as well. Both types of representation can also be integrated as shown by the "hypothesize and match approach" of [Kuipers 87a] and [Kuipers 1989] (see also [Ironi et al. 90] and [Lanzola et al. 90] for an application of a similar approach). An expert system with its compiled heuristic knowledge is used to hypothesize some cause, i.e. a faulty component, to speed up the identification. A qualitative reasoner is used to verify this hypothesis. This can be done by confronting the simulation results of the faulty system with the observed facts:

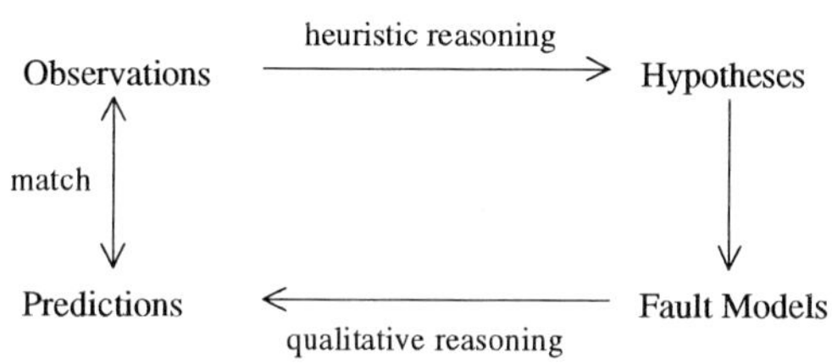

Fig. 64: Integration of structural and compiled knowledge

Qualitative reasoning automatically generates the behavior of a system, its dynamically changing characteristics are an integral part of this approach. Different to classical expert systems, this is based on a structural knowledge representation, which contains both the model components and their local laws. The internal form of implementation, however, may not differ at all, since the models used in qualitative reasoning may also be described by first order logics or some programming language such as Prolog or LISP (as in fact it is done, e.g. [Barrow 84]).

Qualitative reasoning has developed descriptional primitives to represent differential operators which describe the change of values in time, i.e. operators such as d/dt or I. The reasoning mechanism, contrary to the inference engine of expert systems, does not use a forward or backward inference mechanism. It is rather based on independently developed mechanisms which produce trajectories and sequences of states including explanations of their transitions. Thus, these algorithms do not only produce simple Boolean answers but also determine and push the time-dependent calculation - just as it is done in classical simulation. Indeed, contrary to AI, time-dependent behavior was never a problem to simulation. This may now be exploited by qualitative reasoning.

[73] We do not discuss the fact that, in general, the diagnostic process is NP complete. Some heuristics and supplementary knowledge - perhaps in the form of rules similar to classical expert systems - may thus be necessary.

3. Modeling Human Reasoning - a Short Look at Cognitive Science

Qualitative reasoning owes to the desire to fulfill two tasks:

- To build models of physical devices and to derive statements about these devices, which cannot be derived this way or that easy with classical quantitative methods. This may also be called cognitive world modeling. The purpose is to build "better" models. This approach is similar to classical modeling and simulation. Reference models are assumed to exist.
- To understand the reasoning of humans about artifacts and to map this process onto formal representations and, in the long run, onto computer programs. This second task may be called cognitive self-modeling.

The integration of these two tasks may lead to a structure in knowledge representation which contains both the model of a real object and the model of the process of model generation itself. Such a reflexive organization of knowledge is novel. Within such an organization of knowledge several layers and primitives can be distinguished. Humans also use knowledge on different levels of clusters or aggregation, use different methodical primitives to derive new information and structure their knowledge with respect to several epistemological types.

[Hegarty et al. 88] show that, in the understanding of mechanical devices, qualitative processes indeed play a fundamental role. Based on psychological tests in understanding pulley systems, three basic abilities in the correct analysis of mechanical artifacts were identified:

- The separation of relevant attributes from irrelevant ones.
- The consistent application of rules, where rules are defined as relations between identified relevant attributes and the caused physical effort.
- The selective use of quantitative information, i.e. in the case of conflicting rules, the relevant ones are chosen. This is performed by means of an ordered quantity space and relationships between magnitudes, i.e. a representation of variables which resembles the qualitative process theory.

The application of hierarchical models at different levels of aggregation in human thinking is documented by [Collins and Gentner 83]. The question 'Why can a person see his breath on a cold day ?' people answered using three different levels of models. These are macroscopic functional models which link summary features or variables, e.g. temperature, with each other and which characterize masses of elements as a whole. In the following representation they are described using qualitative proportionalities of the process-centered ontology. On a second level, microscopic aggregate models exist which combine the summary variables of the above level to aggregates over space or time of individual particles which behave in a similar way. These models rely on a mapping between functional quantities at the macroscopic level, e.g. temperature of gas, and aggregate quantities at the microscopic level, e.g. average speed of particles in gas. Finally, microscopic molecular models represent the interaction of individual particles. In explaining their reasoning, the test persons interlinked models at these three levels and changed them when necessary. [Collins and Gentner 83] argue that each model of a higher level is supported by one or more models on a lower level. The following table represents these levels and links the respective models with each other, where variable a denotes air, b breath, v water vapor and w water:

Macroscopic models	Aggregate models	Molecular models
temp(v) α_Q temp(a)	Heat Exchange Model	Billiard Ball Model
cond-rate(v) α_Q temp(v)	Aggregation-on-nuclei Model	Dipole Attraction
amount-of(w) α_Q cond-rate(v)	Container Model	Billiard Ball Model
visibility(b) α_Q amount-of(w)	Visibility Model	Absorption & Re-emission

In a correct interpretation the following can be stated: cold air cools the vapor, which leads to a high condensation rate of the water vapor. This in turn leads to a high amount of condensed water, which increases the visibility. The cooling of water corresponds to a heat exchange model on the aggregate level and to billiard ball collisions on the molecular level. Condensation is the aggregation of water molecules around a nucleus, based on dipole electrical attraction. The amount of water in the breath depends on condensation and dispersion at the aggregate level, again based on a billiard ball model. The visibility depends on the ratio of visible particles to the volume of space, in turn depending on the absorption and re-emission of photons at the molecular level. It is reported that - although the test persons did not use these correct models and correspondences in their answers - they always made use of such a three-level argumentation.

Another important property of human reasoning is the use of or even dependence on causal elements. [Forbus and Gentner 86] identified various dimensions of causal reasoning in qualitative physics, corresponding to causal primitives used by humans. This distinction forms the basis of a characterization of existing approaches in qualitative reasoning and allows for the imbedding of new ones. Such distinctions are:

Explicit / implicit mechanisms: Does there exist a separate mechanism which leads from cause to effect ? An example of an explicit mechanism is the concept of process [Forbus 84], which directly relates two phenomena and makes this causation visible. In contrast the concept used in the device-centered ontology of [de Kleer and Brown 84] refers to physical components and their connections, but has no separate and apparent agency besides these elements.

Directed / not-directed connectives: They concern the way how physical laws, i.e. their qualitative description, and their role in causal reasoning are related. One can describe the relationship between variables in the form of a functional dependency, i.e. $y = f(x_1, ..., x_n)$, thus obtaining directed connectives. Not-directed connectives are written in the form of constraints: in the case of n variables and n-1 known values the last value can be derived. Causation cannot be identified in advance. This, for example, motivated [de Kleer and Brown 84] to introduce the notion of mythical causality.

Measurement scenarios: Changes of values of variables can be viewed in four different ways:

Incremental measurement: takes a sequential view of the changes of properties and demands that one change occurs before another, e.g. a row of dominos falls successively when the first one is pushed.

Discrete measurement: looks at the world at two adjacent points of time no matter what happened in between.

Differential measurement: what would a situation look like, if something were different. It compares two different worlds related to each other, they only differ in some properties.

Continuous measurement: considers what is happening during some particular kind of activity.

These distinctions facilitate several conjectures drawn by the authors and based on empirical results:

- The most prototypical class in human reasoning is explicit reasoning with directed connectives.
- Young children and experts constitute two exceptions from the previous statement. According to [Piaget 60] very small children lack the notion of causality at least in areas they are not acquainted with. Experts have options to reason along constraints and are able to use nondirected primitives.
- The incremental view is the most basic measurement scenario. Events occur in a causal chain, each being an effect of its predecessor and the cause of its successor. It seems that humans learn very early to reason in that way.

Human experts use multiple representations of knowledge in complex problem solving tasks, and flexibly switch between these different representations [Bauer and Reiser 90]. Such multiple representation may be, supplementary to the previous mentioned distinctions, differentiated with respect to epistemology. [Brajnik et al. 91] distinguish between knowledge about

structure: This is the system's topology, its components and their interconnections.

behavior: Behaviorial primitives like those already presented describe the behavior of the single components.

function: Components or parts may play certain roles in a specific task. This may relate the behavior to the goal of an artifact.

teleology: Each system is designed for a specific purpose or goal. Although this goal may change, it constitutes an intrinsic feature of a man-made system.

experience: This is associational knowledge based on experience and may link some specific features or parts of the system - as in the form of classical expert systems.

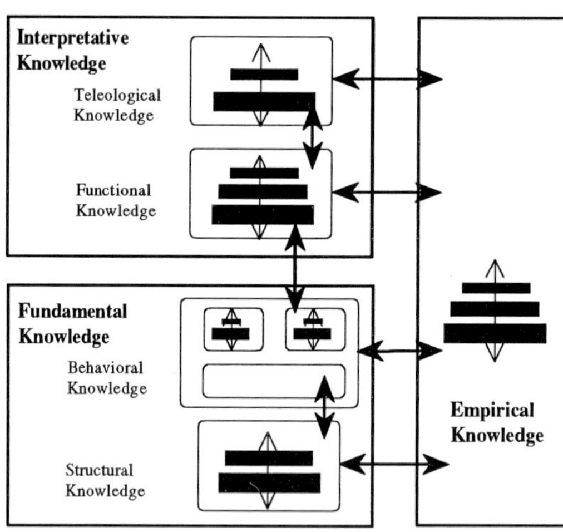

Fig. 65: Organization of knowledge with respect to epistemology

A similar distinction is also drawn by [Sembugamoorthy and Chandresekaran 86]. The links show possible interactions between the representational types, the concept of aggregation is orthogonal to this differentiation. This is indicated by the parts inside the respective classes, connected by thin arrows. Each filled rectangle describes the same model but on a different level of detail. Knowledge can further be classified in a fundamental and interpretative one.

[Chittaro 92] and [Bonarini 92] have developed programs based on this approach. In the reasoning process the system switches - with respect to the task of reasoning - between these representational types and may also interchange the aggregated levels. The goal of the designed artifact constitutes the starting point of the reasoning process.

Qualitative reasoning deals with the description and also formalization of human cognitive processes. Though it does not claim to provide a consistent and complete theory of cognition (which needs contributions of other fields of cognitive science such as AI in general, linguistics, theories in education as well as psychology), it may participate in the formulation of such theories. This is also noted by [Legrenzi and Sonino 91], who underline the contribution of qualitative reasoning to cognitive science. This refers to the discussed representational primitives, the demonstrated emphasis on causal explanations and the classification of knowledge with respect to its usage.

Part V

Modeling in Qualitative Reasoning

The problem of when and how to use a model (or formula) was one of the main motivations in the first works of qualitative reasoning, i.e. the program NEWTON and its application to the roller coaster problem [de Kleer 77]. Thus, this part leads back to one of the initial objectives, i.e. how to build and how to select a proper model. However, the task of modeling is not specific to qualitative reasoning, it is fundamental in every scientific work. A model of the problem has to exist before we can draw conclusions or derive consequences or answer a specific question. But qualitative reasoning offers a specific approach which has one advantage: since it takes a radical point of view, it is satisfied with very little information. Modeling - as a well-identified task distinguished from behavior generation and explanation - represents a major issue and main challenge of qualitative reasoning.

From a historical point of view, in the first research efforts the knowledge about a device, its parts and their relationships was assumed to be given.[74] To proof that a reduced structural and behavioral description was able to produce a consistent, simple and causal explanation, similar or identical to numerical analysis, constituted the main focus of these early works. Though it was always pretended that exact information was lacking, all demonstrated examples were based on known and already well-structured cases. When abandoning the field of pure science - also due to the growing maturity of the field - and entering that of practical applications, the mapping from real world situations to their abstract representations became a real problem and essential. We can observe a shift toward this task in the qualitative reasoning research. The more and the better structured information is put into a problem description, the better the reasoning mechanism can work. Moreover, very often the needed information, for example about the boundaries of specific ranges, actually is available. Thus, taking a historic point of view, the approaches presented in this part may be considered as third generation systems.

Qualitative reasoning shows several advantages, when we look at modeling as the "art" to derive both structural and behavioral primitives from a real system's behavior: a qualitative model is a very vague description, needs far less information and contains far less primitives than a classical numerical model. Complicated procedures in the construction process, such as parameter estimation, are not necessary. Moreover, it provides a valid framework to organize knowledge. Qualitative reasoning - as already outlined - deals with different kinds and layers of knowledge, it makes underlying assumptions explicit and also manages the information about models.[75] This knowledge can be organized in pieces of different size, which may be independent or related. These pieces can be used when necessary or beneficiary. This approach to modeling constitutes a further improvement of qualitative reasoning, which also demonstrates its origins in AI. It clearly distinguishes between the description of a problem and its solution procedure. In principle, we interpret the task of modeling in qualitative reasoning as an attempt to integrate the respective techniques of AI, simulation and cognitive science. It adds time and deep structure to models in AI, brings the notion of a multi-layered

---

[74] We consciously omit here the broad ontological discussion on how to map reality. This discussion was particularly important in the field of naive physics (e.g. the contained-liquid ontology of [Hayes 85b] or the molecular collection ontology of [Collins and Forbus 87]).

[75] This bears some resemblance with the concept of meta-data in the area of data modeling. Therefore, we may use the term "meta-model" for this concept.

and reflexive knowledge representation and its opportunistic use to the simulation community, and takes schemes of causal explanations from cognitive science.

In the first part of this chapter we look at the different prominent approaches to see how they deal with modeling. In a second pass we consider works which build entire model bases. These methods come from AI as well as from simulation theory. This is a further reference to the existence of similar concepts in both areas. While all these approaches work in a deductive way, we also present approaches which proceed in an inductive manner. This chapter attempts to provide an impression of the problems and difficulties encountered. In our opinion, model building remains one of the hard problems and has somehow to be considered as an art based on practical experience.

If we assume an originally existing quantitative model, then the mapping to its qualitative counterpart may be performed along the dimensions of structure (entities and relationships), time and the representation of quantities. In all these dimensions coarser representations produce ambiguity. However, these representations need less information to build the model and to simulate its behavior. In principle, we can distinguish the following relationships between a real object, its "realistic" description in the form of a quantitative model and a qualitative model:[76]

- *one object → several aspects are modeled differently:* a piece of wire, for example, may serve to conduct either temperature or electricity. In this case at least the behavioral description will be different,
- *one function → several models:* a description is related to several different structures which satisfy the same function, e.g. a digital and analog watch, and
- *one or more objects → one qualitative description:* it is the normal case that one qualitative model denotes an entire class of specific devices or situations described by quantitative models.

From the set of the discussed main approaches of qualitative reasoning and their respective successors, we consider the process-centered ontology to deal best with the problem of modeling. It offers descriptional primitives such as objects and processes, and it conceptually distinguishes between general views and process classes and instances which are derived from these general types. In addition, it offers the opportunity for an iterative refinement of object type descriptions with the concept of inheritance. In the device-centered approach modeling is guided by a procedure which assembles different pieces by attaching their interconnections. In an iterative way, hierarchic components can be constructed. Though the-no-function-in-structure principle serves for modularization of the single parts, overall constraints, for example denoting Kirchhoff's laws, have to be respected in the construction of an entire device. The QSIM approach requires a set of known and well-formulated equations. In the qualitative process theory the knowledge structure consists - at least conceptually - of three parts. First, we can identify background knowledge about scenarios and basic laws of the real world. Second, knowledge can be identified about the discussed domain in the form of general views and processes. Finally, the instantiated processes and views exist which deal with a concrete problem.

---

[76] The assumption of a "realistic" model is necessarily wrong, in every modeling step things have to be ignored. The problem is whether a model satisfies a specific task or not, the notion of truth is opportunistic and not absolute.

The operational primitives of the process-centered and the constraint-based view can be considered as very similar, this also results from the chapter which discusses a graph-based representation of models. Both use a similar representation of variables and their primitives, i.e. α_Q and M, I and d/dt, have corresponding interpretations. Based on this similarity, a mapping from the first formalism to the second can be defined [Crawford et al. 90]. Every behavioral mode of [Forbus 84], i.e. a situation with a fixed view and process structure and which also contains a description of its major states, corresponds to an exact set of constraints taken from [Kuipers 86]. When the process and view structure changes, a new description in the form of qualitative differential equations is necessary. In addition, the values of the quantities have to be transferred from the previous to the next overall state structure (see also chapter III.4 about graphs). QSIM may benefit from the modeling power of qualitative process theory through this transformation of the process- and view-based description into its own formalism. We consider this as an empirical proof that modeling is well done in qualitative process theory. However, the qualitative process engine of [Forbus 86] produces an envisionment graph, single trajectories can only be deduced afterwards. Thus, also qualitative process theory may benefit from this transformation, as its structural description can be used to generate single trajectories, as they are generated by QSIM. Following the described procedure of mapping and using a combined notion of both approaches, several levels of representation can be identified. Each level not only subsumes the lower one, but also has a slower change in time:

individual objects and their relationships
views and processes - qualitative constraints
values of variables

The qualitative values of variables change most frequently at every calculation step. These changes define the states and their transitions on the lowest level. On the next level, we can identify the constraining equations which remain constant as long as the view and process structure remains constant. The latter is modified when relationships between objects and their annotated variables change. The existence of concrete objects and their specific relationships, described by the preconditions of processes and views, represent the most constant layer. This layer describes the basic individuals of an entire real world situation. This hierarchy also makes clear that the process-centered ontology provides descriptional primitives which cannot be offered by the constraint-based approach.

a) Deductive Modeling

In the following we discuss some new approaches to model building in qualitative reasoning. In this discussion we concentrate on model bases with multiple models which contain the knowledge about the universe of discourse. Thus, pre-existing knowledge can be used to build or to select a concrete model. In the first of these examples, models on different levels of description of a real world device are assumed to be given. These models, all of which describe the same device, can be organized such that their respective differences, assuming that they are known, can be used to select a proper model candidate. The model representations differ in their level of approximation. Since we can select a model in a dynamic way, i.e. it can be redone several times during the simulation process, we can call such an organization a "fault tolerant" one. Errors made in an initial guess would not be disastrous, since the first choice can be corrected. The domain-dependent graph of models of [Addanki et al. 89] and [Addanki et al. 91] proposes such an organization.

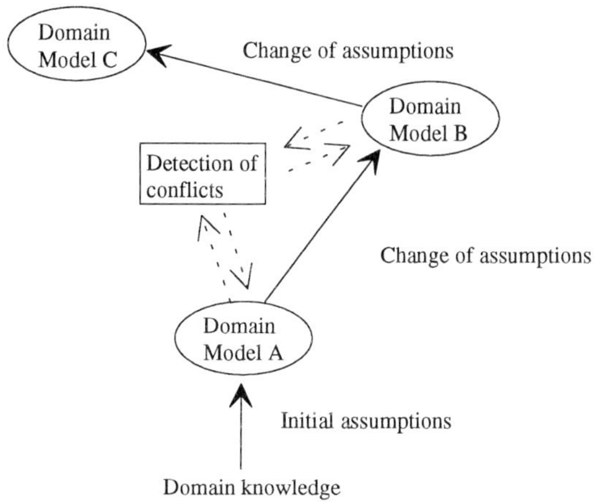

Fig. 66: Dynamic selection of models during simulation

The first model is selected according to some initial assumptions. During simulation a discrepancy may be found either with recorded data or internally defined critical values. It is examined which of the state variables is responsible for such a discrepancy. When this variable is identified, the list of neighboring models is used to determine the model in which the respective variable behaves "better"; it may, for example, remain within some value range. This change in models corresponds to a change in the set of assumptions. The choice of the next best model out of the set of next possible ones is based on a distance metric. This approach does not solve the modeling problem, but it obviously eases the task. A wrong choice of structure may easily be corrected. In the following example a gear train transmission is described by four models [Addanki et al. 89]:

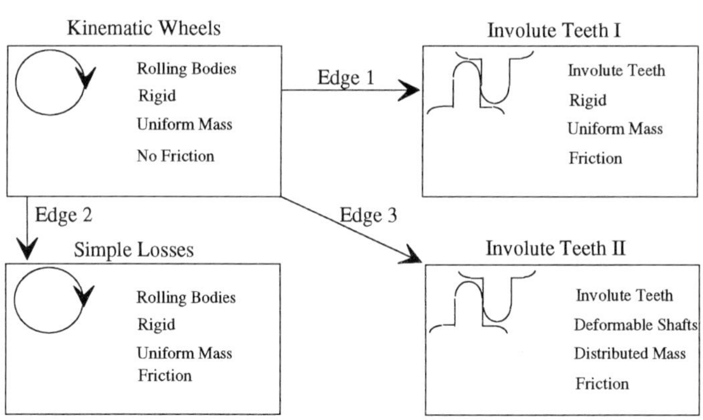

Fig. 67: Four related models of a gear train transmission

These models differ according to their level of description: with or without friction, only rolling bodies or involute teeth, and finally, deformable or not deformable teeth. When we start the simulation with the simplest model, i.e. Kinematic Wheels with no friction, the rotational acceleration will be identified to be higher than indicated by experimentally observed values. This represents an obvious result. A change in the model assumptions has to be identified that guarantees that this rotational acceleration decreases. Such modifications are represented by edges in Fig. 67. [Addanki et al. 89] introduce the concept of a difference (delta) vector, which records all necessary direction of changes to select a better model. In the above case, where variable *r-acc* denotes the rotational acceleration, a delta vector of the form *(r-acc,-)* indicates that *r-acc* has to be reduced. However, if this variable value depends on an error of an intermediate variable, this error has to be propagated to the final variables. For example, if we have *r-acc* = *n-t/in*[77] and the value of the net torque *n-t* is wrong, then the value of *r-acc* will be wrong as well. This type of error leads to a so-called extended delta list in the form *((r-acc,-), (n-t,-))*. Parameter change rules now represent the qualitative effect of a change of assumptions on these parameters of the delta list. The antecedent of such a rule denotes the topical state of the system, its consequent indicates the parameters which and how they change. Therefore, if we apply a rule in order to add friction to the model, i.e. this changes the assumption of model 1, *r-acc* will be corrected. Each of the illustrated edges is associated with some of these rules. The choice of an edge invokes all its rules with the respective parameters r-acc and n-t in their antecedents. The results are stored in an edge satisfaction list which indicates how much each edge contributes to an improvement of the respective parameters in the delta list. The elements of this list are evaluated with regard to some measure and, finally, the candidate with the best result is chosen as the next model. Model Involute Teeth I is chosen in the presented case, i.e. friction is added and another form of transmission mechanism is taken. Thus, this approach allows for the selection of a model with respect to the desired accuracy, dependent on the concrete context. And it offers the opportunity to dynamically change a model, when the initial choice was wrong or the context changes.

This approach suggests some resemblance with the process-centered ontology, as a fixed view and process structure, i.e. state, is comparable to one selected model in the graph of models. However, the process-centered ontology lacks the rules to select the next proper model, when contradictions are encountered. Such contradictions could also be interpreted as discontinuities, bringing the approach of [Addanki et al. 89] close to the variable structure or multi-modeling approach, as described by [Ören 91] or [Zeigler and Louri 93] and developed in the simulation community. This method also allows for the dynamic change of model structures and the handling of discontinuities events.

We interpret models as compiled structures of knowledge. The representation of [Addanki et al. 89] already uses well-defined entire pieces, however, it gives no advice how such basic pieces can be constructed. It does not help, when a new model has to be built from scratch. This question also constitutes an important aspect of reusability. It should be possible to use fragments of knowledge under diverse conditions. It should not be necessary to implement an entire and completely new model for every possible situation. The compositional modeling approach of [Falkenhainer and Forbus 88], described also in [Falkenhainer and Forbus 90] and [Falkenhainer and Forbus 91], and the context-dependent behavior-based modeling approach of [Nayak et al. 91] represent such approaches. Several descriptional elements are associated to each basic model fragment, i.e. compiled piece of knowledge, in the system in order to describe the assumptions of a model's use or to define the context in which it can be reassembled. This additional knowledge can be exploited in the model composition and building process. Such contexts or assumptions describe both structural and behavioral attributes and make the reasoning process more effective and faster. It is possible to restrict the modeling process to these assumptions and contexts instead of using the entire model fragments. However, it is still assumed that, at the very beginning, both the general and the

[77] rotational acceleration = net torque / initial inertia

domain specific knowledge are available and already structured in the necessary form. The chosen organization of this knowledge supports and substantially eases the process of modeling.

The basic idea of compositional modeling, which is based on the process-centered ontology, is that one only needs a model when it is looked for. Therefore, already a query about some behavioral properties of a device may provide additional information to build a model. This view corresponds to the idea that the goal, i.e. objective, of a model should guide the modeling process. It is assumed that there exist

- a domain theory which describes the domain of discourse and consists of domain-dependent model fragments,
- an initial scenario description. A scenario is the specific situation which has to be considered. The description includes at least structural properties of the modeled system and perhaps some statements about its behavior, and
- a query about the behavior of the system.

The result, i.e. model, should be an appropriate scenario model to answer the query. Such a model should be the most relevant one reflecting some optimality criteria, for example with regard to computational overhead.

The model fragments can be described by a tuple $\langle C, A, O, R \rangle$ with
- C: a set of conditions defining the structure to which the model applies: individuals and their interconnection. This corresponds to the preconditions of processes of [Forbus 84],
- A: a set of assumptions which define the model fragment's relevance to the question and contain simplifying assumptions,
- O: a set of operating conditions which define when the respective fragment may become active, corresponding to quantity conditions of views and processes. This set also includes operating assumptions, and
- R: a set of relations imposed by the fragment.

Such a model fragment - additionally to its new features such as simplifying and operating assumptions - looks like a view in the qualitative process theory. In a logical notation a fragment can be described as $C \wedge A \wedge O \rightarrow R$.

Simplifying assumptions explicitly state the model fragment's underlying approximations, perspectives and granularities. Such assumptions have the form Consider(P_Type (system)), which denotes that P_Type is a predicate of the entire object system. Furthermore, such assumptions can be formulated for both the grain size of used elements and approximations regarding the entire system. The assumption Consider(exists(A)) would be of the first type and indicates, that when we reason about some system, the entire component A has to be included, and not some part of A. The second type is of the form Consider (inviscid(flow-A-B)) and denotes that a flow from some point A to a point B can be approximated as not being viscous. Another example is the assumption Consider(no-friction(Kinetic Wheels)), which states that friction can be neglected when we reason about Kinetic Wheels.

Operating assumptions describe local restrictions on quantities and may also define operation modes of the model fragment. An Op-Assumption(greater-than (temp(A), temp(B)), for example, constrains the temperature of A to be higher than that of B. An assumption of the form Mode(switch, OFF) indicates that relations between the model's variables are only valid when the switch is off. Another example of an operating assumption is Steady-State(temp(A)), describing that the temperature of A does not change.

The choice of a model fragment follows the subsequent steps: all model fragments can be instantiated, when their set of individuals satisfies C. Such models are called applicable. If, furthermore, A can be assumed, it can be said that a model is applied to the collection of individuals in C. If, afterwards, its operating conditions hold, then the relations defined in the model fragment become active, i.e.
$C \rightarrow (A \rightarrow (O \rightarrow R))$.

Model fragments are composed by means of shared individuals and their variables, the value passing from one component to another is done through these identical variables. A second alternative to assemble fragments is by means of composable functions which are functions of the type α_Q and I, again using the process-centered ontology. Since in the process-centered ontology models are built by processes and views, at least one process is created by the compositional modeling approach to answer a stated query.

The model composition algorithm works as described below. The implementation is based on the qualitative process engine (QPE) of [Forbus 86]. The dependencies between nodes in an ATMS are used to compute the minimal conjunctions of modeling assumptions needed to produce an appropriate scenario model.

- *Query analysis:* From the content of the query, a set of relevant objects, their associated variables and relationships are identified. An ATMS is used to compute the collection of minimal environments which justify the modeling primitives in the query. However, these environments most probably may not entail a coherent scenario model.
- *Object expansion:* Every environment denotes a set of objects to consider. To ensure coherence, the set of objects may need to be extended by more objects. These new objects can be identified using the part-of hierarchy, which connects objects in this approach. The part-of hierarchy is the only valid structural relationship between any two objects in this modeling approach.
- *Candidate completion:* When all objects are chosen, it might not yet be clear how they should be modeled. The different modeling assumptions, either the simplifying or the operational ones, define their usage. Furthermore, assumptions chosen for one part may determine those for another. The inclusion of new assumptions may also call for a redefinition of the chosen views of the respective parts. This part of the algorithm can also be done by an ATMS, since several assumptions have to be recorded simultaneously. The final result of this step is a list of possible candidate models which may answer the query.
- *Candidate evaluation and selection:* From the list of possible and valid models, each of them composed by single fragments, only one has to be chosen. This is done according to some defined evaluation metric.

The following figure illustrates the different sources of knowledge used in the respective steps of the model composition:

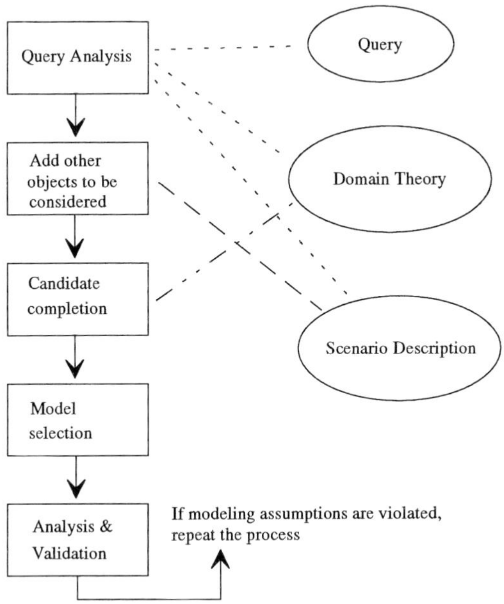

Fig. 68: Modeling steps and the respective sources of knowledge

The constructed model can be used by the qualitative process engine [Forbus 86] to generate an envisionment graph. Its inferred behavior provides the answer to the stated query. The possibility to incorporate also quantitative models on a lower level is a very important enhancement of this approach [Forbus and Falkenhainer 90]. A single model fragment which is qualitatively described may be linked to its quantitative counterpart. This quantitative model is valid for the region of operation which is defined by its qualitative "super-class". This is based on a well-defined list which maps numerical functional dependencies between variables onto their respective qualitative counterparts. This approach represents a promising integration of knowledge on several levels which are necessary in a problem formulation and solution process: knowledge about models, qualitative models and, finally, also quantitative models.

The multifacetted modeling approach described in ([Zeigler 84], [Rozenblit and Zeigler 86] or [Zeigler 89]), with its system entity structure (SES) method, shows a similar organization of knowledge. The knowledge is represented in the form of related model pieces, which can be used to derive a distinct model, i.e. instantiating an object from a prototypical class structure (see also [Zhong and Zeigler 89]; [Rozenblit and Huang 91] describe a rule-based approach to generate models based on the SES concept). The knowledge about the domain is incorporated in little pieces of information, so-called composable model fragments. However, these model fragments only contain quantitative information. The composable model fragments are classified in a strict hierarchic manner by two types of relationships: firstly the *part-of* relationship - called aspect in the original notation - which denotes decomposition, and secondly, the *kind-of* relationship, which denotes the different views a thing can be seen under, similar to the is-a relationship [Brachman 83]. Knowledge is organized in the form of a strict tree, its nodes may be either entities which describe an object, specializations, or decompositions. Entering the tree from above, entities strictly interchange either with *kind-of* or *part-of* nodes. All subparts of a chosen decomposition have to be, and only one specialization can be, taken in the model creation process. Thus, the tree forms a kind of an AND/OR tree. The compiled pieces of knowledge, which finally can be assembled to create a new model, constitute the leaves of the tree. The process of pruning a model, i.e. composing and creating a model, is guided by rules, which may be annotated to each decomposition or specialization node of the classification tree. Specific choices at one point may determine choices at another one. The final structure can be presented as follows, to give an example:

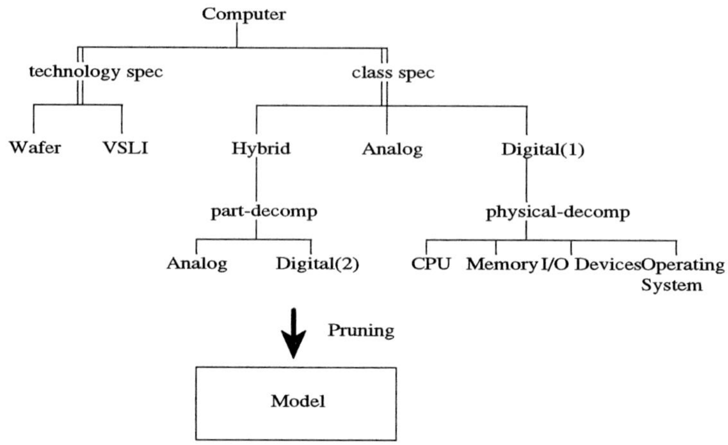

Fig. 69: Example of a system entity structure of [Zeigler 89] and the pruning of a model

Two kinds of specializations may be applied to a computer, one with respect to technology and another with respect to classes of computers. If we choose a computer to be a hybrid one, it has to contain an analog and a digital part. This latter one, when re-entering the tree at the node Digital (1), has to be composed of model fragments for the components CPU, memory, I/O device and operating system. These are - together with the analog computer - the final parts of the model which is created by the pruning process. The property of being VSLI-technology-based - as defined by the second specialization - is also owned by the model due to multiple inheritance. The model of a VLSI hybrid computer can now be used. This process illustrates that the different nodes of the SES have to be treated differently. Arcs leaving a node which denotes an entity may lead to several specializations and / or decompositions. All these successor nodes have to be considered. Handling of the two other node types works as described: all successors of a decomposition node have to be considered, just one successor of a specialization node can be chosen.

A different approach to modeling, which combines also techniques from simulation theory and AI, is described by [Beck and Fishwick 89]. It represents a practical application of natural language processing [Rapaport 88]. If a linguistic description of a situation in the form of some text is given, this method allows for the inference of the structure and the behavioral primitives of a model of the situation. General knowledge is available in the form of objects and their relationships, both described by variables and linguistic phrases. Furthermore, lexical knowledge exists, which links the existing words to each other. Finally, a grammar is defined, which is crucial for the parsing and construction of natural sentences. These different sources of knowledge are used together to analyze a sentence. Sentences are converted into structural descriptions from where - through supplementary mapping - a description in the form of variables, their relationships and equations can be generated. Thus, this approach corresponds to the function which maps $\mathrm{U} \rightarrow \mathrm{U}$, a qualitative input to a quantitative. A context-free grammar to produce first order differential equations - besides other types of equations - is described by [Beck and Fishwick 89] as follows:

equal	→	exp = exp
exp	→	exp + exp
exp	→	exp - exp
exp	→	exp * exp
exp	→	exp / exp
exp	→	d exp / d var
exp	→	(exp)
exp	→	var
exp	→	number

The sentence "the storage rate f_c is proportional to the rate of change e of potential in the community cellular storage capacity C" can be represented by an equation of the form
$f_c = C * de/dt$.

Based on the stored basic elements, i.e. words and concepts of the world organized in a class hierarchy, the following structure can be generated to represent this sentence:

```
proportional
        Superclass: Equal
        Var1: Variable
                Symbol: fc
                Represents: Rate
                Type: Storage
        Var2: Multiply
                Superclass: Binary Operation
                Var1: Constant
                        Symbol: C
                        Represents: Capacity
                        Type: Storage
                Var2: Rate
                        Symbol: e
                        Represents: Potential
                        Type: Change
```

This representation of instantiated object types can directly be translated to a formalism which can be used for calculation. This approach, although based on some available pre-existing knowledge, constructs a model from scratch only by interpreting sentences about the structure and behavioral primitives of real world entities.

b) Inductive Modeling

The approaches to modeling described so far assume the existence of some pre-existing and given knowledge about the domain of discourse, general laws, local behavior or similar things. They work in a deductive manner and deduce a distinct model which satisfies specific needs based on available information. The origin of this initial knowledge is not defined. A completely different approach is used, when one starts with no knowledge at all and iteratively adds information at each step until some final model is obtained. The only pre-existing knowledge is that of an applicable method, which we call inductive modeling in the following. However, after the completed application of this method, there is no further knowledge but the constructed model.

One of the most prominent representatives of this approach is the general system problem solving theory (GSPS) based on General Systems Theory (see [Klir 85], [Cellier 91], and also [Vesanterä and Cellier 89] for an application of this approach). In the following we will discuss GSPS and also present a similar method in qualitative reasoning. These examples again reveal a certain congruence of techniques between qualitative reasoning and simulation theory.

Inductive modeling assumes that the behavior of a system can be observed. Based on these observations, GSPS is able to induce the structure of the model. Modeling is seen as the process of completely identifying the structure, given the behavior. This approach shows that modeling can be seen as the opposite activity of behavior generation. The GSPS framework distinguishes between several layered subsystems, each one subsuming the information of the underlying level. The knowledge becomes richer and denser, when we climb up the hierarchy. The lowest level constitutes the

- *source system:* This is the system as seen by the observer, the relevant variables and their memberships in the respective input or output sets can be identified, i.e. a general causal relationship of variables with respect to their membership in the input and output sets. Furthermore, relevant quantitative or qualitative ranges of the variables can be identified, e.g. switch on - off, perturbation high - medium - low.
- *data system:* This level contains, in addition to the lower source system, the time behavior of the single variables, measured by some external device.
- *behavior system:* In this layer the time-invariant relationships between variables are recorded. These relationships between the variables are induced from the data system through the concept of a generative mask. Since these time-invariant relationships between variables are also valid for the future, they can be used to generate behavior as well.

Such generative masks represent translation rules for variables in the form of a matrix. The dimension of such a matrix is $(d + 1) \times n_{var}$, d denoting the number of sampling intervals and n_{var} the number of variables. The following matrix describes the general relationships between four variables:

	v_1	v_2	v_3	v_4
$t - 2\Delta t$	0	-1	0	0
$t - \Delta t$	-1	0	-2	0
t	0	-4	0	1

Elements are zero, negative or positive, denoting either neutral, generating or generated elements. The matrix corresponds to $v_4(t) = f(v_2(t\text{-}2\Delta t), v_1(t\text{-}\Delta t), v_3(t\text{-}\Delta t), v_2(t))$. The crucial and decisive choice of the number of sampling intervals is left to the modeler and his skills.

[Kraan et al. 91] describe an approach in the area of qualitative reasoning which is, on a semantic level, as previously mentioned, very close to the GSPS theory. This method is based on the notion of the constraint-based approach of [Kuipers 84]. If the description - using this approach - of the behavior of a system is given, a model can be constructed which generates this behavior. Three steps are performed: behavioral data given in a quantitative form are converted to their qualitative representation; secondly, based on these data, constraints are generated which are satisfied by the observed data; and, finally, based on these constraints, one or more models are built. It can be shown, that if a complete description of a consistent set of behaviors is available, then the most constrained model will be built. A description is complete, if all variables of the system are identified, values are given for all time points, and all variables have a correct information about their dimensions. Furthermore, a set of behaviors is consistent, if the dimensions make sense and the relationships between variables are consistent. The obtained model reproduces the observed behavior. In the following example the data description as well as their sequence, already in a qualitative form, of a simple bathtub are given. There is a constant inflow and a constant drain opening:

Variable	Initial Quantity Space	Units
inflow	0, *in1*, ∞	mass/time
outflow	0, ∞	mass/time
netflow	-∞, 0, *net1*, ∞	mass/time
amount	0, ∞	mass

State 0

Variable	Magnitude	Direction of change
inflow	*in1*	*std*
outflow	0	*inc*
netflow	*net1*	*dec*
amount	0	*inc*

State 1

Variable	Magnitude	Direction of change
inflow	*in1*	*std*
outflow	(0, ∞)	*inc*
netflow	(0,*net1*)	*dec*
amount	(0, ∞)	*inc*

State 2

Variable	Magnitude	Direction of change
inflow	*in1*	*std*
outflow	*out1*	*std*
netflow	0	*std*
amount	*amount1*	*std*

The system reaches the point of equilibrium with an amount of *amount1* of liquid corresponding to a level which is below the top of the tub. The constraint generation now examines, whether it can identify functional relationships between variables which can be satisfied. For example, DERIV(x, y) will be valid, when a) the direction of change of x is *inc*, *dec* or *std* and the sign of y is +, - or 0 and b) the dimension of x is the dimension of the variable y divided by time. All possible candidates are produced. Afterwards, the behavior is examined with regard to these constraints.

In the model generation phase the constraints are assembled. In the case that the description of the behavior was both complete and consistent, just one set of constraints is obtained. In the other case, several models are generated. It can now be examined, whether the constraints of these models satisfy the property of pairwise consistency. For example, even without any dimensional information the two constraints ADD(a, b, c) and DERIV(a, b) cannot be consistent. Furthermore, those models which are subsets of others can be eliminated. Due to insufficient information, however, a set of possible models may still contain invalid members. In the example of the bathtub only one model, the correct one, is generated. In the following description of a bathtub the two constraints M^-(outflow, netflow) and M^-(netflow, amount) are redundant:

constant inflow
ADD (outflow, netflow, inflow)
M^- (outflow, netflow)
M^+ (outflow, amount)
M^- (netflow, amount)
DERIV (amount, netflow)

QUALSIM of [Guariso et al. 92] represents a similar approach, at least from a conceptual point of view. Behavioral descriptions serve as the base to produce the structure of a system. [Forbus 87], on the other hand, interprets observations, i.e. behavior, of real world situations by comparing the observed data with a given instantiation of specific processes and views. This work is based on the process-centered ontology. An interpretation of the physical situation becomes possible by confronting the envisionment graph produced by the view and process structure which contains all possible states and state transitions with the observed input data at each qualitative time point, i.e. a point where the system changes state. This approach works backward: beginning from some given state, the sequence of input values is traced back until some initial state is reached. At first glance this approach has little in common with modeling. It seems rather that behavioral data are used to answer specific questions like how and why the current situation happened, which is also an important task of qualitative reasoning. However, since the process starts with observed data, we think that this work of [Forbus 87] to some extent belongs to the class of inductive modeling.

c) Models with Different Time Scales

After this short look at inductive modeling, we will briefly discuss a further problem regarding modeling. When we relate different models, all of them describe the same real objects or at least some objects closely linked with each other. Hence, we may have to consider different time scales. Such related models may work on very different time ranges, which may even differ by some orders of magnitude (see [Kuipers 87a], [Kuipers 87b] and also [Iwasaki 90b]; but also QUALSIM with its local behavior inside a qualitative cell and its "long-term" behavior moving between qualitative cells). Using the notion of the process-centered ontology, two processes which denote the movement of a sliding block on a surface might be described as follows (x denotes the position on a flat axis):

Block-moving-right-process
    effect: dx/dt > 0
    granularity: 0
Block-moving-left-process
    effect: dx/dt < 0
    granularity: 0

The process structure includes the Block-moving-right-process and the Block-moving-left-process. A granularity of 0 indicates the smallest level of time granularity. But now a process may be defined with a slower time level, called

Surface-wearing-out-process
    precondition: a large number of Block-moving-right-processes, Block-moving-left-processes
    effect: dy/dt < 0
    granularity: 4

A decreasing value of y denotes that the block slowly sinks toward the surface, thus both moving processes will be influenced. Reasoning about these two types of processes requires a framework which considers both levels of time granularity. [Kuipers 87a] proposes such an organization by using the fact that models dealing with the same situation at the same moment have to share objects and their respective variables. Therefore, communication can be performed via the sharing of variable values. In the previous situation of a slow and a fast process we assume that both processes incorporate the two common variables a and b, where variable a "causes" a change in variable b. In the fast model the value of variable b will change with some time delay after variable a, whereas in the slower model both variables will change simultaneously, related, for example, through an algebraic constraint. The following figure represents the passing of values between three models working at three different time scales:

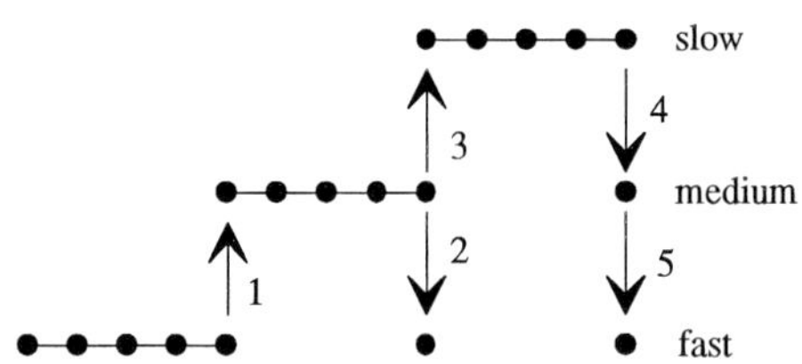

Fig. 70: Communication between three models with three different time scales

Value transfer from the faster to the slower model is done in the following way: if we supply the fast model with an input, then this model will produce some behavior and its final results will be transferred to the respective slower model by means of shared variables. These values of the faster model may serve as initial states of the slower model. Communication in the opposite direction works as follows: when the slow mechanism reaches its final state, the environment of the faster one may have changed as well. However, since the faster model has permanently traced the changes of the slower model through the shared variables, it is always coordinated with the slow model. No explicit communication and value passing mechanism is necessary. In the previous figure this mechanisms are presented by numbers. The result of the fast process is passed as initial value to the medium process (1), the result of this is passed to the slow one (3) and returned automatically to the fast one (2), and so on. The simulation with new values has only to proceed on the respective slower levels.

These considerations lead us back to models as structural representation of knowledge fragments and their relationships. Since these relationships as well as the views of real systems - represented through models - may differ significantly and have a complicated form, a framework which integrates these aspects necessarily becomes very complex. The approach of [Brajnik et al. 91] and [Chittaro et al. 92], discussed to some extent in chapter IV.3, constitutes a first step into this direction. Their approach does not guide model building, the models and their implemented type of knowledge are assumed to be given. A prominent property of this method is its elaborated classification and implementation of knowledge. Knowledge about modeled entities can be distinguished as knowledge about structure, behavior, function and purpose (see also [Sembugamoorthy and Chandresekaran 86]). In the reasoning process these different parts and sources are used and interrelated. A scheduler chooses, in an opportunistic manner, the knowledge which fulfills best its task, this is well-defined by the organization of knowledge. Moreover, this approach to organize knowledge could, at least on a conceptual level, be used also to select proper model pieces. The specific purpose of such a model fragment could be compared with a formulated query, which brings this approach again close to the compositional modeling method of [Falkenhainer and Forbus 91].

This review of different approaches to the problem of modeling reveals the abilities of qualitative reasoning. It is able to manage - in a hierarchic manner - both the model itself and the information about the model. A promising representative is the compositional modeling approach of [Falkenhainer and Forbus 91], which supports the entire process of modeling: from the formulation of the problem in qualitative terms to the generation of qualitative results, which can be further elaborated using properly selected quantitative models. Different aspects, functions and approximations can be treated, and, finally, several quantitative models may be linked to a qualitative one. Thus, it includes all the relationships between an object and its formalized representation, as stated at the beginning of this part. Although this approach represents an important contribution to the task of modeling, it is not able to build models from scratch or to support the process of structure identification, given a sequence of observed data of a real system. This would need to extend this approach and to integrate more elaborate, quantitative methods and concepts of inductive modeling. We think that the complex task of modeling requires a mixture of several methods, among which qualitative reasoning may, indeed, play an important role.

Part VI

Conclusion and Suggestions for Further Research

Our work has clearly revealed the roots of qualitative reasoning in AI in its attempts to formalize and model common-sense physical knowledge as well as human reasoning mechanisms. Since AI - as stated by [Newell 90] - provides a theoretical infrastructure for the study of human cognition, we may also conclude that qualitative reasoning aims at establishing a cognitive theory of "non-numerical" process description and at automating the phase of model building. And AI still constitutes the main background of qualitative reasoning. However, since qualitative reasoning deals with physical systems and their changes in time, basic concepts about dynamic systems such as state diagrams, trajectories, state variables or input - output relations have been introduced. Thus, simulation and system theory constitute a second basis of this approach. This does not seem to be surprising, as they both deal with the modeling of dynamic systems and the generation of their behavior. Nevertheless, although there exists an evident similarity between the semantics of both areas, the structural descriptions as well as the behavior generation mechanisms are derived from AI, based on mathematical concepts. And, as already stated, we can identify cognitive science as a further area close to qualitative reasoning. This is also shown by the discussion about the problem of causality. Because of shortcomings of the early developments - mainly the problem of ambiguity - further knowledge in the form of quantitative information and more elaborated reasoning techniques was integrated. However, these improvements were mainly based on well-known concepts of fields outside AI, as for example the non-crossing rules of trajectories or Markov chains, which we have introduced in this paper. Thus, we can identify qualitative reasoning as an interdisciplinary approach.

Qualitative reasoning in turn influences the areas it descends from: the introduction of deep structure and time into AI and the strengthening of knowledge classification and organization in the simulation and modeling area. Indeed, the introduction of meta-knowledge about knowledge - hence, just what knowledge about modeling is - can be seen as novel. This classification of knowledge may also be important for the process of knowledge acquisition: it is no longer the process of collecting information from different human experts but can be interpreted as modeling as well. We consider qualitative reasoning as a new approach to the problem of modeling which, anyhow, still remains an art. However, qualitative reasoning may give access to models which are easier to build and probably faster to execute, even if "better" quantitative models already exist.

What is specific in qualitative reasoning ? A first point is the radical reduction of the quantity space and the way how both structure and values are described in a qualitative way. Qualitative reasoning is nearly exclusively built upon interval-based value representations, and its method to describe quantities necessarily brings about ambiguous results. Solutions of qualitative reasoning include an entire set of possibilities. We think that its second main result - besides its contribution to modeling - is its ability to draw on the basis of very little information a separation line between the set of feasible and non-feasible behaviors and the possibility to exclude the latter ones.

The qualitative approach to represent quantities and to infer and describe behavior has produced two important mechanisms: the assumption-based truth maintenance system ATMS and the value propagation and filtering algorithm. They are both derived from techniques of AI, but are influenced by simulation as well. They enhance rule-based systems; in addition, they introduce the concept of parallelism, as several assumptions can be handled simultaneously. The necessary introduction of time, basic for the description of real life systems, brings the methods of qualitative reasoning close to traditional simulation algorithms. A main distinction can be drawn between interpretative and constructive approaches within qualitative reasoning. On a higher level, the envisionment of [de Kleer and Brown 84] is interpretative; based on a finite state space it explains how transitions happen. The qualitative differential equations approach [Kuipers 86] is constructive, as it primarily generates a trajectory; the state space may be dynamically enlarged, explanation is based on the resulting trajectory. On a technical level, both methods work in an "interpretative" manner, based on value propagation and generate-test procedures. Values are not calculated straightforward. This gap is filled by approaches based on classical simulation such as [Guariso et al. 92] or [Karp and Friedland 89].

Qualitative reasoning is also close to an object-oriented approach in software engineering and programming languages. It requires a modular implementation and encapsulation of objects. The differentiation into structure and behavior requires both easy assembling of structural components and dynamic extendibility. The existence of class-wide-assumptions as well as modeling as a whole, as demonstrated by the work of both [Addanki et al. 91] and [Falkenhainer and Forbus 91], requires the concept of creating concrete realizations of different basic types, i.e. the concept of instantiation. The discussed approaches in qualitative reasoning as well as in the area of simulation indicate a probable future direction of computer science: along with the object-oriented programming paradigm, the distinction between database design and software engineering may disappear.

Summarizing the following capabilities of qualitative reasoning, we can conclude:
- it can handle situations with incomplete information;
- qualitative models are a level above quantitative models, hence qualitative simulation may both simplify and control numerical simulation;
- qualitative models represent abstractions of entire sets of quantitative models, they may be applied to different as well as novel situations;
- it provides a causal explanation, telling why and how something happens;
- the modeling process is supported by separating different levels and types of knowledge, qualitative reasoning explicitly treats underlying assumptions;
- it constitutes an important step toward the modeling of reasoning processes of people.

However, ambiguity remains a serious problem. This is common to all approaches. If not enough information is available, the tree of possible solutions easily becomes intractable. However, qualitative reasoning provides one advantage: even in the case of very limited information, it enables for distinguishing between feasible and non-feasible solutions. In an iterative approach the qualitatively generated solution space may be investigated by other methods in a second step.

Finally, we will present some speculations about probable further and promising developments, which may also be considered as areas for further research.

a. Modeling Environments

The enrichment of modeling techniques constitutes perhaps the most prominent contribution of qualitative reasoning to both AI and simulation. Crucial for modeling is an appropriate environment, which supports - but not substitutes - all steps from problem formulation to analysis of experiments (see also [Guariso and Werthner 89]). Model bases, although denominated differently, play an important role in qualitative reasoning. A model base has to support the different approaches to look at problems and to combine different views. Furthermore, the iterative enlargement of such a base by new methods has to be supported. The classification of views and relationships still needs to be accomplished to some extent. As a first attempt, we propose the following structure of a multi-dimensional model base, integrating different dimensions:

- *Qualitative abstraction:* Models can be viewed with respect to their qualitative features along the dimensions of qualitative abstraction, i.e. structure, functional operators, description of quantities and time. These levels define the relationships between different models describing the same real system. The different layers of qualitative models may also be connected, perhaps by some kind of an *is-a* relationship. Finally, on a last level, there might exist a completely specified quantitative model.

- *Level of certainty:* In contrast to qualitative abstraction, a qualitative quantity may have a value with some degree of certainty described by means of fuzzy sets. This concept may be extended to relationships and operators as well. Furthermore, models on different levels of certainty may be related to each other.

- *Function:* Several devices and their models - though different in their structure and behavior - may fulfill the same purpose. These devices are designed for the same usage. Their function may play the role of a negotiator between this use and the behavior of the ssystem, just as described by [Brajnik et al. 91].

- *Aspect:* Models can neglect and / or enforce specific features of real objects. A wire, for example, may serve as a conductor for either temperature or electricity or both. This is similar to the class and subclasses relationship, denoted by an *is-a* arc between type nodes.

- *Components:* Models are composed by subparts or components, which, in turn, may be further divided. Thus, a multi-layered *part-of* relationship may be defined. This relationship, in turn, creates a further relationship: parts on the same level of a part-of hierarchy may be connected with each other by interchanging input and output values.

- *Instances and classes:* Finally, such an environment has to contain not only classifications and views of the world which serve in the construction process, but also has to store already solved problems and answered questions. Therefore, instantiated models, responsible for specific problems, have to be stored. Such instances also constitute the final components which have to be assembled to solve a given problem. This forms a kind of an *instance-of* relationship.

Such structures are not only useful in the area of dynamic systems but also for the maintenance of software modules in general. They may support approaches to software reusability as well [Hitz and Werthner 92]. Organized in the form of a graph, each node may denote either a "computable" model or just one of its parts or an entity used for classification and selection. Such a graph is different from approaches based on a pure tree structure and does not require that executable pieces of code be only maintained at the final level of leaves. Such an organization may have a very high degree of complexity, however, this corresponds to the complex relationships between "real" objects. In our proposal this complexity is

The similarity with the process-centered approach could be further exploited. Languages such as Eiffel [Meyer 88] already possess some first concepts to define preconditions of an object to be "called" and the posteffects when leaving an object. This is similar to the process-centered ontology, where at least preconditions and posteffects can be derived, and the approaches to model real systems based on this view. Using these concepts, both the overall behavior and the effect of simple and connected modules could be derived. This should allow to obtain a concise and short description of such objects (shorter than the original code by at least a factor of 50 - 100) and to shortly simulate a module in order to get an idea of its behavior. The sequence of work on a software base could be as follows: one selects a module and looks at its structure; when it satisfies some structural conditions one simulates and checks whether the range of the obtained behavior contains the desired one. The simulation time should be just a fraction of the time which is necessary to run the original code. This approach could not only be used in the selection of modules, but also in the design and diagnostic process. Additionally, this proposal has a further important advantage: modeling can be learned by modeling things that are artificial; thus, when one fails in the process of modeling, one could use a trick and change the object of modeling a little: "For learning nearly everything is allowed".

However, for the application of qualitative reasoning to software reusability severe problems have to be addressed: What are the basic structural and behavioral primitives ? What are the basic types of input and output data of a module ? How is the internal state of a module recorded ? How can a mapping be supplied from a set of elements to just one of its members, for example, how can an operation looking for a maximum in a set of numbers be modeled using "qualitative primitives" ? The central task is not to solve the problem of non-availability of information, but to define a short and concise notation which permits faster reasoning and a better organization than using the original parts of software modules. Future research in this specific area has to classify software pieces and to develop their qualitative structural and behavioral primitives, to design a simulation motor to generate the dynamics of such modules as well as to identify differences to qualitative reasoning.

References

[Abelson and Sussman 87] Abelson H., Sussman G.J.: The Dynamicist´s Workbench I: Automatic Preparation of Numerical Experiments. MIT AI Lab., Memo 955, 1987.

[Abelson et al. 89] Abelson H., Eisenberg M., Halfant M., Katzenelson J., Sacks E., Sussman G.J., Wisdom J., Yip K.: Intelligence in Scientific Computing. Comm. ACM 32, 546-562, 1989.

[Abu-Hanna et al. 91] Abu-Hanna A., Benjamins R., Jansweijer W.: Device Understanding and Modeling for Diagnosis. IEEE Expert 6 (2), 26-32, 1991.

[Addanki et al. 89] Addanki S., Cremonini R., Penberthy J.S.: Reasoning about Assumptions in Graphs of Models. Proc. of IJCAI-89, Detroit, Mich., 1432-1438, 1989.

[Addanki et al. 91] Addanki S., Cremonini R., Penberthy J.S.: Graphs of Models. Artificial Intelligence 51, 145-177, 1991.

[Allen 83] Allen J.F.: Maintaining Knowledge about Temporal Intervals. Comm. ACM 26 (6), 832-843, 1983.

[Aubin 92] Aubin J.P.: Dynamical Qualitative Simulation. Lecture at Comett Matari Programme, Pavia, Italy, p.41, 1992.

[Baily et al. 91] Baily D.A., Kiang Y., Kuipers B., Whinston A.B.: A Theoretical Framework for Modeling Executive Support Systems: A Qualitative and Causal Reasoning Approach. Proc. of DSS and Qual. Reas., Toulouse, France, 1991.

[Barrow 84] Barrow G.H.: Verify: A Program for Proving Correctness of Digital Hardware. Artificial Intelligence 24, 437-491, 1984.

[Bauer and Reiser] Bauer M.I., Reiser B.: Incremental Envisioning: the Flexible Use of Multiple Representations in Complex Problem Solving. Proc. of 12.th Conf. of the Cognitive Science Society; Cambridge, MA, 317 - 324, 1990.

[Beck and Fishwick 89] Beck H.W., Fishwick P.A.: Incorporating Natural Language Descriptions into Modeling and Simulation. Simulation 52 (3), 102-109, 1989.

[Beckman 81] Beckman F.S.: Mathematical Foundations of Programming. Addison Wesley, Reading, MA., 1981.

[Bellman and Zadeh 70] Bellman R.E., Zadeh L.A.: Decision-Making in a Fuzzy Environment. Management Science, 17 (4), 141-164, 1970.

[Berleant 89] Berleant D.: A Unification of Numerical and Qualitative Model Simulation. Workshop on Model Based Reasoning. Proc. of IJCAI-89, Detroit, Mich., 91-96, 1989.

[Berleant and Kuipers 90] Berleant D., Kuipers B.J.: Combined Qualitative and Numerical Simulation with Q3. 4th Int. Workshop on Qualitative Physics, Lugano, CH, 140-152, 1990.

[Bertin et al. 90] Bertin A., Gallanti M., Stefanini A., Tornielle G.: Diagniostic Reasoning Based on Dependency Analysis. CISE Spa, Milan, Italy, 1990.

[Bobrow 1984] Bobrow D.G. (ed.): Qualitative Reasoning about Physical Systems. MIT Press, Cambridge, MA, 1984.

[Bonarini and Sassaroli 92] Bonarini A., Sassaroli P.: Opportunistic Multimodel-Based Diagnosis: Using all the Knowledge We Have. In: Scarl E. (ed.) Proc. of 3rd International Workshop on Principles of Diagnosis, Rosario, WA, 1992.

[Bonczek et al. 81] Bonczek R.H., Holsapple C.W., Whinston A.B.: Foundations of Decision Support Systems. Academic Press, Orlando, Florida, 1981.

[Borrie and Burghes 81] Borrie M.S., Burghes D.N.: Modelling with Differential Equations. Ellis Horwood, Chichester, England, 1981.

[Brachman 83] Brachman R.J.: What IS-A Is and Isn´t: an Analysis of Taxonomic Links in Semantic Networks. IEEE Computer 16 (10), 67-73, 1983.

[Bradshaw 91] Bradshaw J.A.: Using Knowledge of Purpose and Knowledge of Structure as a Basis for Evaluating the Behavior of Mechanical Systems. PhD. Thesis. Technical Report 236, University of Cambridge Computer Laboratory, 1991.

[Bradshaw and Young 91] Bradshaw J.A., Young R.M.: Evaluating Design Using Knowledge of Purpose and Knowledge of Structure. IEEE Expert 6 (2), 33-40, 1991.

[Brajnik et al. 91] Brajnik G., Chittaro L., Guida G., Tasso C., Toppano E.: Functional Knowledge: a Bridge between Behavior and Teleology in the Multi-Modeling Approach. 1st Europ. Workshop on Qualitative Reasoning about Physical Systems, Genova, Italy, 24, 1991.

[Bredeweg and Wielinga 88] Bredeweg B., Wielinga B.: Reasoning about Physical Systems: A Unifying Perspective. Proc. of ECAI-88, Munich, Germany, 287-290, 1988.

[Buchanan and Shortliffe 84] Buchanan B.G., Shortliffe E.H.: Rule-Based Expert Systems: The MYCIN Experiments of the Stanford Heuristic Programming Project. Addison Wesley, Reading, MA, 1984.

[Capelo et al. 91] Capelo A.C., Ironi L., Tentoni S.: An Algorithm for the Automated Generation of Rheological Models. In: Rzevski G., Adey R.A. (eds.) Applications of Artificial Intelligence in Engineering IV. Computational Mechanics Publication. Southampton, 963-979, 1991.

[Capelo et al. 93] Capelo A.C., Ironi L., Tentoni S.: A model-based system for the classification and analysis of materails. To appear in: Int. Systems Engineering (summer issue), 1993.

[Cellier 91a] Cellier F.E.: Continuous System Modeling. Springer, New York, 1991.

[Cellier 91b] Cellier F.E.: GSPS Paradigm for Qualitative Modeling. In: Fishwick P.A., Luker P.A. (eds.) Qualitative Simulation, Modeling and Analysis. Advance in Simulation 5. Springer, New York, 51-71, 1990.

[Chandrasekaran 91] Chandrasekaran B.: Models versus Rules, Deep versus Compiled, Content versus Form, Some Distinctions in Knowledge Systems Research. IEEE Expert 6 (2), 75-79, 1991.

[Chittaro et al. 92] Chittaro L., Guida G., Tasso C., Toppano E.: Functional and Teleological Knowledge in the Multi-modeling Approach for Reasoning about Physical Systems: A Case Study in Diagnosis. Unpublished, Udine, Italy, 57, 1992.

[Chiu 89] Chiu C.: Constructing Qualitative Domain Maps from Quantitative Simulation Models. In: Widman L.E., Loparo K.A., Nielsen N.R. (eds.) Artificial Intelligence, Simulation and Modeling. Wiley, New York, 275-300, 1989.

[Collins and Forbus 87] Collins J.W., Forbus K.D.: Reasoning about Fluids Via Molecular Collections. Proc. of AAAI- 87, Seattle, WA, 590-595, 1987.

[Collins and Gentner 83] Collins A., Gentner D.: Multiple Models of Evaporation Processes. Proc. of 5th Annual Meeting of Cognitive Science Society, Rochester, NY, 1983.

[Conrad 92] Conrad M.: Molecular Computing: The Lock-Key Paradigm. IEEE Computer 25(11), 11-20, 1992.

[Coy et al. 92] Coy W., Nake F., Pflüger J.M., Rolf A., Seetzen J., Siefkes D., Stransfeld R. (eds.): Sichtweisen der Informatik (in German). Vieweg, Braunschweig, 1992.

[Crawford et al. 90] Crawford J., Farquhar A., Kuipers B.J.: QPC: A Compiler from Physical Models into Qualitative Differential Equations. 4th Int. Workshop on Qualitative Physics, Lugano, CH, 31-38, 1990.

[d'Ambrosio 89] d'Ambrosio B.: Extending the Mathematics in Qualitative Process Theory. In: Widman L.E., Loparo K.A., Nielsen N.R. (eds.) Artificial Intelligence, Simulation and Modeling. Wiley, New York, 133-158, 1989.

[Dague et al. 87] Dague P., Raiman O., Deves P.: Troubleshooting: When Modeling is a Trouble. Proc. of AAAI- 87, Seattle, WA, 600-605, 1987.

[Dahl et al. 67] Dahl D.J., Myhrhaug B., Nygaard U.: SIMULA 67, Common Base Language. Norwegian Computing Center, Oslo, Norway, 1967.

[Davis 87] Davis E.: Constraint Propagation with Interval Labels. Artificial Intelligence 32, 281-331, 1987.

[Davis 89] Davis E.: Order of Magnitude Reasoning in Qualitative Differential Equations. Technical Report, New York University Computer Science Department, 1989.

[de Kleer 75] de Kleer J.: Qualitative and Quantitative Knowledge in Classical Mechanics. TR-352, AI Lab., MIT, Cambridge, MA, 1975.

[de Kleer 77] de Kleer J.: Multiple Representation of Knowledge in a Mechanics Problem Solver. Proc. of IJCAI-77, Cambridge, MA, 299-304, 1977.

[de Kleer 79] de Kleer J.: The Origin and Resolution of Ambiguities in Causal Arguments. Proc. of IJCAI-79, tokyo, Japan, 197-204, 1979.

[de Kleer 86a] de Kleer J.: An Assumption-based TMS. Artificial Intelligence 28, 127-162, 1986.

[de Kleer 86b] de Kleer J.: Extending the ATMS. Artificial Intelligence 28, 163-198, 1986.

[de Kleer 86c] de Kleer J.: Problem Solving with the ATMS. Artificial Intelligence 28, 199-224, 1986.

[de Kleer and Bobrow 84] de Kleer J., Bobrow D.G.: Qualitative Reasoning with Higher-order Derivatives. Proc. of AAAI-84, 86-91, 1984.

[de Kleer and Brown 84] de Kleer J., Brown J.S.: A Qualitative Physics based on Confluences. Artificial Intelligence 24, 7-83, 1984.

[de Kleer and Brown 86] de Kleer J., Brown J.S.: Theories of Causal Ordering. Artificial Intelligence 29, 33-61, 1986.

[de Kleer and Williams 87] de Kleer J., Williams B.C.: Diagnosing Multiple Faults. Artificial Intelligence 32, 97 - 130, 1987.

[Dormoy and Raiman 88] Dormoy J.L, Raiman O.: Assembling a Device. Proc. of AAAI-88, Saint Paul, Minn., 330-335, 1988.

[Downing 91] Downing K.: Model Based Diagnosis of Qualitative Physiological Models. Linkoping University, Sweden, 1991.

[Eisenberg 90] Eisenberg M.: Combining Qualitative and Quantitative Techniques in the Simulation of Chemical Reaction Mechanism. In: Webster W., Uttamsingh R. (eds.) AI and Simulation, Theory and Applications. Simulation Series 22, 3, 233-242, 1990.

[Fagin and Halpern 89] Fagin R., Halpern J.Y.: Uncertainty, Belief and Probability. Proc. of IJCAI-89, Detroit, Mich., 1161-1173, 1989.

[Falkenhainer and Forbus 88] Falkenhainer B., Forbus K.D.: Setting up Large-Scale Qualitative Models. Proc. of AAAI-88, Saint Paul, Minn., 301-306, 1988.

[Falkenhainer and Forbus 90] Falkenhainer B., Forbuş K.D.: Compositional Modeling of Physical Systems. 4th Int. Workshop on Qualitative Physics, Lugano, CH, 1-15, 1990.

[Falkenhainer and Forbus 91] Falkenhainer B., Forbus K.D.: Compositional Modeling: Finding the Right Model for the Job. Artificial Intelligence 51, 95-143, 1991.

[Faltings 87] Faltings B.: Qualitative Kinematics in Mechanisms. Proc. of IJCAI-87, Milan, Italy, 437-443, 1987.

[Faltings and Struss 92] Faltings B., Struss P. (eds.): Recent Advances in Qualitative Physics. MIT Press, Cambridge, MA, 1992.

[Fielding, Lee 91] Fielding N.G., Lee R.M. (eds.): Using Computers in Qualitative Research. Sage, London, 1991.

[Fishwick 89] Fishwick P.A.: Qualitative Methodology in Simulation Model Engineering. Simulation 52 (3), 95-101, 1989.

[Fishwick 90] Fishwick P.A.: Invariance and Nominal Value Mapping as Key Themes for Qualitative Simulation. In: Fishwick P.A., Luker P.A. (eds.) Qualitative Simulation, Modeling and Analysis. Advance in Simulation 5. Springer, New York, 72-97, 1990.

[Fishwick and Luker 90] Fishwick P.A., Luker P.A. (eds.): Qualitative Simulation, Modeling and Analysis. Advance in Simulation 5. Springer, New York, 72-97, 1990.

[Fishwick and Zeigler 91] Fishwick P.A., Zeigler B.P.: Qualitative Physics: Towards the Automation of Systems Problem Solving. J. Expt. Theor. Artif. Intell. 3, 219-246, 1991.

[Forbus 80] Forbus K.D.: Spatial and Qualitative Aspects of Reasoning about Motion. Proc. of AAAI-80, Palo Alto, CA, 170-173, 1980.

[Forbus 84] Forbus K.D.: Qualitative Process Theory. Artificial Intelligence 24, 85-168, 1984.

[Forbus 86] Forbus K.D.: The Qualitative Process Engine. Technical Report, University of Illinois, Department of Computer Science, 1986.

[Forbus 87] Forbus K.D.: Interpreting Observations of Physical Systems. IEEE Trans. of SMC 17 (3), 350-359, 1987.

[Forbus 88] Forbus K.D.: Qualitative Physics: Past, Present and Future. In: Shrobe H.E. (ed.) Exploring Artificial Intelligence, Morgan Kaufmann, San Mateo, CA, 239-296, 1988.

[Forbus and Falkenhainer 90] Forbus K.D., Falkenhainer B.: Self-Explanatory Simulations: An Integration of Qualitative and Quantitative Knowledge. 4th Int. Workshop on Qualitative Physics, Lugano, CH, 97-110, 1990.

[Forbus and Gentner 86] Forbus K.D., Gentner D.: Causal Reasoning about Quantities. Proc. of 8th Annual Meeting of Cognitive Science Society, Amherst, MA, 196-207, 1986.

[Forbus et al. 87] Forbus K.D., Nielsen P., Faltings B.: Qualitative Kinematics: A Framework. Proc. of IJCAI-87, Milan, Italy, 430-436, 1987.

[Fouché and Kuipers 91] Fouché Ü., Kuipers B.J.: Introducing Energy into Qualitative Simulation. 1st Europ. Workshop on Qualitative Reasoning about Physical Systems, Genova, Italy, 17, 1991.

[Franke 91] Franke D.W.: Deriving and Using Descriptions of Purpose. IEEE Expert 6 (2), 41-47, 1991.

[Freedmann 71] Freedmann D.: Markov Chains. Holden Day, San Francisco, 1971.

[Gardin and Meltzer 89] Gardin F., Meltzer B.: Analogical Representations of Naive Physics. Artificial Intelligence 38, 139-159, 1989.

[Glymour et al. 89] Glymour C., Scheines R., Spirtes P., Kelly K.: Discovering Causal Structure. Academic Press, San Diego, USA, 1987.

[Govindaraj 87] Govindaraj T.: Qualitative Approximation Methodology for Modeling and Simulation. IEEE Trans. MSC 17 (6), 1987.

[Grossmann and Werthner 93] Grossmann W., Werthner H.: A Stochastic Approach to Qualitative Simulation Using Markov Processes. Proc. of IJCAI-93, Chambéry, France, 1993.

[Guariso and Werthner 89] Guariso G., Werthner H.: Environmental Decision Support Systems. Ellis Horwood, Chichester, Engl., 1989.

[Guariso et al. 89a] Guariso G., Hitz M., Werthner H.: An Intelligent Simulation Model Generator. Simulation 53 (2), 1989.

[Guariso et al. 89b] Guariso, G., Nisoli, L., Rizzoli, A., Werthner, H.: QUALSIM: An Object-Oriented Software Package for Qualitative Modelling and Simulation. In: Iazeolla, G., Lehmann, A., Van den Herik H.J. (eds.) Simulation Methodologies, Languages and Architectures and AI and Graphics for Simulation. Proc. of European Simulation Multiconference 1989, Rome, Italy, June 1989, SCS, 175-180, 1989.

[Guariso et al. 92] Guariso G., Rizzoli A., Werthner H.: Identification of Model Structure via Qualitative Simulation. IEEE Trans. of SMC 22 (5), 1075-1086, 1992.

[Hayes 79] Hayes P.: The Naive Physics Manifesto. In: Michie D. (ed.) Expert Systems in the Microelectronic Age. Edinburgh University Press, 242-270, 1979.

[Hayes 85a] Hayes P.: The Second Naive Physics Manifesto. In: Hobbs J.R., Moore R.C. (eds.) Formal Theories of the Commonsense World. Ablex, Norwood, NJ, 1-36, 1985.

[Hayes 85b] Hayes P.: Naive Physics 1: Ontology for Liquids. In: Hobbs J.R., Moore R.C. (eds.) Formal Theories of the Commonsense World. Ablex, Norwood, NJ, 71-90, 1985.

[Hegarty et al. 88] Hegarty M., Just M.A., Morrison I.R.: Mental Models of Mechanical Systems: Individual Differences in Qualitative and Quantitative Reasoning. Cognitive Psychology 20, 191-236, 1988.

[Hitz and Werthner 92] Hitz M., Werthner H.: A Graph Oriented Approach to Enhance Software Reusability in *-bases. Proc. of WISR´92, 5th Annual Workshop in Software Reuse, Palo Alto, CA, 1992.

[Hodges 92] Hodges J.: Naive Mechanics : A Computational Model of Device Use and Function in Design Improvisation. IEEE Expert 7 (1), 14-27, 1992.

[Hyvönen 89] Hyvönen E.: Constraint Reasoning Based on Interval Arithmetic. Proc. of IJCAI-89, Detroit, Mich., 1193-1198, 1989.

[Ironi et al. 90] Ironi L., Stefanelli M., Lanzola G.: Qualitative Models in Medical Diagnosis. Artificial Intelligence in Medicine 2, 85-101, 1990.

[Ishida 89] Ishida Y.: Using Global Properties for Qualitative Reasoning: A Qualitative System Theory. Proc. of IJCAI-89, Detroit, Mich., 1174-1179, 1989.

[Ishida 92] Ishida Y.: A Graphical Approach to Qualitative Reasoning on Dynamic Systems. Proc. of ECAI-92, Vienna, Austria, 744-748, 1992.

[Iwasaki 88] Iwasaki Y.: Causal Ordering in a Mixed Structure. Proc. of AAAI-88, Saint Paul, Minn., 313-318, 1988.

[Iwasaki 90a] Iwasaki Y.: Causal Ordering Analysis. In: Fishwick P.A., Luker P.A. (eds.) Qualitative Simulation, Modeling and Analysis. Advance in Simulation 5. Springer, New York, 98-118, 1990.

[Iwasaki 90b] Iwasaki Y.: Reasoning with Multiple Abstraction Models. 4th Int. Workshop on Qualitative Physics, Lugano, CH, 183-193, 1990.

[Iwasaki and Bhandari 88] Iwasaki Y., Bhandari I.: Formal Basis for Commonsense Abstraction of Dynamic Systems. Proc. of AAAI-88, Saint Paul, Minn., 307-312, 1988.

[Iwasaki and Simon 86a] Iwasaki Y., Simon H.A.: Causality in Device Behavior. Artificial Intelligence 29, 3-32, 1986.

[Iwasaki and Simon 86b] Iwasaki Y., Simon H.A.: Theories of Causal Ordering: Reply to de Kleer and Brown. Artificial Intelligence 29, 63-72, 1986.

[Karp and Friedland 89] Karp P.D., Friedland P.: Coordinating the Use of Qualitative and Quantitative Knowledge in Declarative Device Modeling. In: Widman L.E., Loparo K.A., Nielsen N.R. (eds.) Artificial Intelligence, Simulation and Modeling. Wiley, New York, 189-206, 1989.

[Keuneke 91] Keuneke A.M.: Device Representation: The Significance of Functional Knowledge. IEEE Expert 6 (2), 22-25, 1991.

[Kirby and Hunter 91] Kirby I., Hunter J.: Further Progress in Qualitative Modeling of Cardiac Electrophysiology. Dept. of Computing Science, University of Aberdeen, Scottland, 1991.

[Kiriyama et al. 91] Kiriyama T., Tomiyama T., Yoshikawa H.: Model Generation in Design. Dept. of Precision Machinery, The University of Tokyo, Japan, 1991.

[Klir 85] Klir G.J.: Architecture of Systems Problem Solving. Plenum Press, New York, 1985.

[Kraan et al. 91] Kraan I.C., Richards B.L., Kuipers B.J.: Automatic Abduction of Qualitative Models. 5th Int. Workshop on Qualitative Reasoning about Physical Systems, Austin, TX, 295-301, 1991.

[Kuipers 84] Kuipers B.J.: Commonsense Reasoning about Causality: Deriving Behavior from Structure. Artificial Intelligence 24, 169-203, 1984.

[Kuipers 85] Kuipers B.J.: The Limits of Qualitative Simulation. Proc. of IJCAI-85, Los Angeles, Cal., 128-136, 1985.

[Kuipers 86] Kuipers B.J.: Qualitative Simulation. Artificial Intelligence 29, 289-388, 1989.

[Kuipers 87a] Kuipers B.J.: Qualitative Simulation as Causal Explanation. IEEE Trans. SMC 17 (3), 432-444, 1987.

[Kuipers 87b] Kuipers B.J.: Abstraction by Time-Scale in Qualitative Simulation. Proc. of AAAI-87, Seattle, WA, 621-625, 1987.

[Kuipers 89] Kuipers B.J.: Qualitative Reasoning with Causal Models in Diagnosis of Complex Systems. In: Widman L.E., Loparo K.A., Nielsen N.R. (eds.) Artificial Intelligence, Simulation and Modeling. Wiley, New York, 257-274, 1989.

[Kuipers and Berleant 88] Kuipers B.J., Berleant D.: Using Incomplete Quantitative Knowledge in Qualitative Reasoning. Proc. of AAAI-88, Saint Paul, Minn., 324-329, 1988.

[Kuipers and Chiu 87] Kuipers B.J., Chiu C.: Taming Intractible Branching in Qualitative Simulation. Proc. of IJCAI-87, Milan, Italy, 1079-1085, 1987.

[Kuipers et al. 91] Kuipers B.J., Chiu C., Dalle Molle D.T., Throop D.R.: Higher-order Derivative Constraints in Qualitative Simulation. Artificial Intelligence 51, 343-379, 1991.

[Lanzola et al. 90] Lanzola G., Stefanelli M., Barosi G., Magnani L.: NEOANEMIA: A Knowledge-Based System Emulating Diagnostic Reasoning. Computers and Biomedical Research 23, 560-582, 1990.

[Lee and Kuipers 88] Lee W.L., Kuipers B.J.: Non-Intersection of Trajectories in Qualitative Phase Space: A Global Constraint for Qualitative Simulation. Proc. of AAAI-88, Saint Paul, Minn., 286-290, 1988.

[Legrenzi and Sonino 91] Legrenzi P., Sonino M.: The Formal Representation of Naive Physics. 1st Europ. Workshop on Qualitative Reasoning about Physical Systems, Genova, Italy, 33, 1991.

[Leitch and Shen 92] Leitch R., Shen Q.: Being Committed to Qualitative Simulation. Workshop on Model Based Reasoning at ECAI 92, Vienna, Austria, 51- 58, 1992.

[Leyval and Ledoux 91] Leyval L., Ledoux A.: Qualitative Simulation for the Supervision of a Nuclear Reprocessing Plant. Commisariat a l'Energie Atomique, CEN VALRHO, Cedex, France, 1991.

[Mavrovouniotis and Stephanopoulos 87] Mavrovouniotis M.L, Stephanopoulos G.: Reasoning with the Orders of Magnitude and Approximate Relations. Proc. of AAAI-87, Seattle, WA, 626-630, 1987.

[Mavrovouniotis and Stephanopoulos 88] Mavrovouniotis M.L, Stephanopoulos G.: Formal Order-Of-Magnitude Reasoning in Proecess Engineering. Computer Chemical Engineering 12, 867-880, 1988.

[Meyer 88] Meyer B.: Object-oriented Software Construction. Prentice Hall, New York, 1988.

[Milne and Travé-Massuyès 92] Milne R., Travé-Massuyès L.: Applied Qualitative Reasoning. Tutorial at ECAI-92, Vienna, Austria, 1992.

[Minsky 81] Minsky M.: A Framework for Representing Knowledge. In: Haugeland J. (ed.) Mind Design. MIT Press, Massachusetts, 95-128, 1981.

[Nayak et al. 91] Nayak P.P, Joskowicz L., Addanki S.: Automated Model Selection Using Context-Dependent Behaviors. 5th Int. WS on Qualitative Reasoning about Physical Systems, Austin, TX, 10-23, 1991.

[Newell 90] Newell A.: Unified Theories of Cognition. Harvard University Press. Cambridge, Massachusetts, 1990.

[Nielsen 88] Nielsen P.: A Qualitative Approach to Mechanical Constraint. Proc. of AAAI-88, Saint Paul, Minn., 270-275, 1988.

[Odum 71] Odum P.: Fundamentals of Ecology. W.B. Saunders Co., Philadelphia, PA, 1971.

[Ören 84] Ören T.I.: GEST - A Modeling and Simulation Language Based on System Theoretic Concepts. In: Ören T.I., Zeigler B.P., Elzas M.S. (eds.) Simulation and Model-based Methodologies: An Integrative View. Springer, Berlin, Heidelberg, New York, 281-336, 1984.

[Ören 91] Ören T.I.: Dynamic Templates and Semantic Rules for Simulation Advisors and Certifiers. In: Fishwick P.A., Modjeski R.B. (eds.) Knowledge-Based Simulation: Methodology and Application. Springer, Berlin, Heidelberg, New York, 53-76, 1991.

[Ören et al. 84] Ören T.I., Zeigler B.P., Elzas M.S. (eds.): Simulation and Model-based Methodologies: An Integrative View. Springer, Berlin, Heidelberg, New York, 1984.

[Oyeleye and Kramer 89] Oyeleye O.O., Kramer M.A.: The Role of Causal and Noncausal Constraints in Steady-state Qualitative Modeling. In: Widman L.E., Loparo K.A., Nielsen N.R. (eds.) Artificial Intelligence, Simulation and Modeling. Wiley, New York, 47-73, 1989.

[Pearl 86] Pearl J.: Fusion, Propagation and Structuring in Belief Networks. Artificial Intelligence 29, 241-288, 1986.

[Peot and Shachter 91] Peot M.A., Shachter R.D.: Fusion and Propagation with Multiple Observations in Belief Networks. Artificial Intelligence 48, 299-218, 1991.

[Pflug 86] Pflug G.: Stochastische Modelle in der Informatik (in German). B.G. Teubner, Stuttgart, 1986.

[Piaget 60] Piaget J.: The Children's Conception of Physical Causality. Littlefield, Adams, Co., Paterson, New Jersey, 1960.

[Pichler 75] Pichler F.: Mathematische Systemtheorie (in German). De Gruyter, Berlin, 1975.

[Price and Lee 88] Price C.J., Lee M.H.: Why Do ExpertSystems Need Deep Knowledge. Proc. of ECAI-88, Munich, Germany, 264-266, 1988.

[Raiman 88] Raiman O.: Order of Magnitude Reasoning. Proc. of AAAI-88, Saint Paul, Minn., 100-104, 1988.

[Raiman 91] Raiman O.: Order of Magnitude Reasoning. Artificial Intelligence 51, 11-38, 1991.

[Rajagopalan 86] Rajagopalan R.: Qualitative Modeling and Simulation: A Survey. In: Kerckhoffs E.J.H., Vansteenkiste G.C., Zeigler B.P. (eds.) AI Applied to Simulation. Simulation Series 18, No.1, SCS, 9-26, 1986.

[Rapaport 88] Rapaport W.J.: Syntactic Semantics: Foundations of Computational Natural Language Understanding. In: Fetzer J.H. (ed.) Aspects of Artificial Intelligence, Kluwer Academic Publishers, Dordrecht, 81-132, 1988.

[Reiter 87] Reiter R.: A Theory of Diagnosis from First Principles. Artificial Intelligence 32, 57 - 95, 1987.

[Ritschard 83] Ritschard G.: Computable Qualitative Comparative Techniques. Econometrica 51, 1145 - 1168, 1983.

[Robinson 66] Robinson A.: Non-Standard Analysis. North-Holland, Amsterdam, 1966.

[Roddis and Martin 92] Roddis K. W. M., Martin L.J.: Qualitative Reasoning about Fatigue and Fracture in Steel Bridegs. IEEE Expert 7 (4), 41-48, 1992.

[Rozenblit and Huang 91] Rozenblit J.W., Huang Y.M.: Rule-Based Generation of Model Structures in Multifacetted Modelling and System Design. ORSA Journal on Computing, 3(4), 330-344, 1991.

[Rozenblit and Zeigler 86] Rozenblit J.W., Zeigler B.P.: Entity-based Structures for Modeling and Experimental Frame Construction. In: Elzas M.S., Ören T.I., Zeigler B.P. (eds.) Modeling and Simulation Methodology in the Artificial Intelligence Era. North-Holland, Amsterdam, 195-210, 1986.

[Sacks 87] Sacks E.: Piecewise Linear Reasoning. Proc. of AAAI-87, Seattle, WA, 649-654, 1987.

[Sacks 90a] Sacks E.: A Dynamic Systems Perspective on Qualitative Reasoning. Artificial Intelligence 42, 349-362, 1990.

[Sacks 90b] Sacks E.: Automatic Qualitative Analysis of Ordinary Differential Equations Using Piecewise Linear Approximations. Artficial Intelligence. Artificial Intelligence 41, 313-364, 1990.

[Scheines et al. 91] Scheines R., Spirtes P., Glymoure C.: A Qualitative Approach to Causal Modeling. In: Fishwick P.A., Luker P.A. (eds.) Qualitative Simulation, Modeling and Analysis. Advance in Simulation 5. Springer, New York, 72-97, 1990.

[Sembugamoorthy and Chandresekaran 86] Sembugamoorthy V., Chandresekaran B.: Functional Representation of Devices and Compilation of Diagnostic Problem-Solving Systems. In: Kolodner J.L., Riesbeck C.K. (eds.) Experience, Memory and Reasoning. Lawrence Erlbaum Associates, Hillsdale, New Jersey, 1986.

[Shen and Leitch 90] Shen Q., Leitch R.: Integrating Commonsense and Qualitative Simulation by the Use of Fuzzy Sets. 4th Int. Workshop on Qualitative Physics, Lugano, CH, 221-232, 1990.

[Shen and Leitch 91] Shen Q., Leitch R.: Extending the Quantity Space in Qualitative Reasoning. 1st Europ. Workshop on Qualitative Reasoning about Physical Systems, Genova, Italy, 13, 1991.

[Shortliffe 76] Shortliffe E.H.: Computer-Based Medical Consultations: MYCIN. Elsevier,New York, 1976.

[Simmons 86] Simmons R.: "Commonsense" Arithmetic Reasoning. Proc. of AAAI-86, Philadelphia, PA, 118-124, 1986.

[Simon 52] Simon H.A.: On the Definition of the Causal Relation. Journ. Philosophy 49, 517-528, 1952.

[Skorstad 90] Skorstad G.: Clustered Causal Ordering. 4th Int. Workshop on Qualitative Physics, Lugano, CH, 290-299, 1990.

[Spriet and Vansteenkiste 82] Spriet J.A., Vansteenkiste G.C.: Computer-aided Modelling and Simulation. Int. Lecture Notes in Computer Science, Academic Press, London, 1982.

[Sticklen and Bond 91] Sticklen J., Bond W.E.: Functional Reasoning and Functional Modeling, Introduction. IEEE Expert 6 (2), 20-21, 1991.

[Strawson 59] Strawson F.: Individuals: An Essay of Descriptive Methaphysics. Methuen, London, 1959.

[Struss 87] Struss P.: Problems of Interval Based Qualitative Reasoning. Technical Report Siemens #INF2ARM-87, 18, 1987.

[Struss 88] Struss P.: Global Filters for Qualitative Behaviors. Proc. of AAAI-88, Saint Paul, Minn., 275-279, 1988.

[Struss and Dressler 89] Struss P., Dressler O.: "Physical Negation" - Integrating Fault Models into the General Diagnostic Engine. Proc. of IJCAI-89, Detroit, MI, 1318-1323, 1989.

[Sugaya 89] Sugaya H.: Qualitative Modeling for Industrial Applications. ASEA Brown Boveri Corporate Research, Knowledge Systems Group, CH, 1989.

[Travé and Kaszkurewicz 86] Travé L., Kaszkurewicz E.: Qualitative Controllability and Observability of Linear Dynamical Systems. In: IFAC/IFOR Symposium on Large Scale Systems, Pergamon Press, 1986.

[Travé-Massuyès 92] Travé-Massuyès L.: Qualitative Reasoning over Time: History and Current Prospects. The Knowledge Engineering Review 7 (1), 1-18, 1992.

[Vesanterä and Cellier 89] Vesanterä P.J., Cellier F.E.: Building Intelligence into an Autopilot Using Qualitative Simulation to Support Global Decision Making. Simulation 52 (3), 111-121, 1989.

[Vescovi 91] Vescovi M.R.: Self-Explanatory Simulations from Structural Equations. 1st Europ. Workshop on Qualitative Reasoning about Physical Systems, Genova, Italy, 12, 1991.

[Vilain et al. 86] Vilain M., Kautz H., Beek P.: Constraint Propagation Algorithms for Temporal Reasoning. Proc. of AAAI-86, Philadelphia, PA, 377-382, 1986.

[Waltz 75] Waltz D.: Understanding Line Drawings of Scenes with Shadows, In: P. Whinston (ed.) The Psychology of Computer Vision. McGraw-Hill, New York, 1975.

[Weld 88] Weld D.S.: Exaggeration. Proc. of AAAI-88, Saint Paul, Minn., 291-296, 1988.

[Weld and de Kleer 90a] Weld D.S., de Kleer J.: Qualitative Reasoning about Physical Systems, Introduction. Morgan Kaufmann Publishers, San Mateo, Cal., 1-11, 1990.

[Weld and de Kleer 90b] Weld D.S., de Kleer J.: Qualitative Reasoning about Physical Systems, Chapter 9. Morgan Kaufmann Publishers, San Mateo, Cal., 611-616, 1990.

[Wellman 88] Wellman M.P.: Qualitative Probabilistic Networks for Planning under Uncertainty. In: Lemmer J.F., Kanal L.N. (eds.) Uncertainty in Artificial Intelligence 2. Machine Intelligence and Pattern Recognition 5. North - Holland, Amsterdam, 197-208, 1988.

[Wiederhold et al. 92] Wiederhold G., Wegner P., Ceri S.: Toward Megaprogramming. Comm. ACM 35, 89-99, 1992.

[Williams 84] Williams B.C.: Qualitative Analysis of MOS Circuits. Artificial Intelligence 24, 281-346, 1984.

[Williams 86] Williams B.C.: Doing Time: Putting Qualitative Reasoning on Firmer Ground. Proc. of AAAI-86, Philadelphia, PA.,105-113, 1986.

[Williams 88] Williams B.C.: MINIMA: A Symbolic Approach to Qualitative Algebraic Reasoning. Proc. of AAAI-88, Saint Paul, Minn., 264-270, 1988.

[Williams 91] Williams B.C.: A Theory of Interaction: Unifying Qualitative and Quantitative Algebraic Reasoning. Artificial Intelligence 51, 39-94, 1991.

[Williams and de Kleer 91] Williams B.C., de Kleer J.: Qualitative Reasoning about Physical Systems, a Return to Roots. Artificial Intelligence 51, 1-9, 1991.

[Yager et al. 87] Yager R.R., Ovchinnikov S., Tong R.M., Nguyen H.T.: Fuzzy Sets and Applications: Selected Papers by L.A. Zadeh. Wiley, New York, 1987.

[Yip 88] Yip K.: Generating Global Behaviors using Deep Knowledge of Local Dynamics. Proc. of AAAI-88, Saint Paul, Minn., 163-169, 1988.

[Zeigler 76] Zeigler B.P.: Theory of Modelling and Simulation. John Wiley, New York, 1976.

[Zeigler 84] Zeigler B.P.: Multi-Facetted Modelling and Discrete Event Simulation. Academic Press, New York, 1984.

[Zeigler 89] Zeigler B.P.: Object-Oriented Simulation with Hierarchical, Modular Models: Intelligent Agents and Endomorphic Systems. Academic Press, New York, 1989.

[Zeigler et al. 79] Zeigler B.P., Klir G., Elzas M., Ören T.I.: Methodology in Systems Modelling and Simulation. North-Holland, Amsterdam, 1979.

[Zeigler and Louri 93] Zeigler B.P., Louri A.: A Simulation Environment for Intelligent Machine Architectures. Journal on Current and Distributed Processing, 1993.

[Zhong and Zeigler 89] Zhong G., Zeigler B.P.: The SES: Knowledge Representation for Simulation Models and Design. In: Widman L.E., Loparo K.A., Nielsen N.R. (eds.) Artificial Intelligence, Simulation and Modeling. Wiley, New York, 47-73, 1991.

Index

Z